The Exchange Rate in a
Behavioral Finance Framework

The Exchange Rate in a Behavioral Finance Framework

Paul De Grauwe

Marianna Grimaldi

Princeton University Press

Princeton and Oxford

Copyright © 2006 by Princeton University Press

Published by Princeton University Press,
41 William Street, Princeton, New Jersey 08540

In the United Kingdom: Princeton University Press,
3 Market Place, Woodstock, Oxfordshire OX20 1SY

ISBN-13: 978-0-691-12163-X
ISBN-10: 0-691-12163-X
Library of Congress Control Number: 2006920668

A catalogue record for this book is available from the British Library

This book has been composed in Times and typeset by T&T Productions Ltd, London
Printed on acid-free paper ⊗
www.pup.princeton.edu

Printed in the United States of America

10 9 8 7 6 5 4 3 2 1

Contents

Preface

The study of exchange rates has undergone large fluctuations, very much like the exchange rates themselves. During the 1970s, when the exchange rates of the major currencies were made flexible, exchange rate economics became a booming field of research. The best and the brightest were attracted, and major advances were made in our understanding of the determinants of the exchange rate. Or so we thought. In the early 1980s, Meese and Rogoff showed conclusively that our cherished models from the 1970s could not stand the test of empirical verification. The publication of Meese and Rogoff's empirical analysis produced a crash in exchange rate economics. For the next ten years economists shunned the field. Theoretical analysis of exchange rates became unpopular.

The 1990s saw a renaissance of the field. Several factors contributed to this renewed interest. First, macroeconomic analysis became gripped by the microfoundation school, i.e., the desire to firmly base all macroeconomic modeling on the hypothesis of rational agents who continuously optimize their utility in an intertemporal framework. This also led to a rewriting of open-economy macroeconomics, including exchange rate economics. This rewriting, which was initiated by Obstfeld and Rogoff, became hugely popular in the academic community. It is no exaggeration to say that it took over the whole of macroeconomics, relegating to the dustbin macroeconomic models that did not explicitly start from the paradigm of the optimizing individual agent. The troublesome aspect of this development is that, while great effort was exerted to refine the theoretical models, there was a conspicuous absence of similar efforts to test the empirical relevance of these models. The result was that a large theoretical literature developed that became increasingly dissociated from economic reality.

A second factor boosting the popularity of exchange rate economics originated from empirical analysis of the exchange markets. As in other asset markets, economists detected an increasing number of empirical puzzles in the foreign exchange markets, i.e., empirical regularities that could not be explained by the rational-expectations–efficient-market model. This led to different directions in theoretical research. One was led by Evans and Lyons, who stressed the need to incorporate the microstructure of the exchange markets, i.e., the institutional detail that surrounds agents when they make decisions to buy or sell foreign currencies. This analysis was very useful, especially for our understanding of the short-term behavior of the exchange rates.

The mounting evidence of empirical anomalies in the asset markets led to an increasing popularity of theories that incorporate insights from psychology and brain research in economic analysis. Influenced by the research of Kahneman, Tversky, Thaler, and others, a whole new field emerged. This new field was commonly labeled "behavioral finance." It stressed that, when confronted with risk, agents do not conform to some of the postulates of the rational agent paradigm. In addition, when these agents are confronted with complex information problems, they tend to use simple behavioral rules. All this led to a burgeoning literature analyzing the stock markets.

Surprisingly, relatively few spillovers of this behavioral finance literature are to be found in exchange rate economics. The aim of this book is to bridge this gap, and to model the foreign exchange market using some notions from behavioral finance. In particular, we will introduce the idea that agents who are confronted with complex information will use simple rules to guide their behavior, putting these rules to a fitness test *ex post*. We will use this paradigm of "bounded rationality" in a consistent way to model the exchange market. As will be seen, such a paradigm leads to a surprisingly complex and realistic dynamics of the exchange rates.

We started the research underlying this book in 2000. The period of five years since then has been one of intense research and exciting discoveries. It has also been a period of intense communication and countless seminars and conferences. This communication has been extremely rewarding, helping us to sharpen our ideas. A great number of people have helped us along the road to the finished book you are holding. Here are some of them: Michel Beine, Volker Bohm, Yin-Wong Cheung, Vincenzo Costa, Casper de Vries, Hans Dewachter, Roberto Dieci, Marc Flandreau, Cars Hommes, Tor Jacobson, Philip Lane, Anna Lindahl, Thomas Lux, Richard Lyons, Marco Lyrio, Agnieszka Markiewicz, Ronald McDonald, Patrick Minford, Michael Moore, Yvonne Neese, Assaf Razin, Piet Sercu, Peter Sinclair, Jan Tuinstra, Jurgen von Hagen, and Peter Westaway. We are very grateful to them, for the support, insights, and the criticism we received. We owe a special word of thanks to Roberto Dieci, with whom we have collaborated intensely and who advised us on how to solve the more difficult mathematical problems (see Sections 2.4, 2.7, and 3.4.1). We also thank our colleagues at the Department of Economics of the University of Leuven and at the Sveriges Riksbank, respectively, for the many discussions that very often led to new ideas. Finally, Marianna Grimaldi is grateful to her husband, Marten Blix, for both his professional advice and his unyielding support.

The Exchange Rate in a
Behavioral Finance Framework

1
The Need for a New Paradigm

1.1 The Rational Representative Agent Paradigm

Since the start of the rational-expectations revolution in the mid 1970s, macroeconomic analysis has been dominated by the assumption of the rational representative agent. This assumption has now become the main building block of macroeconomic modeling, so much so that macroeconomic models without a microfoundation based on the rationality assumption are simply no longer taken seriously.

The main ingredients of the rational representative agent model are well-known. First, the representative agent is assumed to continuously maximize his utility in an intertemporal framework. Second, the forecasts made by this agent are rational in the sense that they take all available information into account, including the information embedded in the structure of the model. This implies that agents do not make systematic errors in forecasting future variables. The great attractiveness of the rational-expectations model is that it imposes consistency between the agent's forecasts (the subjective probability distribution of future variables) and the forecasts generated by the model (the objective probability). Third, the model implies that markets are efficient, i.e., asset prices (including the exchange rate that will be the focus of our analysis in this book) reflect all relevant information about the fundamental variables that determine the value of the asset. The mechanism that ensures efficiency can be described as follows: when rational agents value a particular asset, they compute the fundamental value of that asset and price it accordingly. If they obtain new information, they will immediately incorporate that information in their valuation of the asset. Failure to arbitrage on that new information would imply that they leave profit opportunities unexploited. Rational agents will not do this.[1]

The efficient-market implication of the model is important because it generates a number of predictions that can be tested empirically. The main empirical prediction of the rational representative agent model is that changes in the price of an asset must reflect unexpected changes (news) of the fundamental variables. The corollary of

---

[1] The foundations of the efficient-market theory were laid long ago by the French mathematician Bachelier (1900). It was rediscovered by Samuelson, and popularized by Friedman (1953) and Fama (1965, 1970). Since then it has formed the cornerstone of asset pricing and financial theory.

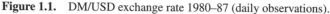

Figure 1.1. DM/USD exchange rate 1980–87 (daily observations).

this prediction is that when there is no news about the underlying fundamentals the price cannot change. Thus, only if the fundamentals change unexpectedly should one observe movements in the asset price.[2]

There is no doubt that the rational-expectations–efficient-market (REEM) model is an elegant intellectual construction that continues to exert a strong attraction to many economists enamored by the beauty of its logical consistency.

1.2 Cracks in the REEM Construction

A scientific theory, unlike religious belief or works of art, should not be judged by its elegance but by its capacity to withstand empirical testing. It is now increasingly recognized that the main empirical predictions of the REEM model have not been borne out by the facts.

A major shock to the theory came when spectacular bubbles and crashes occurred both in the stock markets and in the foreign exchange markets.[3] We show two episodes of such bubbles and crashes in the foreign exchange market. Figure 1.1 shows the DM/USD exchange rate during the period 1980–87. We observe that during the first half of the 1980s the dollar experienced a strong upward movement, so that by 1985 it had doubled in value against the German mark. In 1985 the crash

---

[2] Note that efficient-market theory says only that current exchange rate changes are related to unpredicted current changes in the fundamentals (news). The theory does not imply that exchange rate changes are related to observed changes in the fundamentals. The part of the observed current changes in the fundamentals that were predicted will not lead to changes in the current exchange rate.

[3] See Shiller (1989) for an analysis of the stock market crash of 1987. In 2000 Shiller predicted that the stock market bubble of the late 1990s would crash (Shiller 2000).

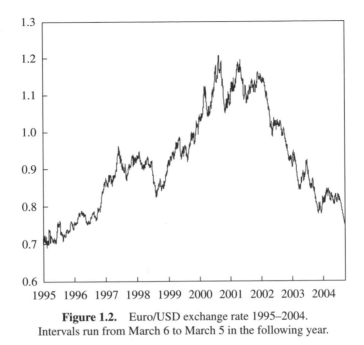

Figure 1.2. Euro/USD exchange rate 1995–2004.
Intervals run from March 6 to March 5 in the following year.

came, and in the following two years the dollar halved in value again against the mark. Something similar occurred during the period 1996–2004. Figure 1.2 shows the euro/USD rate during that period.[4] From 1996 to 2001 the dollar increased by more than 70% against the euro (DM). In 2001 it started a spectacular decline, such that by the end of 2004 it was at approximately the same level as it was at the start of the bubble. Thus, it appears that, since the start of flexible exchange rates in 1973, the dollar has been involved in two major bubbles and crashes, each of which has lasted eight to nine years. To put it another way, since 1973 the dollar was caught by a bubble-and-crash dynamics for about half of the time.

Defenders of the REEM model will of course have difficulty in accepting this bubble-and-crash interpretation of the dollar exchange rate movements.[5] They will typically argue that these movements can be explained by a series of fundamental shocks. For example, it can be argued that the upward movement of the dollar during the period 1980–85 was due to a series of positive shocks in U.S. fundamentals, to be followed after 1985 by a series of negative news about U.S. fundamentals for two years. A similar interpretation of the dollar movements could be given during the period 1996–2004. The trouble with this interpretation is that there was simply not enough positive news to account for the long upward movements. Similarly,

---

[4] Note that, prior to 1999, the euro did not exist. We used the DM/dollar rate from 1996 to 1998, converting the DM into euro at the official conversion rate used on December 31, 1998, when the euro was launched.

[5] See Garber (2000) in the context of famous bubbles in history.

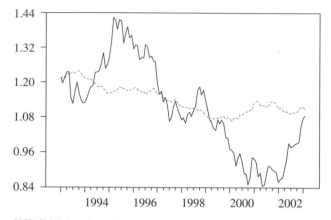

Figure 1.3. USD/DM (euro) exchange rate, market and fundamental, 1993–2003. Dashed gray line denotes fundamental rate; solid black line denotes US/DM (euro) exchange rate. (Source: Ehrmann and Fratzscher (2005).)

there was not enough negative news to explain the crashes afterward (see Frankel and Froot 1986, 1990).

The lack of sufficient news in the fundamentals to explain the wide swings of the exchange rates is made very visible in a recent study of Ehrmann and Fratzscher (2005). These authors looked carefully at a whole series of fundamental variables (inflation differentials, current accounts, output growth) in the United States and in the Eurozone and computed an index of news in these fundamentals. We show the result of their calculation in Figure 1.3, together with the USD/euro rate during the period 1993–2003.[6] It is striking to find that there is very little movement in the news variable, while the exchange rate is moving wildly around this news variable. In addition, quite often the exchange rate moves in the opposite direction to that expected if it were driven by fundamental news. For example, it can be seen from Figure 1.3 that during the period 1999–2001 the news about the euro was relatively more favorable than the news about the dollar (see De Grauwe (2000) for additional evidence), and yet the euro declined spectacularly against the dollar.

This lack of correlation between news in the fundamentals and the exchange rate movements has been documented in many other studies. For example, using high-frequency data, Goodhart (1989) and Goodhart and Figliuoli (1991) found that most of the time the exchange rate moves when there is no observable news in the fundamental economic variables. This result was also confirmed by Faust et al. (2002). Thus, the empirical evidence that we now have is that the exchange rate movements are very much disconnected from movements in the fundamentals. This finding for the foreign exchange market is consistent with similar findings in

---

[6] Note that the exchange rate in this figure is defined as the inverse of the exchange rate in Figures 1.1 and 1.2.

the stock markets (see Cutler et al. 1988; Shiller 1989; Shleifer 2000). It has led Obstfeld and Rogoff to identify this "disconnect puzzle" as the major unexplained empirical regularity about the exchange rates (Obstfeld and Rogoff 1996).

One possible rationalization of the large cyclical movements of the exchange rate around its fundamental could be found in the celebrated Dornbusch (1976) model. This model, which continues to be very popular in the classroom, incorporates the efficient-market hypothesis but adds some rigidities in the prices of goods.[7] As a result, it produces the overshooting phenomenon, i.e., the exchange rate overreacts to news in the fundamentals (it overshoots) and then moves back over time to its fundamental value. The Dornbusch model has sometimes been seen as the model that rescues the efficient-market model because it shows that temporary movements away from the fundamental need not imply that markets are inefficient. The trouble with this rescue operation is that the dynamics of the Dornbusch model does not conform with the dynamics observed in the foreign exchange market. The Dornbusch model predicts that news in the fundamentals leads to an instantaneous jump in the exchange rate and a slow movement back to the fundamental afterwards. But this is not what we observe in reality. When the exchange rate is involved in a bubble and crash, it appears that the bubble phase is quite long, while the crash is typically shorter. This is exactly the opposite of the dynamics in the Dornbusch model. In addition, in order for the Dornbusch model to explain the bubbles of 1980–85 and of 1996–2001 one would need a long series of positive news in the dollar fundamentals, each of which leads to positive jumps in the exchange rate. As we showed above, there were simply not enough positive shocks in the fundamentals to do the trick. On one occasion, i.e., during the period 1999–2001, the exchange rate movements were even going in a direction opposite to the news.

Other empirical anomalies have been discovered that invalidate the REEM model. We will discuss these anomalies in greater detail in this book. Here we mention the phenomenon of volatility clustering, i.e., it has been found that the volatility of the exchange rate is autocorrelated. This means that there are tranquil and turbulent periods. These periods of tranquillity and turbulence alternate in an unpredictable fashion. We show some descriptive evidence of this in Figure 1.4, which presents the daily changes (the returns) in the DM/USD rate during the period 1986–95. It can clearly be seen that periods of small and large changes in the exchange rate tend to cluster. If one adheres to the REEM model, the only way one can explain this volatility clustering is to assume that the volatility in the news about fundamental variables is clustered, so that the volatility clustering in the exchange rate just reflects volatility clustering in the news. Explaining volatility clustering in the exchange rate by volatility clustering in the news, however, is a "Deus ex machina" explanation that shifts the need to explain these phenomena to a higher

---

[7] A well-known empirical implementation of the Dornbusch model is Frankel (1979).

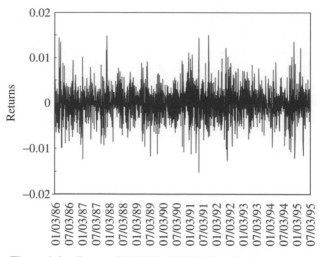

Figure 1.4.   Returns DM/USD (1986–95) daily observations.

level. In other words, the REEM model has no explanation for the widespread empirical observation that the volatility of asset prices, including the exchange rate, tends to be clustered.

Figure 1.4 reveals another empirical phenomenon observed in the exchange rate data. This is that the returns[8] are not normally distributed.[9] We can see from Figure 1.4 that there were quite often daily changes in the DM/USD rate that are several times the standard deviation during the sample period (1986–95). We observe that at three occasions the daily change was 0.015 or more, which is five times the standard deviation of 0.0029. Such a large change has a chance of occurring only once every 7000 years, if the returns are normally distributed. The fact that we find three such large changes during a sample period of ten years rules out the possibility that these returns are normally distributed. In order to show the contrast with normally distributed returns, we present a series of artificially generated returns that are normally distributed in Figure 1.5. The contrast between these normally distributed returns and observed exchange rate returns is striking.[10]

The evidence that the exchange rate returns are not normally distributed leads to a similar problem for the REEM model. In order to explain the nonnormality of exchange rate changes, the news in the fundamentals must be nonnormally distributed. As in the previous case, this interpretation shifts the need to explain the

---

[8] These are defined as the first differences of the logarithm of the exchange rate.

[9] Mandelbrot (1963) was the first to notice this phenomenon in the commodity markets. It has been found in many other asset markets.

[10] In Chapter 8 we will subject the return series to more rigorous tests to detect whether they are normally distributed. It will be shown that, typically, the observed exchange rate changes are not normally distributed. It should be stressed that this phenomenon has been observed in other financial markets. See Mandelbrot (1963), who was one of the first to analyze this phenomenon.

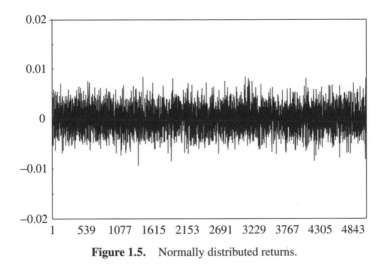

Figure 1.5. Normally distributed returns.

phenomenon to another level. In other words, the REEM model has no explanation for the widely observed fact that returns are not normally distributed,[11] and has to rely on a "Deus ex machina" explanation.[12]

The reaction of economists to the accumulating evidence against the REEM model has gone in two directions. One reaction has been to invoke technical reasons why the empirical evidence is unfavorable for the REEM model. For example, tests of the existence of bubbles and crashes and of a disconnect puzzle have often been dismissed by arguing that these tests are based on a misspecification of the underlying model of the fundamental variables. This criticism, however, has become less and less credible, as researchers have specified many different models producing similar results, i.e., that asset prices and exchange rates in particular are only loosely related to underlying fundamentals. Quite paradoxically, the increasing empirical evidence against the REEM model has led to retrenchment into a more rigorous microfoundation of macroeconomic models (see Obstfeld and Rogoff (1996), who have done this very systematically in open-economy macroeconomics). This

---

[11] It could be argued that the overshooting feature of the Dornbusch model can explain the nonnormality of the returns. We have argued, however, that this model fails to account for another prediction of the Efficient Market Hypothesis model, i.e., that the exchange rate is dissociated from its fundamental so often. In addition, the Dornbusch overshooting feature that can be invoked to account for the nonnormality of the returns has its origin in an assumption of market imperfection in the *goods* market (price rigidity). In this sense it is not an explanation that finds its origin in the workings of the financial markets. Similar explanations have been provided recently in the context of microfounded open-economy macromodels. For example, Moore and Roche (2005) assume habit formation by consumers in a microfounded open-economy macromodel. Unsurprisingly, since such an assumption introduces a rigidity in the goods market, the nominal exchange rate is forced to jump when shocks occur in the fundamental.

[12] Note that we do not claim that the REEM model implies that returns have to be normally distributed. What we claim is that the REEM model has no good explanation for the widespread empirical evidence that returns are not normal.

retrenchment into theoretical analysis has as yet led to few empirical propositions that can be refuted by the data.

The second reaction to the empirical failure of the REEM model has been to look for alternative modeling approaches. This reaction has been greatly stimulated by the emergence of a new branch of economic thinking introduced first by Simon (1957) and later by Kahneman and Tversky, Thaler, Shleifer, and others. In the next section we summarize the main ideas behind this school of thought that is sometimes called "behavioral economics" and, when applied to financial markets, "behavioral finance."[13]

1.3   Behavioral Finance: A Quick Survey

The starting point of this school of thought is the large body of evidence that has accumulated over time indicating that individuals do not behave in the way described by the rational agent paradigm. Many anomalies have been found by different researchers. Pathbreaking research was done by Kahneman and Tversky. (For a nice survey of this research the reader is referred to the Nobel lecture of Kahneman (2002).) We mention just a few of these anomalies here. The first one is called "framing" (Tversky and Kahneman 1981). One of the major tenets of the rational agent model is that the individual's preferences are not affected by the particular way a choice is presented. However, it appears that agents' preferences are very much influenced by the way a choice is "framed." A famous example of such a framing effect is the Asian disease problem, which shows how the way a choice is formulated leads agents to choose differently. In an appendix (see Section 1.5) we discuss this Asian disease framing effect in greater detail.

A second anomaly has also been researched thoroughly by Kahneman and Tversky. This anomaly challenges the expected utility theory that is at the center of the REEM model. This theory was first formulated by the great mathematician Bernoulli in 1738. It assumes that rational agents who maximize the utility of their wealth only take into account the utility of their final asset position. Their initial wealth position does not affect the value they attach to that final asset position. Kahneman and Tversky found that this assumption is rejected by agents' behavior. This was found in both experimental and observational studies (Kahneman and Tversky 2000). It appears from these studies that agents' evaluation of their final asset position does depend on the initial wealth. This finding led Kahneman and Tversky to propose another theory of choice under uncertainty. In this theory, called prospect theory, the carriers of utility are gains and losses (changes in wealth rather than states of wealth). One of the important insights of this theory is that agents

---

[13] There are other modeling approaches that have been pursued. One is the development of models that take into account the microstructure of the markets (see Evans and Lyons 1999; Lyons 2001). Another modeling approach that departs from rational expectations has been pioneered by Evans and Honkapohja (2001) in which agents learn about the underlying model using statistical tools.

attach a different utility value to gains and losses (Kahneman and Tversky 1973). We will use and further expand this theory in Chapter 5.

Other anomalies that challenge the rational agent model were discovered (see Thaler (1994) for spirited discussions of many anomalies). We just mention "anchoring" effects here, whereby agents who do not fully understand the world in which they live are highly selective in the way they use information and concentrate on the information they understand or the information that is fresh in their minds. This anchoring effect explains why agents often extrapolate recent movements in prices.

These empirical anomalies lead to the conclusion that agents do not conform to the rational agent model. But let us pause here for a while. The view that many agents do not behave rationally (in the sense in which rationality is defined in the REEM model) does not necessarily invalidate that model. Proponents of the REEM model have countered that, for markets to be efficient, it is sufficient that some agents are rational.[14] To see this, suppose that agents are driven by anchoring effects and are using extrapolative forecasting rules. This will drive the exchange rate away from its fundamental value. The rational agents will recognize that there are profit opportunities to exploit. They will therefore be willing to arbitrage, i.e., to sell the currency when it is overpriced, and to buy it when it is underpriced. This arbitrage activity by the rational agents then ensures that the exchange rate always reflects its fundamental value. Thus, even if the world is populated by a lot of irrational agents, it will be sufficient to have a few rational agents for the markets to conform to the REEM predictions. The market outcome will make it appear as if all agents are rational, while only a few actually are. This has led to the idea that the rational agent assumption is an "as-if" proposition.

The trouble with this criticism of behavioral finance theory is that it is not borne out by the empirical evidence discussed in the previous section. The empirical rejection of market efficiency can now be interpreted in two ways. It means that either the rational agent as defined in the REEM model simply does not exist, or there exist such superior individuals but for some reason they are prevented from exploiting the profit opportunities created by the behavior of the irrational agents. In this second interpretation it is as if these rational agents do not exist.[15] Whichever interpretation is correct, we have to look for a modeling approach other than that based on the rational agent model. This alternative approach will have to take into account the departures from rationality that have been documented in the behavioral finance literature.

---

[14] The most eloquent statement of this view is to be found in Friedman (1953).

[15] In Chapter 5 we return to this issue, for it could be that under certain conditions these rational agents are prevented from exploiting profit opportunities created by irrational agents, while under other conditions they may be able to exploit these opportunities. Identifying these conditions will be the subject of Chapter 5.

1.4   The Broad Outlines of an Alternative Approach

In this book we will use the main ideas that have been developed in the framework of the behavioral finance approach, and we will try to formalize it. The broad outlines of this approach can be summarized as follows. First, agents experience a cognitive problem when they try to understand the world in which they live. They find it difficult to collect and to process the complex information with which they are confronted. As a result, they use simple rules ("heuristics") to guide their behavior. They do this not because they are stupid or irrational, but rather because the complexity of the world is overwhelming, making it pointless to try to understand it completely. Thus, the agent we will assume is very different from the rational agent assumed to populate our economic models who is able to comprehend the full complexity of the world, i.e., who has a brain that can contain and process the information embedded in the world in its full complexity. This is rather an unreasonable assumption. It is tantamount to assuming that humans are godlike creatures.

The second component in our modeling approach will be to discipline the behavior of our agents, i.e., to impose some criterion that allows some behavioral rules to survive and others to disappear. Thus, in this second stage we will assume that agents regularly evaluate the behavioral rules they use. We will do this by assuming that agents compare the utility of the rule they are using with the utility of other rules and that they are willing to switch to another rule if it turns out that this other rule gives them more satisfaction. Thus, behavioral rules will have to pass some fitness criterion. In this sense, one can say that rationality is introduced in the model. Rationality should, however, be understood in a different way than in the REEM model. It is a selection mechanism based on trial and error, in which imperfectly informed agents decide about the best behavior based on their past experiences. We claim that this trial-and-error strategy is the best possible one in a very uncertain world.

This two-stage modeling approach can also be interpreted in the context of modern theories about how human brains function. It is now increasingly recognized by psychologists and brain scientists that there are two (interacting) cognitive processes at work in our brains. These have been called system 1 and system 2 by Stanovitch and West (2000) (see also Epstein 1994; Hammond 1996; Kahneman 2002; Sloman 2002; Damasio 2003). System 1 is based on intuition and emotion; it is associative and difficult to control, or even to express verbally; it is automatic, fast, and effortless. System 2 is based on explicit reasoning; it is slow, effortful, and potentially rule-governed. It also functions as a monitoring process evaluating the quality of the mental processes as a whole (Gilbert 2002; Stanovitch and West 2002). The structure we impose on the decision process of our agents is similar to this dual structure existing in our brains, albeit in a very simplified version.

The two-stage approach proposed here comes closer to a correct microfoundation of macroeconomics. Conversely, based on what we now know about the functioning of the brain, we can conclude that the microfoundation of macroeconomics that is present in the REEM model has no scientific basis. Humans certainly do not make decisions using the process of reasoning (system 2) in isolation. The emotional process is of crucial importance for allowing the reasoning process to lead to rational decisions (see Damasio (2003) for an elegant analysis of the interaction of emotional and rational processes).

1.5   Appendix: The Asian Disease Problem

This problem vividly illustrates how the framing of a problem has an influence on decisions of individual agents.

Suppose there is an outbreak of an influenza epidemic coming from Asia. Scientists predict that if nothing is done 10 000 people will die in the United States. They have, however, devised two different programs to reduce the number of victims. The members of Congress have to decide which program to adopt. If the first program is adopted, 4000 people will be saved; if the second program is adopted, there is a 40% probability that 10 000 people will be saved and a 60% probability that nobody will be saved.

When respondents are asked which of the two programs they prefer a large majority typically chooses the first program. This implies that most respondents are risk averse.

But let us now assume that the two programs are "framed" differently and that they are presented in the following way: if the first program is adopted, 6000 people will die; if the second program is adopted, there is a 40% probability that nobody will die, and a 60% probability that 10 000 people will die.

When this time respondents are asked which of the two programs they prefer a large majority chooses for the second program. This suggests that most respondents are risk seekers. It should be clear, however, that the two decision problems are identical. Only the way the programs are presented (are framed) differs. The framing of the problem appears to have a significant effect on the decisions.

This framing problem has been found to exist even when the agents who have to decide are highly trained professionals. There is a famous framing effect involving experienced physicians who had to decide between surgery or radiation therapy and who decided very differently depending on whether the outcome statistics were formulated in terms of mortality rates or survival rates (see Kahneman 2002).

2

A Simple Behavioral Finance Model
of the Exchange Rate

2.1 Introduction

In the previous chapter we argued that the rational-expectations–efficient-market (REEM) model of the foreign exchange market does not do well in empirical testing. We need a different model. In this chapter we present such an alternative. We will proceed in two steps. In the first step, we present a model of the exchange rate with a minimal structure. This will be done in the present chapter. It will enable us to concentrate on the information rules agents use when they make forecasts. In a second step (Chapter 3) we will add more structure to the exchange rate model and analyze the interaction with the information rules that agents use.

How to model the way agents form their expectations? As pointed out in the previous chapter, we should start from the observation that the information is so complex that no single agent is capable of fully understanding it. In fact, the complexity of the world surpasses by far the capacity of any individual's brain to store and process this information. An individual can only store and process a tiny part of the information that is relevant to him.

Agents are aware of the exceptional complexity of the world in which they live. They will therefore follow a different forecasting strategy than the one the rational-expectations model assumes, in which individual agents can store and process all relevant information in their brain. Instead, the strategy they follow consists of two steps. First, agents apply simple forecasting rules, often referred to as "heuristic rules" in the psychological literature. By necessity, they only use small parts of the full (but too complex) information set available in the world.

Second, although agents have only a limited capacity for understanding the world, they are not fools. They want to find out whether the rule they use is a good one. The way they do this is by checking *ex post* how profitable the rule is compared with other available rules. If they find out that the rule is less profitable, they will consider switching to the better rule. If not, they stick to their initial rule.

This trial-and-error strategy is a very basic one. We find it in many different areas of human behavior. For example, most technological developments are the result of trial-and-error strategies, in which agents try some innovation. If this turns out to be profitable, it is kept. If not, it is discarded. Such trial-and-error strategies, in fact, are based on deep-seated evolutionary rules that are found in nature quite generally. It seems that trial-and-error strategies are favored by individual agents who face an environment that they do not understand well and who are trying to learn its complexity. In this sense, trial and error is a learning strategy.[1]

As stressed in the previous chapter, this way of modeling information processing is very different from the rational-expectations informational assumption, in which an individual agent is capable of understanding the complex underlying economic structure and uses that information *ex ante*, i.e., prior to making a decision. In the world we model here, agents are "boundedly rational," i.e., we assume that because individual agents have a limited ability to process and to analyze the available information, they are forced to select simple forecasting rules. This is the "bounded" part in their rationality. These agents, however, exhibit rational behavior in the sense that they check the profitability of these rules *ex post* and are willing to switch to the more profitable rule. Thus, they use the best possible strategies within the confines of their limited ability to analyze and to use the available information. This assumption of bounded rationality was first proposed by Simon (1957). It was later taken over and further developed by researchers of the "behavioral economics" school, which merges insights obtained from psychology with economic analysis. Pathbreaking research was done by Tversky and Kahneman (see, for example, Tversky and Kahneman (1981) and Kahneman (2002) for an overview of the major insights). This research has been very influential in the development of a new school in finance, the so-called "behavioral finance" school. Representative authors are Thaler (1994), Shleifer (2000), Barberis and Thaler (2002), and Johansen and Sornette (1999).

2.2   The Model

In this chapter we develop a simple exchange rate model using these insights. We start by defining the fundamental exchange rate. This is the exchange rate that is consistent with equilibrium in the real part of the economy. In a very simple model this could be the purchasing-power-parity (PPP) value of the exchange rate. In more elaborate models (e.g., the monetary model, or the model of Williamson (1994), this fundamental exchange rate could be determined by the interaction of more variables than the price levels. The modeling of the fundamental exchange rate is outside the scope of this chapter. We will return to this when we add structure to the model. Here we assume that the fundamental exchange rate, s_t^*, is exogenous

---

[1] Recently economists have introduced into their models learning strategies based on the idea that agents use econometric tools to learn about the underlying model, as if they are econometricians (Sargent 1993; Evans and Honkapohja 2001).

and that it behaves like a random walk without drift. This implies that

$$s_t^* = s_{t-1}^* + \varepsilon_t, \tag{2.1}$$

where ε_t is a white-noise error term.

We now model the way agents make forecasts about the future exchange rates. We assume that agents can use two types of simple forecasting rule.[2] One type of forecasting rule will be called "fundamentalist," and agents who use such a rule will be called fundamentalists for short. (This does not mean that these agents have an inherent "fundamentalist" nature, for as we will see they will happily switch to the other rule if the latter is more profitable.) The second type of rule will be called "chartist," and the agents who use this rule will be labeled chartists. We will also use the term "technical analysts" for the latter.

The fundamentalists are assumed to know the fundamental exchange rate. They compare the present market exchange rate with the fundamental rate and they forecast the future market rate to move towards the fundamental rate. In this sense they follow a negative feedback rule. This leads us to specify the following rule for the fundamentalists:

$$E_{f,t}(\Delta s_{t+1}) = -\psi(s_t - s_t^*), \tag{2.2}$$

where $E_{f,t}$ is the forecast made in period t by the fundamentalists using information up to time t, s_t is the exchange rate in period t, Δs_t is the change in the exchange rate, and $\psi > 0$ measures the speed with which the fundamentalists expect the exchange rate to return to the fundamental one. This parameter is presumably related to the speed of adjustment of prices in the goods market, but we do not specify its precise link with this speed of adjustment.[3] Note that throughout this book we define the exchange rate to be the price of the foreign currency in units of the domestic currency. Thus, an increase in the exchange rate is equivalent to a depreciation of the domestic currency (an appreciation of the foreign currency).

The chartists are assumed to follow a positive feedback rule, i.e., they extrapolate past movements of the exchange rate into the future. We will use the simplest possible hypothesis here: we assume that chartists extrapolate only last period's exchange rate into the future. Thus, we assume them to have a very short memory. In Section 2.10 we will return to the importance of memory and assume in that case that chartists have a longer memory. The chartists' forecast is written as

$$E_{c,t}(\Delta s_{t+1}) = \beta \Delta s_t, \tag{2.3}$$

where $E_{c,t}$ is the forecast made by the chartists using information up to time t, and β is the coefficient expressing the degree with which chartists extrapolate the

---

[2] Frankel and Froot (1986, 1990) were the first to propose such a modeling approach for the exchange market.

[3] In a rational-expectations model agents are assumed to know this speed of adjustment and a precise link can be made. This is the case in the Dornbusch model, for example.

past change in the exchange rate; we assume that $0 < \beta < 1$ to ensure dynamic stability.[4]

Note that the chartists do not take into account information concerning the fundamental exchange rate. In this sense they can be considered to be noise traders (see De Long et al. 1990).

The reader may ask why we introduce such a rule here. There is a lot of empirical evidence that chartism (technical analysis) is used widely to make forecasts (see Taylor and Allen (1992), Menkhoff (1997, 1998), Cheung and Chinn (2001), Cheung et al. (2004), and Schulmeister (2005), who document that technical analysis is in fact the main forecasting method used in the main foreign exchange markets). The rules used by technical analysts are generally more complicated than the simple one we postulate in equation (2.3).[5] As we will show later, the use of a very simple forecasting rule can create great complexity in the dynamics of the foreign exchange market. If we were to introduce complex forecasting rules here, there would be little surprise in the finding that the dynamics of the exchange rate is complex.

Economists have generally been scornful about chartism and technical analysis. It does not make sense to extrapolate the past exchange rate movements, without taking into account other bits of information. Yet the evidence is that many agents do just that. Does this mean that these people are crazy? Not necessarily. We will have to analyze whether such "crazy" rules are profitable. If they are, and if they remain profitable for long periods of time, then maybe there is something in these rules that makes them particularly fit to survive in a turbulent environment that escapes the comprehension of individual agents. If that is the case, there is no reason to dismiss these rules because they do not follow the dogma of rational behavior as economists usually define it.

The next step in our analysis is therefore to specify how agents evaluate the usefulness of these two forecasting rules. The general idea that we will follow is that agents use one of the two rules, compare their profitability *ex post*, and then decide whether to keep the rule or switch to the other one.

In order to implement this idea we use a fitness criterion which is based on discrete-choice theory in the spirit of Brock and Hommes (1997, 1998).[6] This means

---

[4] Recently, heterogeneity of agents has also been introduced in rational-expectations models (see, for example, Bacchetta and van Wincoop 2003). The implication of rational expectations in models with heterogeneous agents is that it creates "infinite regress," i.e., the exchange rate depends on the expectations of other agents' expectations, which depend in turn on the expectations of the expectations of other agents' expectations, and so on, ad infinitum. This leads to intractable mathematical problems except under very restrictive simplifying assumptions. Although this approach is intellectually satisfying, it is unclear that it is a good representation of what agents do in the exchange market. It requires these agents to solve a mathematical problem to which mathematicians have as yet been unable to give a general solution. This seems to us as imposing too large an informational burden on individual agents.

[5] For more information on technical analysis and chartism see James (2003).

[6] This specification is often applied in discrete-choice models. For an application in the markets for differentiated goods, see Anderson et al. (1992). There are other ways to specify a rule that governs the

that the fractions of the total population of agents using chartist and fundamentalist rules are a function of the relative (risk-adjusted) profitability of these rules. We specify this procedure as

$$w_{f,t} = \frac{\exp(\gamma \pi'_{f,t})}{\exp(\gamma \pi'_{f,t}) + \exp(\gamma \pi'_{c,t})}, \qquad (2.4)$$

$$w_{c,t} = \frac{\exp(\gamma \pi'_{c,t})}{\exp(\gamma \pi'_{f,t}) + \exp(\gamma \pi'_{c,t})}, \qquad (2.5)$$

where $w_{f,t}$ and $w_{c,t}$ are the fractions of the population who use fundamentalist and chartist forecasting rules, respectively. Obviously, $w_{f,t} + w_{c,t} = 1$. The variables $\pi'_{f,t}$ and $\pi'_{c,t}$ are the (risk-adjusted) profits realized by the use of chartists' and fundamentalists' forecasting rules in period t, i.e., $\pi'_{f,t} = \pi_{f,t} - \mu \sigma^2_{f,t}$ and $\pi'_{c,t} = \pi_{c,t} - \mu \sigma^2_{c,t}$ and $\pi_{f,t}$ and $\pi_{c,t}$ are the profits made in forecasting, while $\sigma^2_{f,t}$ and $\sigma^2_{c,t}$ are variables expressing the risks chartists and fundamentalists incur when making forecasts. As a measure of this risk we will take the variance of the forecast errors. Finally, μ is the coefficient of risk aversion. The reader will note that this specification of the risk-adjusted profits is very much influenced by utility maximization in a mean-variance framework, in which the expected utility of an investment is positively affected by the expected return and negatively by the risk of the investment.[7] Note also that agents only take into account the last period's profits. In Section 2.10 we will relax this assumption and allow agents to remember profits (and losses) they made in the more distant past.

Equations (2.4) and (2.5) can now be interpreted as follows. When the risk-adjusted profits of the technical traders' rule increase relative to the risk-adjusted profits of the fundamentalists' rule, then the share of agents who use technical trader rules in period t increases, and vice versa. The parameter γ measures the intensity with which the technical traders and fundamentalists revise their forecasting rules. With an increasing γ, agents react strongly to the relative profitability of the rules. In the limit $\gamma \to \infty$, all agents choose the forecasting rule which proves to be more profitable. When $\gamma = 0$ agents are insensitive to the relative profitability of the rules. In the latter case the fraction of technical traders and fundamentalists is constant and equal to 0.5. Thus, γ is a measure of inertia in the decision to switch to the more profitable rule.[8]

One objection to the switching rules (2.4) and (2.5) could be that when, say, the chartist rule is the more profitable one, all agents will use that rule. In other words

---

selection of forecasting strategies. One was proposed by Kirman (1993); another was formulated by Lux and Marchesi (1999).

[7] The expression $\pi_{i,t} - \mu \sigma^2_{i,t}$ is also related to the Sharpe ratio (see also Pratt 1964).

[8] The logic of the switching rule is in the same spirit of the adaptive learning rules that are now used in game theoretic models (see, for example, Cheung and Friedman 1997; Fudenberg and Levine 1998). In these models, actions that did better in the observed past tend to increase in frequency, while actions that did worse tend to decrease in frequency.

we should set $\gamma = \infty$. The psychological literature, however, reveals that there is a "status quo bias" in decision making (see Kahneman et al. 1991). In other words, the existing psychological evidence suggests that agents find it difficult to change a decision rule they have been using for some time. They need time to do so. The way we formalize this idea is to set $0 < \gamma < \infty$.

We now go into the problem of defining with more precision the profits and the risk associated with them. We define the profits as the one-period earnings of investing \$1 in the foreign asset. More formally,

$$\pi_{i,t} = [s_t(1+r^*) - s_{t-1}(1+r)]\,\text{sgn}[(1+r^*)E^i_{t-1}(s_t) - (1+r)s_{t-1}],\quad (2.6)$$

where

$$\text{sgn}[x] = \begin{cases} 1 & \text{for } x > 0, \\ 0 & \text{for } x = 0, \\ -1 & \text{for } x < 0, \end{cases}$$

and $i = \text{c}, \text{f}$.

Thus, when agents forecast an increase in the exchange rate (the price of the foreign currency) and this increase is realized, their per-unit profit is equal to the observed increase in the exchange rate (corrected for the interest differential). If instead the exchange rate declines, they make a per-unit loss which equals this decline (because in this case they have bought foreign assets which have declined in price).

In contrast with Brock and Hommes (1997, 1998) we use a concept of profits per unit invested, and not the total profits realized by agents. We do this for two reasons. First, equations (2.4) and (2.5) select the fittest rules. They do not select agents. To make this clear, suppose that technical traders happen to have more wealth than fundamentalists, so that their total profits exceed the fundamentalists' profits despite the fact that the technical rule happens to be less profitable (per unit invested) than the fundamentalist rule. In this case, our switching rule will select the fundamentalists' rule although the agents who use this rule make less profit (because their wealth happens to be smaller) than agents using chartist rules. Second, in our definition of profits, agents must use only publicly available information, i.e., the forecasting rules and the observed exchange rate changes. They do not have to know their competitor's profits (which depend on their wealth).

Finally, we specify the risk variables in the following way. As mentioned earlier, we define the risk associated with forecasting to be the variance of the forecast error. In the logic of the short-run memory hypothesis used in this section, we assume that agents just look at the last period's squared forecast error. (In Section 2.10 we relax this assumption about the memory of agents.) Thus, we have

$$\sigma^2_{i,t} = [E^i_{t-1}(s_t) - s_t]^2. \quad (2.7)$$

In the previous sections we have specified how agents make forecasts in a bound-edly rational way. We now aggregate these forecasts to obtain the aggregate market forecast. The market forecast of the exchange rate change can be written as a weighted average of the expectations of chartists and fundamentalists, i.e.,

$$E_t \Delta s_{t+1} = -w_{f,t} \psi (s_t - s_t^*) + w_{c,t} \beta \Delta s_t, \tag{2.8}$$

where $w_{f,t}$ and $w_{c,t}$ are defined in (2.4) and (2.5).

The realized change in the market exchange rate in period $t+1$ equals the market forecast made at time t plus some white-noise errors, ϵ_{t+1}, occurring in period $t+1$ (i.e., the news that could not be predicted at time t). We obtain

$$\Delta s_{t+1} = -w_{f,t} \psi (s_t - s_t^*) + w_{c,t} \beta \Delta s_t + \epsilon_{t+1}. \tag{2.9}$$

We now have all the equations of the model, and we can start analyzing its characteristics.

2.3 Stochastic Simulation of the Model

The nonlinear structure of our model does not allow for a simple analytical solu-tion. As a result, we have to use numerical simulation methods. One drawback of this approach is that we cannot easily derive general conclusions. We will com-pensate for this drawback by presenting sensitivity analyses of the numerical solu-tions. The simulations we perform are stochastic. Stochastic shocks occur in the model because the fundamental exchange rate is driven by a random walk (see equation (2.1)) and because there is noise in the process determining the market exchange rate (see equation (2.9)). We will assume that ε_t and ϵ_t are normally dis-tributed with means equal to 0, and standard deviation equal to 0.1. (Later we will introduce a different regime in which the variance of the white-noise disturbances is increased. It will be shown that these variances are quite important.)

We present two examples of stochastic simulations that are quite typical for the kind of dynamics predicted by our model (see Figure 2.1). In Chapter 8 we will calibrate the model, i.e., we will choose the parameters of the model in such a way that it replicates the statistical features of observed exchange movements most closely. We will see that these are parameters that come very close to those we use here. Parts (a) and (b) of Figure 2.1 show the simulated market and fundamental exchange rates obtained in two different simulation runs, using the same parameter configurations. Parts (c) and (d) show the corresponding shares of the chartists.

The most striking features of these simulations are the following. First, it appears that the exchange rate is very often disconnected from the fundamental exchange rate. This means that the market exchange rate follows movements that are dissoci-ated from the fundamental rate. This is especially obvious in the first simulation run (parts (a) and (c)), where we find that the exchange rate is disconnected from the

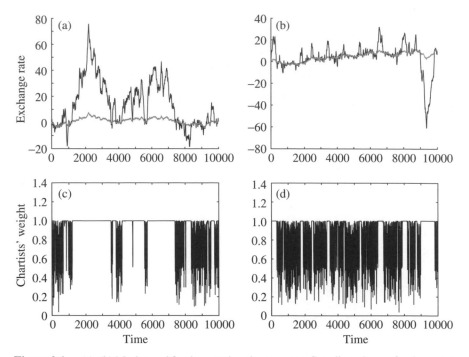

Figure 2.1. (a), (b) Market and fundamental exchange rates. Gray lines denote fundamental rate; black lines denote exchange rate. (c), (d) Weight of chartists. In all four parts, $\psi = 0.2$, $\beta = 0.9$, $\gamma = 5$.

fundamental most of the time. In parts (b) and (d) there are periods of disconnection, but these are less frequent. This leads to a second feature of these exchange rate movements. There appear to be two types of regime. In one regime the exchange rate follows the fundamental exchange rate quite closely. These "fundamental regimes" alternate with regimes in which the fundamental does not seem to play a role in determining the exchange rate. We will call these "nonfundamental regimes." We will also call the latter ones "bubble regimes." The nature of the latter can be seen in Figure 2.1(c),(d). Nonfundamental regimes are characterized by situations in which the chartists' weights are very close to 1. In contrast, fundamental regimes are those during which the chartists' weights are below 1 and are fluctuating significantly. These two regimes appear to correspond to two types of equilibrium. Thus, a fundamental regime seems to occur when the exchange rate stays within the basin of attraction of a fundamental equilibrium. In such a regime, the exchange rate movements stay very close to the fundamental exchange rate. Conversely, a nonfundamental regime seems to occur when the exchange rate moves within the basins of attraction around bubble equilibria. We will analyze the existence and the nature of these two equilibria in more detail in Sections 2.4 and 2.5. In an appendix

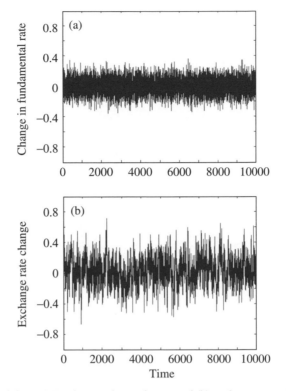

Figure 2.2. (a) Fundamental rate change and (b) exchange rate change.
$\psi = 0.2, \beta = 0.9, \gamma = 5.$

(see Section 2.14) we show the same simulations for different stochastic realizations of the fundamental variable. We find that the results are independent of these different realizations.

We also note from Figure 2.1 that fundamental and nonfundamental regimes alternate in unpredictable ways. The left-hand panels (parts (a) and (c)) show a simulation during which bubble regimes tend to dominate, while the right-hand panels (parts (b) and (d)) show a simulation during which fundamental regimes are more frequent. The two simulations, however, were run with exactly the same parameters. The only difference is the underlying stochastics of the fundamental exchange rate. We will return to this feature again and show that it has something to do with the discontinuities that characterize the border between fundamental and nonfundamental equilibria.

A third feature of Figure 2.1 is the existence of excess volatility, i.e., the exchange rate is subject to much more short-term volatility than the fundamental exchange rate. In addition, it appears that the exchange rate is occasionally subject to very large changes. We can show these features in a more precise way by plotting the one-period changes of the simulated exchange rate and of the fundamental rate that are

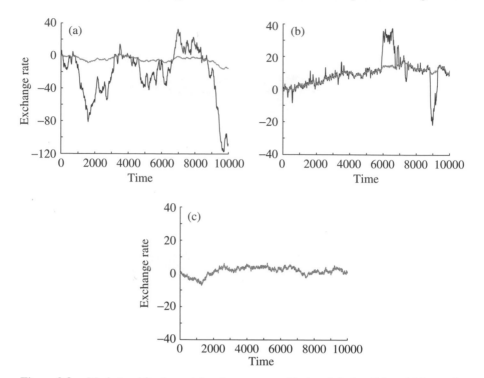

Figure 2.3. Market and fundamental exchange rates with $\psi = 0.2$, $\beta = 0.9$, and (a) $\gamma = 5$, (b) $\gamma = 3$, and (c) $\gamma = 1$. Gray lines denote fundamental rate; black lines denote exchange rate.

obtained from Figure 2.1. This is done in Figure 2.2. Panel (a) shows the one-period changes of the fundamental rate. Since the fundamental rate follows a random walk, the one-period changes are normally distributed. As a result most changes are located in a given band, and there are few large outliers. This is very different from panel (b), which shows the one-period changes of the simulated market exchange rate. These changes are larger on average but, more importantly, there are regularly very large outliers. This suggests that the changes in the market exchange rate are not normally distributed. The structure of these changes strikingly resembles real-life changes observed in the foreign exchange markets (see Figure 1.4). We will return to this feature of the exchange rate dynamics in Chapter 8, where we analyze the statistical properties of exchange rate changes in more detail. We will argue that the exchange rate dynamics simulated by our model closely mimics those observed in reality.

As mentioned earlier, the numerical solutions are sensitive to the parameter values chosen. We illustrate this sensitivity by presenting simulations assuming different parameter values. Figure 2.3 shows the results of stochastic simulations of the model for different values of γ. Remember that γ measures the sensitivity of the

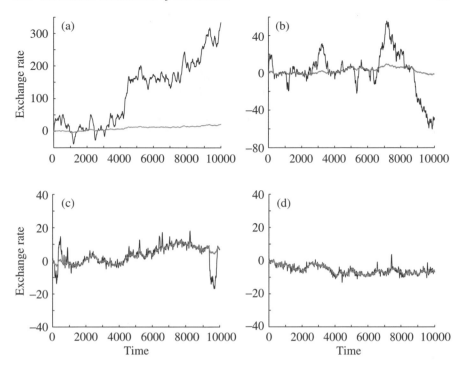

Figure 2.4. Market and fundamental exchange rates with $\psi = 0.2$, $\gamma = 5$, and (a) $\beta = 0.95$, (b) $\beta = 0.9$, (c) $\beta = 0.85$, and (d) $\beta = 0.8$. Gray lines denote fundamental rate; black lines denote exchange rate.

switching rule to risk-adjusted profits. Thus, when γ is high, agents react strongly to changing profitabilities of the forecasting rules they have been using. Conversely, when γ is small, they do not let their forecasting rules depend much on these relative profitabilities. The results shown in Figure 2.3 are quite remarkable. We find that when γ is large, the exchange rate tends to deviate strongly from the fundamental value most of the time. Thus, when γ is high the exchange rate seems to be attracted most of the time by nonfundamental equilibria. Conversely, when agents are not very sensitive to relative profitabilities (low γ) the exchange rate follows the fundamental rate closely, suggesting that it is then attracted by the fundamental equilibrium most of the time. This result is quite surprising. It implies that when agents come closer to being rational, i.e., they always select the most profitable forecasting rule, the exchange rate deviates most strongly from the fundamental. In other words, when agents are very rational the market exchange rate becomes a poor reflection of the underlying fundamental value.

Another important parameter of the model is the degree of extrapolation, β, used in chartist forecasting rules. We therefore simulated the model with different values of β. The results are shown in Figure 2.4. Unsurprisingly, we find that when β is high the exchange rate is strongly attracted by nonfundamental equilibria.

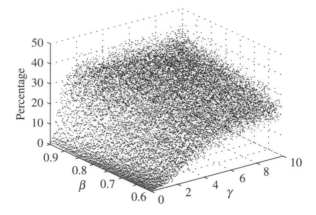

Figure 2.5.   Percentage of the time in which bubbles occur: $T = 1000$ and $\mu = 1$.

As a result, the exchange rate wanders away from its fundamental value for long periods of time. When β is small (i.e., 0.8 or less) the forces of attraction of the fundamental variable are very strong, so that the exchange rate remains very close to its fundamental value.

In order to be a little more systematic about the sensitivity of the results of the model with respect to the parameters, we performed the following experiment. We simulated the model for different values of the parameters γ and β. In each simulation of 10 000 periods, we computed the percentage of the time that the exchange rate deviated from the fundamental by more than three standard deviations of the fundamental variable during twenty consecutive periods or more. The presumption is that, if the exchange rate diverges for so long and by so much, it is attracted by a nonfundamental equilibrium. This conclusion may not be clear to the reader now, but it will become so when we have analyzed the deterministic part of the model. We show the result of this exercise in the three-dimensional Figure 2.5. On the x- and y-axes we set out the parameters γ and β, respectively. On the vertical axis we show the percentage of the time that the exchange rate was attracted by a nonfundamental equilibrium, as defined previously. Each point corresponds to one simulation of 10 000 periods for a particular combination of γ and β. We find that, when γ increases, the probability that the exchange rate is attracted by a nonfundamental equilibrium increases. The same conclusion holds for increases in β. The implication of the latter result is that, when chartists extrapolate past changes with more intensity, the exchange rate is likely to diverge from its fundamental for longer periods of time.

While our model is inherently stochastic, it will be useful to analyze the deterministic part of the model. This will enable us to better understand its structure and to identify the sources of the results presented here. We perform such an analysis in the next section.

2.4 The Steady State of the Model

This section profited a great deal from our collaboration with Roberto Dieci, who worked out the analytical characterization of the steady state. As mentioned earlier, the nonlinear structure of the model does not allow for an analytical solution. We can, however, analyze its steady-state characteristics, by stripping it from its stochastic component. An analysis of the deterministic component of the model will help us to understand the results reported in the previous section. The first step in the analysis is to eliminate the error term in (2.1). Thus, we now assume that the fundamental variable is constant. In addition, for the sake of convenience, we set the fundamental rate, $s_t^* = s^* = 0$. As a result, the exchange rate movements can be interpreted as deviations from its fundamental value.

The assumption of a constant fundamental changes the nature of the model. A confrontation of the deterministic (riskless) version of the model with the stochastic (risky) version will enable us to obtain better insights into the dynamics of the stochastic model.

We rewrite equation (2.9) for Δs_t as follows:

$$s_t = s_{t-1} - w_{f,t-1}\psi s_{t-1} + w_{c,t-1}\beta(s_{t-1} - s_{t-2}), \tag{2.10}$$

where

$$w_{f,t-1} = \frac{\exp[\gamma(\pi_{f,t-1} - \mu\sigma_{f,t-1}^2)]}{\exp[\gamma(\pi_{c,t-1} - \mu\sigma_{c,t-1}^2)] + \exp[\gamma(\pi_{f,t-1} - \mu\sigma_{f,t-1}^2)]}. \tag{2.11}$$

Equations (2.7), defining the variance terms, can also be rewritten as follows:

$$\sigma_{c,t-1}^2 = [E_{t-2}^c(s_{t-1}) - s_{t-1}]^2, \tag{2.12}$$

$$\sigma_{f,t-1}^2 = [E_{t-2}^f(s_{t-1}) - s_{t-1}]^2. \tag{2.13}$$

Using the definition of the forecasting rules (2.2) and (2.3), this yields

$$\sigma_{c,t-1}^2 = [-\beta s_{t-3} + (1+\beta)s_{t-2} - s_{t-1}]^2, \tag{2.14}$$

$$\sigma_{f,t-1}^2 = [(1-\psi)s_{t-2} - s_{t-1}]^2. \tag{2.15}$$

With suitable changes of variables it is possible to write these equations as a three-dimensional system. Set

$$u_t = s_{t-1} \quad \text{and} \quad x_t = u_{t-1} = s_{t-2}.$$

The three dynamic variables are (s_t, u_t, x_t). The state of the system at time $t-1$, i.e., $(s_{t-1}, u_{t-1}, x_{t-1})$, determines the state of the system at time t, i.e., (s_t, u_t, x_t), through the following three-dimensional dynamical system:

$$s_t = [1 + \beta - w_{f,t-1}(\psi + \beta)]u_t - (1 - w_{f,t-1})\beta x_t, \tag{2.16}$$

$$u_t = s_{t-1}, \tag{2.17}$$

$$x_t = u_{t-1}, \tag{2.18}$$

where

$$w_{f,t-1} = \frac{\exp[\gamma(\pi_{f,t-1} - \mu\sigma^2_{f,t-1})]}{\exp[\gamma(\pi_{c,t-1} - \mu\sigma^2_{c,t-1})] + \exp[\gamma(\pi_{f,t-1} - \mu\sigma^2_{f,t-1})]}, \quad (2.19)$$

$$\sigma^2_{c,t-1} = [-\beta x_{t-1} + (1+\beta)u_{t-1} - s_{t-1}]^2, \quad (2.20)$$

$$\sigma^2_{f,t-1} = [(1-\psi)u_{t-1} - s_{t-1}]^2, \quad (2.21)$$

$$\pi_{c,t-1} = (s_{t-1} - u_{t-1})\,\mathrm{sgn}[\beta(u_{t-1} - x_{t-1})], \quad (2.22)$$

$$\pi_{f,t-1} = (s_{t-1} - u_{t-1})\,\mathrm{sgn}[-\psi u_{t-1}], \quad (2.23)$$

and we have assumed that $r = r^* = 0$.

It can now be shown that the model produces two types of steady-state solution. We analyze these consecutively.

2.4.1 The Exchange Rate Equals Its Fundamental Value

Since we have normalized the fundamental exchange rate s^*_t to be 0, the fundamental solution implies that $s_t = 0$. As a result, the variance terms go to 0.

The steady state of the system is now obtained by setting

$$(s_{t-1}, u_{t-1}, x_{t-1}) = (s_t, u_t, x_t) = (\bar{s}, \bar{u}, \bar{x})$$

in the dynamical system (2.16)–(2.18).

There is a unique steady state where

$$\bar{s}, \bar{u}, \bar{x} = 0. \quad (2.24)$$

Notice also that, at the steady state,

$$\bar{w}_c = \tfrac{1}{2}, \qquad \bar{w}_f = \tfrac{1}{2}, \qquad \bar{\pi}_f = 0, \qquad \bar{\pi}_c = 0, \qquad \bar{\sigma}^2_f = 0, \qquad \bar{\sigma}^2_c = 0,$$

i.e., the steady state is characterized by the exchange rate being at its fundamental level, by zero profits and zero risk, and by fundamentalist and technical trader fractions equal to $\tfrac{1}{2}$.

2.4.2 The Exchange Rate Equals a Nonfundamental Value

The model allows for a second type of steady-state solution. This is a solution in which the exchange rate is constant and permanently different from its (constant) fundamental value. In other words, the model allows for a constant nonzero exchange rate in the steady state.

The existence of such an equilibrium can be shown as follows. We use equation (2.10) and set $s_t = s_{t-1} = s_{t-2} = \bar{s}$, so that

$$-w_{f,t}\psi\bar{s} = 0.$$

It can now easily be seen that if $w_{f,t} = 0$, any constant exchange rate will satisfy this equation. From the definition of $w_{f,t}$ in (2.19) we find that, when $\sigma^2_{f,t} \to \infty$, $w_{f,t} \to 0$.

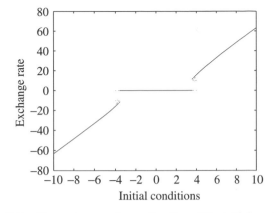

Figure 2.6. The exchange rate as a function of the initial conditions:
$\psi = 0.2$, $\beta = 0.9$, $\gamma = 1$.

We will call this nonfundamental equilibrium a bubble equilibrium. We call it a bubble equilibrium because it is an equilibrium in which fundamentalists exert no influence on the exchange rate. The reason is that fundamentalist rules are no longer being used (their weight $w_{f,t} = 0$). Mathematically, this can only happen for forecast errors that are infinitely high. However, as will be shown in the numerical simulations, we can come quite close to such a nonfundamental equilibrium for reasonable values of the fundamentalist forecasting errors.

With this dynamical system it is not possible to perform the local stability analysis of the steady state with the usual techniques, based upon the analysis of the eigenvalues of the Jacobian matrix evaluated at the steady state. The reason is that the "map" whose iteration generates the dynamics is not differentiable at the steady state.

2.5 Numerical Analysis of the Deterministic Model

The strong nonlinearities make an analysis of the model's global stability impossible. Therefore, we use numerical techniques to analyze the solutions of the model in this deterministic setup. We select "reasonable" values of the parameters, i.e., those that come close to empirically observed values. In an appendix (see Section 2.13) we present a table with the numerical values of the parameters of the model and the lags involved. As we will show later (in Chapter 8), these are also parameter values for which the model replicates the observed statistical properties of exchange rate movements. We will also analyze how sensitive the solution is to different sets of parameter values.

In Figure 2.6 we show the solutions for the exchange rate for different initial conditions. On the horizontal axis we set out the different initial conditions. These are initial shocks to the exchange rate in the period before the simulation is

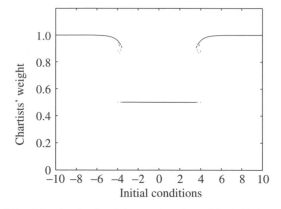

Figure 2.7. The chartists' weight as a function of the initial conditions:
$\psi = 0.2, \beta = 0.9, \gamma = 1.$

started.[9] The vertical axis shows the solutions for the exchange rate corresponding to these different initial conditions. These were obtained by simulating the model over 10 000 periods. We found that after such a long period the exchange rate had stabilized to a fixed point (a fixed attractor). As mentioned earlier, the fundamental exchange rate was normalized to 0. We find the two types of fixed-point solution that we discussed in the previous section. First, for small disturbances in the initial conditions, the fixed-point solutions coincide with the fundamental exchange rate. As suggested in the previous section, we call these solutions the *fundamental solutions*. Second, for large disturbances in the initial conditions, the fixed-point solutions diverge from the fundamental. We call these solutions (attractors) *nonfundamental solutions (attractors)*. We will also refer to the latter as "bubble[10] equilibria." It will become clear why we label these attractors in this way. The larger the initial shock in the exchange rate, the farther the attractors are removed from the fundamental exchange rate. The different nature of these two types of fixed-point attractor can also be seen from an analysis of the technical traders' weights that correspond to these different fixed-point attractors. We show these technical traders' weights as a function of the initial conditions in Figure 2.7.

First, we find that, for small initial disturbances, the technical traders' weight converges to 50% of the market. Thus, when the exchange rate converges to the fundamental rate, the weights of the technical traders and the fundamentalists are equal to 50%. For large initial disturbances, however, the technical traders' weight converges to 1. Thus, when the technical traders take over the whole market, the

---

[9] There are more lags in the model, i.e., five. Thus, we set the exchange rate with a lag of more than one period before the start equal to 0. This means that the initial conditions are one-period shocks in the exchange rate prior to the start of the simulation. All the other lagged dynamic variables are set equal to 0 when the simulation is started.

[10] We use the word "bubble" in a different way than in the rational-expectations literature. We discuss this in Chapter 3.

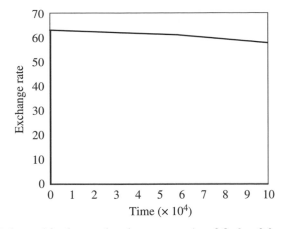

Figure 2.8. Market and fundamental exchange rates: $\psi = 0.2$, $\beta = 0.9$, $\gamma = 1$. Black line denotes exchange rate. The fundamental rate coincides with the x-axis (it is zero throughout).

exchange rate converges to a nonfundamental (bubble) attractor. The meaning of a bubble attractor can now be better understood. It is an exchange rate equilibrium that is reached when the number of fundamentalists has become sufficiently small (the number of chartists has become sufficiently large) so as to eliminate the effect of the mean-reversion dynamics. It will be made clearer in the next section why fundamentalists drop out of the market. Here it suffices to understand that such equilibria exist.

It is important to understand the nature of these nonfundamental (bubble) attractors. In contrast to the fundamental equilibria they are not really fixed-point solutions. When the exchange rate reaches a bubble attractor after an initial shock, it starts a return movement towards the fundamental that is exceedingly slow. Numerical simulations show that it takes several hundred thousand periods for the exchange rate to return to its fundamental value. We show an example of this exceedingly slow return movement in Figure 2.8. This shows the evolution of the simulated exchange rate in the time domain when the initial shock to the exchange rate is $+10$. This shock brings the exchange rate into a nonfundamental attractor, after which the exchange rate starts declining. After 100 000 periods less than 10% of the adjustment has taken place. The exchange rate is then declining at a rate of 0.000 07 per period. The weight of the chartists corresponding with the exchange rate in Figure 2.8 remains extremely close to 1. Even after 100 000 periods, the chartist weight has declined to just 0.999 999 1. Thus, the nonfundamental attractors can be considered to be "quasi-constant." In stochastic simulations such as those reported in the previous section, where there are disturbances every period, it is as if these nonfundamental attractors are fixed-point equilibria.

The idea behind this result is the following. When the exchange rate is in a nonfundamental equilibrium, the share of fundamentalists is almost equal to zero.

Because the share of fundamentalists is so close to zero, it is as if the fundamentalists are absent from the market. As a result, the influence fundamentalists exerts on the exchange rate is practically zero, and the movement of the exchange rate is also practically zero. Thus, for all practical purposes we can treat this nonfundamental equilibrium as a fixed-point equilibrium. In this sense, the technical traders' expectations are then model consistent, i.e., technical traders who extrapolate the past movements forecast no (visible) change. At the same time, since the fundamentalists have all but left the market, there is no (visible) force acting to bring back the exchange rate to its fundamental value. Thus, two types of equilibrium exist: a fundamental equilibrium, where technical traders and fundamentalists coexist, and a nonfundamental equilibrium, where the technical traders have crowded out the fundamentalists. In both cases, the expectations of the agents in the model are consistent with the model's outcome. We will return to this issue in the next chapter, when we expand the model. This will enable us to analyze the conditions under which these nonfundamental equilibria are truly constant. We will show that these equilibria can be truly fixed points.

2.6 Sensitivity Analysis of the Deterministic Model

In this section we perform a sensitivity analysis of the deterministic model. This will enable us to describe how the space of fundamental and bubble equilibria is affected by different values of the parameters of the model. In this section we concentrate on two parameters, i.e., β (the extrapolation parameter of technical traders) and γ (the sensitivity of technical traders and fundamentalists to relative profitability).

2.6.1 Sensitivity with Respect to β

We show the result of a sensitivity analysis with respect to β. We construct a three-dimensional version of Figure 2.6. We show this in Figure 2.9(a). The fixed attractors (i.e., the solutions of the exchange rate) are shown on the vertical axis. The initial conditions are shown on the x-axis and the different values for β on the z-axis. Thus, the two-dimensional Figure 2.6 in Section 2.5 is a "slice" of Figure 2.9(a) obtained for one particular value of β (0.9 in Figure 2.6). We observe that, as β increases, the plane which represents the collection of the fundamental equilibria narrows. At the same time the space taken by the bubble equilibria increases, and these bubble equilibria tend to increasingly diverge from the fundamental equilibria. Thus, as the extrapolation parameter increases, smaller and smaller shocks in the initial conditions push the exchange rate into the space of bubble equilibria. In other words, as β increases, the probability of obtaining a bubble equilibrium increases.

Figure 2.9(b) shows a similar three-dimensional picture, where we have used a higher value for the parameter γ, i.e., $\gamma = 5$. Remember, γ measures the sensitivity of fundamentalists and chartists to relative profitability of the forecasting rules.

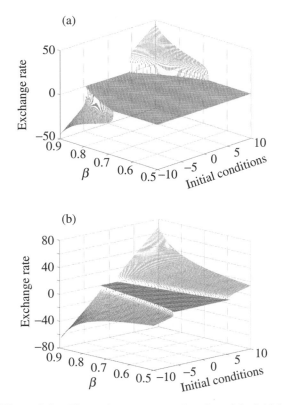

Figure 2.9.   The exchange rate as a function of the initial conditions and β: (a) $\psi = 0.2$, $\gamma = 1$; (b) $\psi = 0.2$, $\gamma = 5$.

We find, quite strikingly, that the plane of fundamental equilibria has narrowed considerably. Thus, the same initial shocks that, in the previous figure, did not lead to bubble equilibria now do so. Note again that, as β increases, the plane collecting the fundamental equilibria narrows.

Note also that the boundary between the fundamental and the bubble equilibria is discontinuous. We will return to this later in order to analyze the nature of this boundary.

2.6.2   Sensitivity with Respect to γ

From the preceding analysis it appears that the parameter γ is important in determining whether fundamental or bubble equilibria will prevail. This can also be shown by constructing Figure 2.10, which presents a similar three-dimensional figure relating the fixed attractors to both the initial conditions and the values of γ. We find that for γ equal to or close to 0, all equilibria are fundamental. Thus, when agents are not sensitive to changing profitabilities of forecasting rules, the exchange rate will always converge to the fundamental equilibrium, whatever the

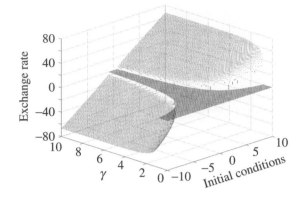

Figure 2.10. The exchange rate as a function of the initial
conditions and γ: $\psi = 0.2$, $\beta = 0.9$.

initial condition. As γ increases, the space of fundamental equilibria shrinks. With
sufficiently high values of γ, small initial disturbances (noise) are sufficient to push
the exchange rate into a bubble equilibrium. In other words, as γ increases, the probability of obtaining a bubble equilibrium increases. Finally, as in the case of β, we
also observe that the boundary between the bubble and fundamental equilibria is
discontinuous.

There is another useful way to analyze the nature of these two types of equilibrium. This consists in drawing the "basins of attraction" around these two types of
equilibrium. We do this in the next section.

2.7 Basins of Attraction

Analysis of the basins of attraction is often used in nonlinear dynamical analysis.[11]
When applied to our model, it consists in collecting the initial conditions that will
lead to a fundamental equilibrium and those that will lead to bubble equilibria and
plotting them in one graph. We present examples of such an exercise in Figure 2.11.
On the horizontal axis we set out the exchange rate one period before the start of the
simulation ($s(-1)$); on the vertical axis we set out the exchange rate two periods
before the start of the simulation ($s(-2)$). (The initial exchange rates with longer
lags are set equal to zero.) We then collect all the combinations of these two initial
conditions that lead to a fundamental equilibrium and give these points a dark color.
Similarly we collect all these initial conditions that lead to bubble equilibria and
give these points a lighter color. We do this for several values of the parameters of the
model. The left-hand panels of Figure 2.11 are arranged in increasing values of the
parameter γ (keeping β fixed at 0.9); the right-hand panels are arranged in increasing value of β (keeping γ fixed at 5). We observe that, as γ increases, the basin of

---

[11] See De Grauwe et al. (2005) for another application. We are grateful to Roberto Dieci for his advice
on constructing basins of attraction.

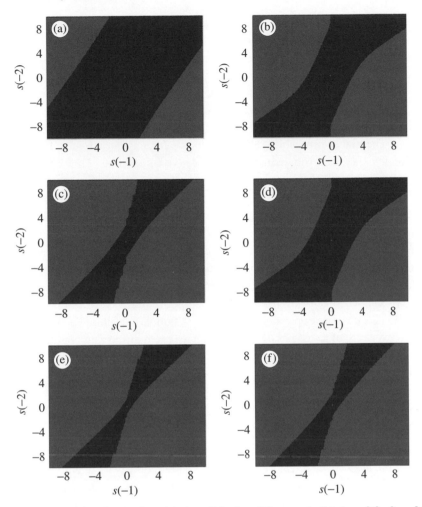

Figure 2.11. Basin of attraction: (a) $\psi = 0.2$, $\beta = 0.9$, $\gamma = 1$; (b) $\psi = 0.2$, $\beta = 0.7$, $\gamma = 5$; (c) $\beta = 0.9$, $\gamma = 5$; (d) $\psi = 0.2$, $\beta = 0.8$, $\gamma = 5$; (e) $\psi = 0.2$, $\beta = 0.9$, $\gamma = 10$; and (f) $\psi = 0.2$, $\beta = 0.95$, $\gamma = 5$.

attraction around the fundamental equilibrium shrinks. At the same time the basin of attraction around the bubble equilibria expands. This confirms what we found in the previous section. A similar phenomenon is observed in the right-hand panels of Figure 2.11: when β increases, the basin of attraction around the fundamental equilibrium shrinks, while the basins of attraction around the bubble equilibria expands.

From this analysis of the deterministic part of the model we have learned that there exist two kinds of attractor in the model. First, there is a fundamental attractor. This is a fixed-point equilibrium that is reached if the initial shocks to the system are not too large. When the system is in a fundamental equilibrium both chartists and fundamentalists coexist. Second, there are many nonfundamental quasi-equilibria that can be reached if the initial shocks are large enough. A characteristic of these quasi-equilibria is that the share of fundamentalists is so low that for all practical purposes they do not influence the market price anymore. It is as if they do not exist. These quasi-equilibria, which we have also called bubble equilibria, are reached in a self-fulfilling way. That is, when a sequence of shocks occurs that drives the exchange rate, say, upwards, those who use extrapolative forecasting make more money. The higher profitability of extrapolative forecasting attracts other agents, the fundamentalists, who switch to extrapolative forecasting. This reinforces the upward movement. This process stops when all (i.e., practically all) agents have switched to chartism.

In a way it can be said that these bubble equilibria are made possible because of a failure of arbitrage. Agents who use fundamentalists' forecasting rules recognize that a profit opportunity arises when the exchange rate deviates from its fundamental value. However, because of the losses they incur and the large forecast errors they make during a bubble phase, these risk-averse fundamentalists switch to safer and more profitable forecasting rules. Arbitrage opportunities exist, but everybody is afraid to take up these opportunities. As a result, bubble equilibria become possible.

The existence of two types of attractor creates many surprising features once we allow for stochastic shocks. In the previous section we showed that in a stochastic environment the model generates switches from one type of equilibrium to the other, creating cyclical movements around the fundamental. There are other features of the model worth analyzing, to which we now turn.

2.8   The Stochastic Model: Sensitivity to Initial Conditions

One of the most striking features generated by the model is its sensitivity to initial conditions. This feature is often found in nonlinear models. It means that very small changes in the initial conditions lead to very different future paths of the exchange rate.[12] In Figure 2.12 we illustrate this feature in a stochastic simulation of the model. Let us concentrate first on panel (a), which is obtained by simulating the exchange rate under two different initial conditions. The solid line is obtained by setting all initial exchange rates equal to zero; the dotted line is obtained by setting $s(-1) = 0.01$ while keeping the other initial exchange rates equal to zero. The fundamental variable in the two simulations is assumed to be exactly the same random walk. Thus, the departure of the two exchange rates that we observe at some point is not due to differences in the underlying fundamental. Figure 2.12(b) shows a similar simulation for another realization of the fundamental variable. In this simulation, which uses the same parameters as in panel (a), the sensitivity to

---

[12] In Chapter 10 we will perform a more rigorous analysis of the conditions under which sensitivity to initial conditions occurs. We will link this feature to the existence of chaotic dynamics.

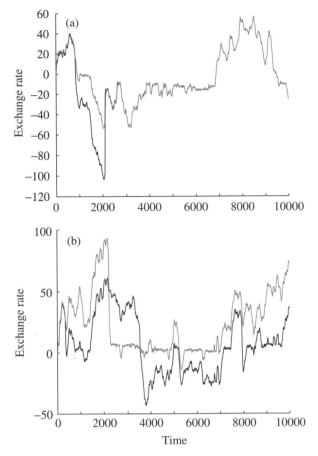

Figure 2.12. Exchange rate sensitivity to initial conditions: $\psi = 0.2$, $\beta = 0.9$, $\gamma = 5$. Black line, without shock; gray line, with shock.

initial conditions is quite spectacular, leading to a totally different time path of the two exchange rates. Thus, our model produces sensitivity to initial conditions. However, at the same time, the occurrence of sensitivity is quite unpredictable. In many simulation runs it does not occur at all, while in others it is very strong.

2.9 Why "Crashes" Occur

An important feature of the exchange rate dynamics obtained in the model is that it generates persistent movements towards a nonfundamental (bubble) equilibrium. However, invariably, once in a bubble equilibrium, the exchange rate at some point returns to a fundamental equilibrium, i.e., it "crashes." While the initial movement away from the fundamental can easily be understood, the "crash" is not. Why is it

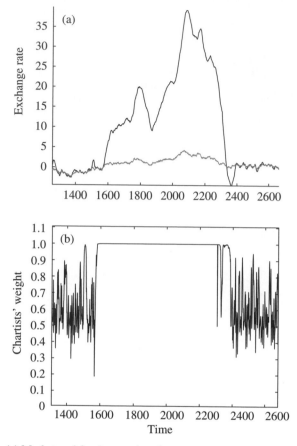

Figure 2.13. (a) Market and fundamental exchange rates (black line, exchange rate; gray line, fundamental rate) and (b) weight of chartists. In both cases, $\psi = 0.2$, $\beta = 0.9$, $\gamma = 5$.

that, once in a nonfundamental equilibrium, the exchange rate returns to its fundamental value? In order to understand this better, we analyze the anatomy of the two stages: the movement away from the fundamental and the return movement (the crash).[13] We do this in Figure 2.13, where we look at a typical bubble-and-crash scenario as simulated by the model. We show the market exchange rate and its fundamental in Figure 2.13(a), and the corresponding chartist's weight in Figure 2.13(b). The upward movement (let us call this the bubble phase) is characterized by a sudden increase in the share of chartists towards 1. The mechanism that produces this bubble phase can be described as follows. At a certain moment, due to a series of stochastic shocks, the exchange rate is moving in one direction. This tends to increase the profitability of extrapolating forecasting made by chartists. This in

---

[13] The description we provide of bubbles and crashes has very much the same ingredients as the classical historical analysis that was made by Kindleberger (1978).

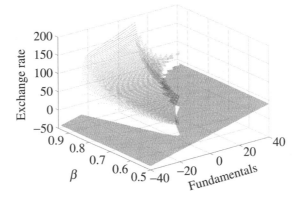

Figure 2.14. The exchange rate as a function of β and the fundamentals, $\psi = 0.2$, $\gamma = 5$, with initial conditions $s(-1) = 10$ and $s(-2) = -10$.

turn attracts more agents towards the use of extrapolating forecasting, which reinforces the upward movement. This "bandwagon" effect leads to a situation in which (almost) everybody uses extrapolative forecasting. We have reached a bubble equilibrium. Note that this bubble equilibrium is reached because of the self-fulfilling nature of the profitability of extrapolative forecasting. As more agents are attracted towards extrapolative forecasting the upward movements in the exchange rate are reinforced, increasing the profitability of this kind of forecasting. At the same time, during this bubble phase, fundamentalist forecasting is increasingly loss making, i.e., the fundamentalist rule predicts increasingly strong declines, which do not arise, leading to large losses for the fundamentalists.[14]

When the exchange rate is in a bubble equilibrium, there is an absence of mean-reverting (fundamentalist) forecasting, so the exchange rate wanders aimlessly, unmoved by fundamentalist forces. This situation, however, does not last. At some point movements in the fundamental exchange rate will start attracting the exchange rate, leading to a crash. The crash phase is typically shorter than the bubble phase, due to the fact that during the crash both the chartists and the fundamentalists forecast a decline in the exchange rate.

One can show the importance of shocks in the fundamental rate in triggering a crash phase by returning to the deterministic version of the model. We performed the following experiment. We fixed the initial condition at some value ($s(-1) = +10$ and $s(-2) = -10$) that produces a bubble equilibrium (for a given parameter configuration).[15] We then introduced permanent changes in the fundamental value (ranging from -40 to $+40$) and computed the attractors for different values of β.

---

[14] Risk also matters in this dynamics of a bubble and crash, i.e., the risk perception of chartists and fundamentalists changes during the bubble. We will analyze the importance of risk and risk aversion in Chapter 4.

[15] As can be seen from Figure 2.11, these are initial conditions that produce a bubble equilibrium, and are located deep inside the basins of attraction around the bubble equilibria.

We show the results of this exercise in Figure 2.14. On the x-axis we show the different fundamental values of the exchange rate, while on the y-axis we have the different values of β. The vertical axis shows the attractors (exchange rate solutions). The upward sloping plane is the collection of fundamental equilibria. It is upward sloping (45%) because an increase in the fundamental rate by, say, 10 leads to an equilibrium exchange rate of 10. For small values of β we always have fundamental equilibria. This result matches the results of Figure 2.9, where we found that for low β values all the initial conditions lead to a fundamental equilibrium.

The major finding of Figure 2.14 is that when permanent shocks in the fundamental are small relative to the initial (temporary) shocks, we obtain bubble equilibria. The corollary of this result is that when the fundamental shock is large enough relative to the noise, we obtain a fundamental equilibrium. Thus, if an initial temporary shock has brought the exchange rate into a bubble equilibrium, a sufficiently large fundamental shock will lead to a crash. In a stochastic environment in which the fundamental rate is driven by a random walk (permanent shocks), any bubble must at some point crash because the attractive forces of the fundamental accumulate over time and overcome the temporary dynamics of the bubble.

The interesting aspect of this result is that the crash occurs irrespective of whether the fundamental shock is positive or negative. Since we have a positive bubble, it is easy to understand that a negative shock in the fundamental can trigger a crash. A positive shock has the same effect though. The reason is that a sufficiently large positive shock in the fundamental increases the value of forecasting rules that use fundamental information. As a result, fundamentalist forecasting becomes more profitable, thereby increasing the number of fundamentalists in the market and leading to a crash (to the new and higher fundamental rate). In other words, while in the short run chartists exploit the noise to start a bubble, in the long run, when the fundamental rate inexorably moves in one or the other direction, fundamentalists' forecasting becomes attractive.

It is also interesting to note that, as β increases, the size of the shocks in the fundamental necessary to bring the exchange rate back to its fundamental rate increases. In a stochastic environment this means that bubbles will be stronger and longer lasting when β increases.

The previous experiment selected an initial bubble equilibrium that is located relatively far from the basin of attraction around the fundamental equilibrium. We repeated the same experiment choosing bubble equilibria that are located closer to the basin of attraction around the fundamental (see Figure 2.11). We show two examples in Figure 2.15. Panel (a) shows the results for initial conditions $s(-1) = 8$, and $s(-2) = 0$. It can be seen that smaller shocks in the fundamental exchange rate will lead the exchange rate to return to its fundamental value. Panel (b) shows the result when the initial condition is $s(-1) = 4$ and $s(-2) = 0$, which is very

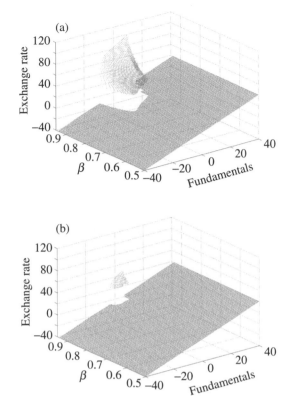

Figure 2.15. The exchange rate as a function of β and the fundamentals, $\psi = 0.2$, $\gamma = 5$, with (a) initial conditions $s(-1) = +8$ and (b) initial conditions $s(-1) = +4$.

close to the basin of attraction around the fundamental (see Figure 2.11). The shocks needed to bring the exchange rate to its fundamental value have now become very small.

The structure of the deterministic version of the model allows us to understand why, in a stochastic environment, the exchange rate will switch back and forth between the fundamental and the nonfundamental attractor, and why therefore the exchange rate appears to cycle around the fundamental variable.

2.10 The Role of Memory

Memory plays an important role in the model. By that we mean that when agents make forecasts they use the past as their guide. In addition, when checking the profitability of their forecasting rules they remember past profits and past forecasting errors they made. Thus, past experiences influence both their forecasting rules and their evaluation of these rules. The question then is: how far back do they go? In other words, how much do they remember. In this section we analyze how the memory of agents affects the results of our model. We first concentrate on the memory of the chartists, and then study the memory in the evaluation of the rules (the fitness criterion).

2.10.1 The Memory of Chartists

Until now we have assumed that chartists extrapolate the last period's exchange rate change into the future. Clearly, chartists are more sophisticated than this. They have a longer memory. In order to take memory into account we now specify their forecasting rule as follows:

$$E_{c,t}(\Delta s_{t+1}) = \beta \sum_{i=0}^{\infty} \rho_i \, \Delta s_{t-i}.$$

Thus, the chartists compute a moving average of the past exchange rate changes and they extrapolate these changes into the future exchange rate change. We will set $\rho_i = (1 - \rho)\rho^i$. Thus, we will assume an exponential decay in the weights given to the past exchange rate changes. This allows us to rewrite equation (2.3) as a partial adjustment equation:

$$E_{c,t}(\Delta s_{t+1}) = \rho E_{c,t-1}(\Delta s_t) + (1 - \rho)\beta \Delta s_{t-1}. \tag{2.25}$$

The parameter ρ in equation (2.25) can be interpreted as reflecting the memory of chartists. If $\rho = 0$, chartists remember only the last period's exchange rate change, and they extrapolate this into the future. When ρ increases, the weight given to exchange rate changes farther removed in the past increases. In other words, the chartists' memory becomes longer. We will allow ρ to vary between 0 (chartists suffer from complete loss of memory) and 1 (chartists have an infinite memory).

We first present some stochastic simulations for different values of the memory parameter ρ in Figure 2.16. We find that for small values of the memory parameter we obtain the results that we have found in previous sections, i.e., that the exchange rate switches between fundamental and nonfundamental attractors in an unpredictable way. For some sufficiently high value of ρ, this feature completely disappears and the exchange rate remains tightly linked to its fundamental value, as in Figure 2.16(c), where the exchange rate and its fundamental coincide almost completely. Thus, when agents have a very long memory, the occurrence of bubbles and crashes disappears.

As before, we also analyze the deterministic version of the model. We proceed as before and compute a bifurcation diagram in which we set the initial conditions on the x-axis, the memory parameter ρ on the y-axis, and the exchange rate solution on the vertical axis. The result is shown in Figure 2.17. We find that, as the memory of the chartists increases, the size of the fundamental space increases. When memory is very large, all solutions turn out to be fundamental equilibria. However, the transition is highly nonlinear. When ρ remains between 0 and 0.8, changes in ρ

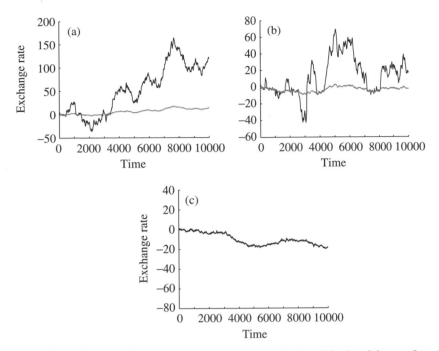

Figure 2.16. Market and fundamental exchange rates with $\psi = 0.2$, $\beta = 0.9$, $\gamma = 5$, and (a) $\rho = 0$, (b) $\rho = 0.5$, (c) $\rho = 0.9$. (a), (b) Black line, exchange rate; gray line, fundamental rate. In (c) both lines are very close.

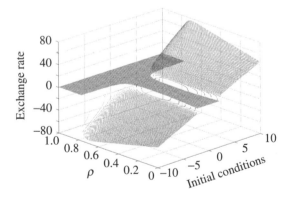

Figure 2.17. The exchange rate as a function of the initial conditions and ρ, with $\psi = 0.2$, $\beta = 0.9$, and $\gamma = 5$.

have very little influence on the size of the fundamental space. In that range, the equilibria are almost completely insensitive to increases in memory. When a critical value is exceeded (here around 0.8), all bubble equilibria suddenly disappear. Thus, memory matters. However, it matters in a very nonlinear way. Chartists need a very long memory to eliminate the occurrence of bubble equilibria.

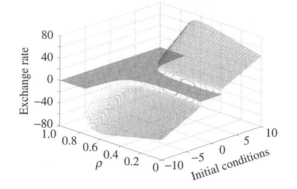

Figure 2.18.   The exchange rate as a function of the initial conditions and ρ,
with $\psi = 0.2$, $\beta = 0.9$, and $\gamma = 5$.

2.10.2   Remembering Profits and Risk

Until now we have assumed that agents choose the forecasting rules based on the
relative (risk-adjusted) profitabilities of these rules in the previous period. This
implies that agents have a very short memory; they only remember the last period's
profits and the last period's risk. It is probably more realistic to assume that agents
look at the past risk-adjusted profits while giving an increasingly smaller weight to
observations far in the past. We implement this idea now, and we assume that agents
compute a weighted average of past profits where the weights are exponentially
declining. Thus, they compute the following profits:

$$\pi_{f,t}'^* = (1 - \rho) \sum_{i=0}^{\infty} (\rho^i \pi_{f,t-i}'),$$

$$\pi_{c,t}'^* = (1 - \rho) \sum_{i=0}^{\infty} (\rho^i \pi_{c,t-i}'),$$

where ρ can, as before, be interpreted as the memory parameter, i.e., when ρ
increases, the weight given to faraway observations increases. When $\rho = 0$, agents
only remember the last period's risk-adjusted profit. Note that we assume that agents
have the same memory parameter when remembering past risk-adjusted profits as
when they use a chartist forecasting rule. We then substitute $\pi_{f,t}'^*$ and $\pi_{c,t}'^*$ into the
fitness rules (2.4) and (2.5) and obtain the new model that we simulated.[16]

The effect of introducing memory into the fitness criterion is shown in Figure 2.18. We show a three-dimensional bifurcation diagram similar to the previous
one. We now have the memory parameter ρ on the y-axis. We find a very similar

---

[16] Note that by introducing memory into the model we come closer to the adaptive learning models
that have become increasingly popular in game theoretic models (see Cheung and Friedman 1997,
1998; Fudenberg and Levine 1998). In these models, agents learn to use certain actions based on their
profitability observed in the past. This is what agents do in our model too.

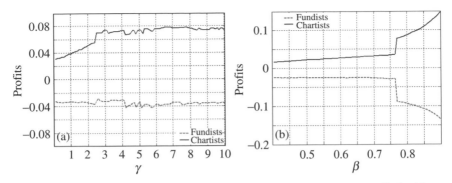

Figure 2.19. Profits of fundamentalists (lower line) and chartists (upper line) with (a) $\psi = 0.2$, $\beta = 0.8$ and (b) $\psi = 0.2$, $\gamma = 1$.

result, as in the previous section, i.e., as the memory in the fitness criterion increases the size of the fundamental space increases. Thus, memory has a stabilizing force, which is not surprising as it adds inertia to the system. However, the pattern is nonlinear. Within the range $0 < \rho < 0.8$ changes in ρ have very little impact on the nature of the equilibria. Only when ρ exceeds 0.8 do we obtain a very marked increase in the size of the fundamental equilibria. Thus, we need a very strong memory to eliminate the bubble equilibria.

2.11 Is Chartism Evolutionarily Stable?

An important issue is whether chartism is sufficiently profitable to survive in the long run. As mentioned earlier, traditional economic analysis has been rather scornful about chartism and technical analysis. These strategies appear to be "irrational." In efficient markets such strategies should disappear in the long run because they cannot be persistently profitable.[17] In contrast to these theoretical conclusions, the empirical evidence strongly suggests that technical analysis is profitable, and that the use of these forecasting rules has no tendency to disappear. Our model predicts that chartism is indeed profitable and remains so in the long run.

In order to analyze the profitability of chartist forecasting rules we simulated the model stochastically over 5000 periods and we computed the average profits (per unit invested) of chartist and fundamentalist forecasting rules. We did this for different values of the parameters γ and β. The results are shown in Figure 2.19. We show the average profits (per unit invested) made by the use of chartist and fundamentalist rules for different values of γ and β. Some results are noteworthy. First, for all parameter values, chartist forecasting rules turn out to be more profitable than fundamentalist rules. Second, when γ and β increase, the profitability of chartist rules increases relative to the profitability of fundamentalist rules. This result is related to the fact that, as these parameters increase, the probability of the

---

[17] This argument was defended forcefully by Friedman (1953).

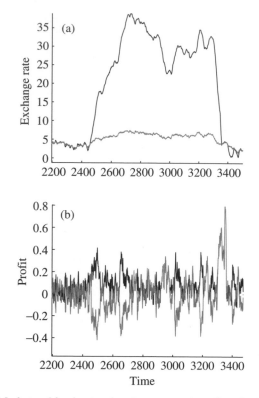

Figure 2.20.   (a) Market and fundamental exchange rates (gray line, fundamental rate; black line, exchange rate) and (b) profits of chartists and fundamentalists. In both parts, $\psi = 0.2$, $\beta = 0.9$, and $\gamma = 5$.

occurrence of bubbles increases (see Section 2.6, where we show this). Chartist forecasting rules become more profitable in an environment of turbulence during which the exchange rate deviates from its fundamental. We show this feature in Figure 2.20, where we simulate the model in the time domain. We compare the profits of the use of chartist and fundamentalist rules during one particular bubble-and-crash phase. It can clearly be seen that, during the bubble phase of the exchange rate movement, agents who use chartist rules make large profits, while agents who use fundamentalist rules make large losses. In an environment in which these bubble-and-crash phases become more frequent, chartist rules become more profitable on average.

One noteworthy aspect of the previous results is that fundamentalist rules appear to be loss making on average. Does this mean that, instead of chartists, the fundamentalists are in danger of extinction? It is important to stress here that we measure the profitability of forecasting rules. We do not measure the profits and losses of agents who use these rules. During the bubble phases we observe that the use of chartist rules is very profitable, while the use of fundamentalist rules is loss making. As a result, most agents switch to the use of chartist rules and few, if any, agents continue to use fundamentalist rules during these bubble phases. In other words, the results of Figures 2.19 and 2.20 say nothing about the evolution of the wealth position of agents over time, because clever agents will have switched frequently from one rule to the other. Only the agents who are stupid enough to stick to the same fundamentalist rule during the whole period make the losses reported in Figure 2.19. The model, however, predicts that few, if any, agents will do this.

2.12 Conclusion

Humans find it difficult to understand the world in which they live. The complexity of the information is so vast that the individual brain cannot hope to understand but a tiny part of it.[18] The rational-expectations paradigm that dominates macroeconomics today fails to take this into account. It has been based on the view that the representative agent's brain is fully capable of understanding the complex world. In other words, it has started from the proposition that there is a one-to-one correspondence between the information set embedded in the world and the information set that can be stored and processed in each individual's brain. This is an extraordinary assumption, which is tantamount to assuming that each individual agent is a godlike creature. In fact, monotheistic religions have typically defined God to be a creature capable of mastering the full complexity of the world. Such an extraordinary assumption could still have a scientific value if it allowed us to make good empirical predictions. It does not, however, and should therefore be discarded, which is what we did in this chapter. We assumed that agents are boundedly rational, i.e., they use simple forecasting rules that do not incorporate all the available information. However, these agents are willing to learn and will switch to other rules if it turns out that these rules are more profitable than the rule they have been using.

Such trial-and-error learning strategies create a surprisingly rich dynamics in the foreign exchange market. First, two types of equilibrium are generated (a fundamental equilibrium and a nonfundamental equilibrium) to which the exchange rate is attracted. Second, the existence of these two types of equilibrium leads in a stochastic environment to large swings of the exchange rate around its fundamental value. It is as if the trial-and-error learning strategies lead to a never-ending groping of the market towards the fundamental exchange rate. Third, these boundedly rational strategies create turbulence that appears to be nonnormally distributed, despite the

---

[18] This is also the starting point of Hayek's famous analysis of the use of information in society (Hayek 1945). He argued that, because individual agents can only grasp a tiny little part of the existing information, markets are necessary to coordinate their decisions. Today's rational-expectation macroeconomic theories assume that the sum of all the information is concentrated in the brains of individuals. In Hayek's view, in such an informational environment, markets are superfluous.

fact that the news coming from the fundamental is normally distributed. Thus, the nonnormality of the exchange rate changes comes out of the model endogenously. We will return to this feature in later chapters, in order to analyze it in greater detail. Fourth, there is sensitivity to initial conditions, i.e., trivially small disturbances can change the whole future path of the exchange rate. This feature will turn out to have important implications for the ability to forecast the exchange rate and for the effectiveness of intervention policies. The latter will be analyzed in Chapter 9. Finally, extrapolative forecasting rules that do not take into account information about the fundamental exchange rate do surprisingly well, and on average create more profits than fundamental-based forecasting rules. The reason why this happens is that these extrapolative rules create noise that in turn generates additional profits in a self-fulfilling way. As a result, these are forecasting strategies that can survive in the long run.

In the following chapter we introduce more structure in the underlying exchange rate model and analyze the extent to which this changes the dynamics of the exchange rate.

Table 2.1. Numerical values of parameters.

Parameters	Values	Sensitivity analysis
ψ	0.2	No
β	0.9	Yes
γ	5	Yes
r and r^*	0	No

2.13 Appendix: Numerical Values of the Parameters Used in the Base Simulation

In Table 2.1 we present the numerical values of the model. In the first column we list the parameters of the model, and in the second we present the numerical values in the base simulations. The third column indicates whether or not we have performed a sensitivity analysis on these numerical values. If not, we use the same numerical value in all simulations.

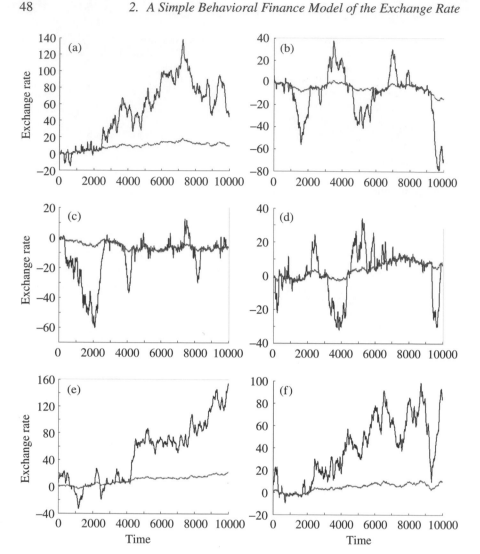

Figure 2.21. Market and fundamental exchange rates with $\psi = 0.2$, $\beta = 0.9$, and $\gamma = 5$ for all parts. Gray line, fundamental rate; black line, exchange rate.

2.14 Appendix: Simulations of the Base Model with Different Stochastic Realizations

In this appendix we show the results of simulating the base model, i.e., the model with the parameter configuration of Figure 2.1 assuming different stochastic realizations of the fundamental variable. These are shown in Figure 2.21. We find that the results are comparable with those obtained in Figure 2.1.

3

A Slightly More Complex
Behavioral Finance Model

3.1 Introduction

In the previous chapter we developed a very simple exchange rate model with minimal structure. In the present chapter we add more structure to that model. We do this for two reasons. First, we want to be sure that the results we obtained in the previous chapter are not dependent on the simplicity of the structure of the underlying exchange rate model. Second, the additional structure of the model will enable us to analyze issues that we could not address in the previous chapter. For example, it will make it possible to study how the exchange rate affects the real side of the economy, and how official interventions in the foreign exchange market affect the exchange rate.

The model is based on the choice that agents make between a risky and a risk-free asset. The risky asset will be the foreign one; the risk-free asset will be the domestic one. Each agent has a given wealth and allocates her wealth between these two types of asset. In order to make the best possible choice, she maximizes a utility function that consists of two elements: the expected return and the risk involved in holding the risky asset.

We will superimpose on this model the same assumptions about the way these agents forecast the future exchange rate. Thus, agents select simple forecasting rules and check *ex post* the (risk-adjusted) profitability of these rules. We now turn to the equations describing the model.

3.2 The Model

The model consists of three building blocks. The first one describes how agents select their optimal portfolio using a mean-variance utility framework. The other two blocks are based on the same assumptions as those we made in the previous chapter about the way agents make their forecasts.

3.2.1 The Optimal Portfolio

Each agent can invest in two assets, a domestic (risk-free) asset and a foreign (risky) asset. The agents' utility function can be represented by the following equation:

$$U(W_{t+1}^i) = E_t(W_{t+1}^i) - \tfrac{1}{2}\mu V^i(W_{t+1}^i), \tag{3.1}$$

where W_{t+1}^i is the wealth of agent i at time $t+1$, E_t is the expectation operator, μ is the coefficient of risk aversion, and $V^i(W_{t+1}^i)$ represents the conditional variance of the wealth of agent i. Agent i is characterized by the fact that she uses a particular forecasting rule. We could also call the latter a "belief." Thus, agent i has a particular type of belief, which we call a type-i belief. Equation (3.1) is a standard mean-variance utility function that is often used in the theory of finance. It is also used to derive the best-known model in the theory of finance: the capital asset pricing model.

The wealth of agent i is specified as follows:

$$W_{t+1}^i = (1+r^*)s_{t+1}d_{i,t} + (1+r)(W_t^i - s_t d_{i,t}), \tag{3.2}$$

where r and r^* are respectively the domestic and the foreign interest rates (which are known with certainty), s_{t+1} is the exchange rate at time $t+1$, and $d_{i,t}$ represents the holdings of the foreign assets by agent i at time t. Thus, the first term on the right-hand side of (3.2) represents the value of the (risky) foreign portfolio expressed in domestic currency at time $t+1$, while the second term represents the value of the (riskless) domestic portfolio at time $t+1$.[1]

The substitution of equation (3.2) into (3.1) and maximization of the utility with respect to $d_{i,t}$ enable us to derive the standard optimal holding of foreign assets by agent i:[2]

$$d_{i,t} = \frac{(1+r^*)E_t^i(s_{t+1}) - (1+r)s_t}{\mu\sigma_{i,t}^2}, \tag{3.3}$$

where $\sigma_{i,t}^2 = (1+r^*)^2 V_t^i(s_{t+1})$. The optimal holding of the foreign asset depends on the expected excess return (corrected for risk) of the foreign asset. The market demand for foreign assets at time t is the sum of the individual demands, i.e.,

$$\sum_{i=1}^{N} n_{i,t}d_{i,t} = D_t, \tag{3.4}$$

where $n_{i,t}$ is the number of agents of type-i belief.

Market equilibrium implies that the market demand is equal to the market supply, Z_t. The market supply is determined by the net current account and by the

---

[1] The model could be interpreted as an asset pricing model with one risky asset (e.g., shares) and a risk-free asset. Equation (3.2) would then be written as

$$W_{t+1}^i = (s_{t+1} + y_{t+1})d_{i,t} + (1+r)(W_t^i - s_t d_{i,t}),$$

where s_{t+1} is the price of the share in $t+1$ and y_{t+1} is the dividend per share in $t+1$.

[2] If the model is interpreted as an asset pricing model of one risky asset (shares) and a risk-free asset, the corresponding optimal holding of the risky asset becomes

$$d_{i,t} = \frac{E_t^i(s_{t+1} + y_{t+1}) - (1+r)s_t}{\mu\sigma_{i,t}^2}.$$

sales or purchases of foreign exchange of the central bank. In a first stage we will assume both to be exogenous. (In Chapter 4 we will endogenize the current account; in Chapter 9 we will analyze how foreign exchange market interventions affect Z_t.) Thus,

$$Z_t = D_t. \tag{3.5}$$

Substituting the optimal holdings into the market demand and then into the market equilibrium equation and solving for the exchange rate s_t yield the market clearing exchange rate:

$$s_t = \left(\frac{1+r^*}{1+r}\right) \frac{1}{\sum_{i=1}^{N} w_{i,t}/\sigma_{i,t}^2} \left[\sum_{i=1}^{N} w_{i,t} \frac{E_t^i(s_{t+1})}{\sigma_{i,t}^2} - \Omega_t Z_t\right] + \epsilon_t, \tag{3.6}$$

where

$$w_{i,t} = \frac{n_{i,t}}{\sum_{i=1}^{N} n_{i,t}}$$

is the weight (share) of agents with type-i belief,

$$\Omega_t = \frac{\mu}{(1+r^*)\sum_{i=1}^{N} n_{i,t}}, \tag{3.7}$$

and ϵ_t is a white noise error term.

Thus, the exchange rate is determined by the expectations of the agents, E_t^i, about the future exchange rate. These forecasts are weighted by their respective variances $\sigma_{i,t}^2$. When agent i's forecasts have a high variance, the weight of this agent in the determination of the market exchange rate is reduced. In the following we will set $r = r^*$.

3.2.2 The Forecasting Rules

Agents form their expectations of the future exchange rate in the same way as in the previous chapter. For the sake of convenience we repeat the equations here.

As before, we assume that two types of forecasting rule are used. The agents using a fundamentalist rule, the "fundamentalists," base their forecast on a comparison between the market and the fundamental exchange rates, i.e., they forecast the market rate to return to the fundamental rate in the future:

$$E_t^f(\Delta s_{t+1}) = -\psi(s_{t-1} - s_{t-1}^*), \tag{3.8}$$

where $0 < \psi < 1$ and s_{t-1}^* is the fundamental exchange rate at time $t-1$. This fundamental exchange rate is related to the current account. At this stage of the analysis, however, we will consider s_t^* to be an exogenous variable, like the current account.

The timing of the forecasts is important. When fundamentalists forecast the future exchange rate, they use publicly available information up to period $t-1$. This implies that fundamentalists make their forecasts before the market clearing exchange rate s_t has been revealed to them. This assumption is in the logic of the model used here in which agents do not know the full model structure. As a result, they cannot compute the market clearing exchange rate of time t, that is, the result of their forecasts made in period t. In a rational-expectations environment, agents know the underlying model and are capable of making such calculations. As a result, in a rational-expectations model, agents use information about the exchange rate at time t. The timing assumption underlying the agents' forecasts in (3.8) allows us to derive the market clearing exchange rate in (3.6) as a unique price for which demand equals supply (Brock and Hommes 1998). An issue that arises here is how this timing assumption can be made consistent with the optimization process described in the previous section. There we assumed that, when computing their optimal holdings of foreign assets in period t, agents have information about the exchange rate in period t. The inconsistency is only superficial. The optimal holdings derived in equation (3.3) can be interpreted as a Marshallian demand curve in which an auctioneer announces a price. Agents then decide on their optimal holdings conditioned on this announced price. The auctioneer then collects the bids and computes the market clearing price. The latter is not in the information set of the agents when they make their forecasts for the exchange rate in period $t + 1$.

Note also that the timing assumption in equation (3.8) appears to be different from that used in the previous chapter (see equation (2.2)). This is because in Chapter 2 we used a model in which the exchange rate in period $t + 1$ is determined by the forecast agents made in period t plus an unforeseen random disturbance occurring in period $t + 1$. Thus, information up to period t was in the information set of agents when they made their forecast in period t.

The agents using technical analysis, the "technical traders," forecast the future exchange rate by extrapolating past exchange rate movements. Their forecasting rule can be specified as

$$E_t^c(\Delta s_{t+1}) = \beta \sum_{k=1}^{\infty} \rho(1 - \rho)^k \Delta s_{t-k}. \tag{3.9}$$

Thus, the technical traders compute a moving average of the past exchange rate changes and extrapolate this into the future exchange rate change. The degree of extrapolation is given by the parameter β. As before, the parameter ρ can be interpreted as the memory parameter.

We now analyze how fundamentalists and technical traders evaluate the risk of their portfolio. The risk is measured by the variance terms in equation (3.6), which we define as the weighted average of the squared (one period ahead) forecasting errors made by technical traders and fundamentalists, respectively. Thus,

$$\sigma_{i,t} = \sum_{k=1}^{\infty} \rho(1 - \rho)^k [E_{t-k-1}^i(s_{t-k}) - s_{t-k}]^2, \tag{3.10}$$

where $i = \mathrm{f}, \mathrm{c}$.

3.2.3 Fitness of the Rules

We use the same fitness criterion to select the forecasting rules, as in the previous chapter. Thus,

$$w_{c,t} = \frac{\exp(\gamma \pi'_{c,t})}{\exp(\gamma \pi'_{c,t}) + \exp(\gamma \pi'_{f,t})}, \tag{3.11}$$

$$w_{f,t} = \frac{\exp(\gamma \pi'_{f,t})}{\exp(\gamma \pi'_{c,t}) + \exp(\gamma \pi'_{f,t})}, \tag{3.12}$$

where $\pi'_{c,t}$ and $\pi'_{f,t}$ are the risk-adjusted net profits made by technical traders and fundamentalists forecasting the exchange rate in period t, using information up to $t-1$, i.e., $\pi'_{c,t} = \pi_{c,t} - \mu \sigma^2_{c,t}$ and $\pi'_{f,t} = \pi_{f,t} - \mu \sigma^2_{f,t}$. We will use the same measure of risk as in equation (3.10).

Profits are defined as the one period return, i.e.,

$$\pi_{i,t} = [s_{t-1}(1+r^*) - s_{t-2}(1+r)] \operatorname{sgn}[(1+r^*)E^i_{t-1}(s_t) - (1+r)s_{t-1}], \tag{3.13}$$

where

$$\operatorname{sgn}[x] = \begin{cases} 1 & \text{for } x > 0, \\ 0 & \text{for } x = 0, \\ -1 & \text{for } x < 0 \end{cases}$$

and $i = c, f$.

Given that we assume $r = r^*$, we obtain

$$\pi_{i,t} = [(1+r)\Delta s_{t-1}] \operatorname{sgn}[E^i_{t-1}(\Delta s_t)]. \tag{3.14}$$

Note the timing assumption in the definition of profits: $\pi_{i,t}$ is the profit that agent i computes in period t using information of the exchange rate up to time $t-1$. This is in the same logic as the timing assumption in the forecasting rules. Agents do not observe the exchange rate in period t because this exchange rate will be the outcome of their decisions. Since they do not have rational expectations they cannot compute this equilibrium exchange rate in advance. In (3.14) it is assumed that agents evaluate their last forecast, i.e., the one made in period $t-1$. This is a forecast made for Δs_t. However, s_t is not yet observed. In principle they would have to wait one more period to evaluate the forecast made in $t-1$. They do not want to wait so long. So they compare that forecast to the last available change in the exchange rate, i.e., Δs_{t-1}. One way to interpret this timing assumption is to view the agent as making a forecast in $t-1$ and to buy a futures contract if she expects an increase (or to sell a futures contract if she expects a decline). In period t, when she evaluates her forecast, her futures contract will have increased in value if $\Delta s_{t-1} > 0$ has the same sign as the change forecasted in $t-1$.

3.3 Stochastic Simulation of the Model

As in the previous chapter, we first present the results of a stochastic simulation
of the model which assumes that the fundamental exchange rate is driven by a
random-walk process. We contrast the results of the mean-variance model with
those obtained with the simple model in the previous chapter. We show the results
in Figure 3.1 for a particular parameter combination. Two features stand out. First,
as in the previous chapter, we find that the exchange rate is disconnected from
its fundamental for much of the time. Periods in which the exchange rate stays
close to its fundamental alternate with periods in which it wanders away from
its fundamental. The latter periods are those during which the chartists dominate
the market (see Figure 3.1(c),(d)). Second, the periods during which the exchange
rate departs from its fundamental and during which the chartists dominate appear
to be more protracted in the mean-variance model than in the simple model of
the previous chapter. This suggests that in the mean-variance model the attraction
exerted by the nonfundamental equilibria seems to be stronger than in the simple
model. This feature is found for most parameter configurations.

In order to better understand these features it will be useful to study the deterministic version of the model in the same way as we have done in Chapter 2.

3.4 Solution of the Deterministic Model

In this section, we investigate the properties of the solution of the deterministic
version of the model that we obtained by setting the stochastic error terms equal
to 0. The model consists of equations (3.6)–(3.13).

3.4.1 The Steady State

We analyze the steady state of the simplified version of the model.[3] As in Chapter 2,
we assume that technical traders take only one lag into account.[4] In addition, we
set $Z = 0$, and normalize the fundamental rate, $s_t^* = s^* = 0$. We can then write
equation (3.6) as follows:

$$s_t = s_{t-1} - \Theta_{f,t}\psi s_{t-1} + \Theta_{c,t}\beta(s_{t-1} - s_{t-2}), \tag{3.15}$$

where

$$\Theta_{f,t} = \frac{w_{f,t}/\sigma_{f,t}^2}{w_{f,t}/\sigma_{f,t}^2 + w_{c,t}/\sigma_{c,t}^2} \tag{3.16}$$

---

[3] We are grateful to Roberto Dieci for his help in working out the analytical representation of the
steady state (see also De Grauwe et al. 2005).

[4] One can easily add additional lags without altering the steady-state analysis.

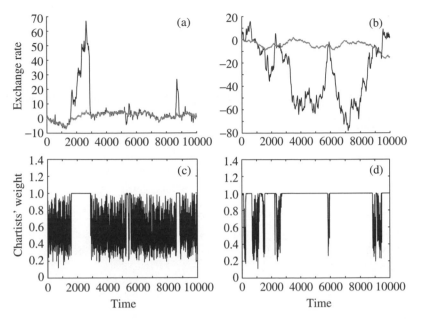

Figure 3.1. Comparison between (a), (c) the simple model in Chapter 2 and (b), (d) the mean-variance model. Parts (a) and (b) show the market and fundamental exchange rates (gray line, fundamental rate; black line, exchange rate). Parts (c) and (d) show the chartists' weights. $\psi = 0.2$ $\beta = 0.9$, $\gamma = 5$, and $\rho = 0.5$.

and

$$\Theta_{c,t} = \frac{w_{c,t}/\sigma_{c,t}^2}{w_{f,t}/\sigma_{f,t}^2 + w_{c,t}/\sigma_{c,t}^2} \tag{3.17}$$

are the risk-adjusted weights of fundamentalists and technical traders, and

$$w_{f,t} = \frac{\exp[\gamma(\pi_{f,t} - \mu\sigma_{f,t}^2)]}{\exp[\gamma(\pi_{c,t} - \mu\sigma_{c,t}^2)] + \exp[\gamma(\pi_{f,t} - \mu\sigma_{f,t}^2)]}. \tag{3.18}$$

Note that we obtain an important difference between the basic exchange rate equation in this chapter (equation (3.15)) and that obtained in the previous chapter (see equation (2.10)). Here the weights given to the fundamentalist and chartist forecasts in the exchange rate equation are the risk-adjusted shares of these two types of forecasting rule, while these shares were not adjusted for risk in the previous chapter. Thus, in the present version of the model, forecasting rules that are very risky (i.e., have a large forecasting error) are given a low weight in the determination of the market clearing exchange rate.

Equations (3.10), defining the variance terms, can be rewritten as follows:

$$\sigma_{c,t}^2 = (1 - \rho)\sigma_{c,t-1}^2 + \rho[E_{t-2}^c(s_{t-1}) - s_{t-1}]^2, \tag{3.19}$$

$$\sigma_{f,t}^2 = (1 - \rho)\sigma_{f,t-1}^2 + \rho[E_{t-2}^f(s_{t-1}) - s_{t-1}]^2. \tag{3.20}$$

Using the definition of the forecasting rules (3.8) and (3.9), this yields

$$\sigma_{c,t}^2 = (1 - \rho)\sigma_{c,t-1}^2 + \rho[(1 + \beta)s_{t-3} - \beta s_{t-2} - s_{t-1}]^2, \tag{3.21}$$

$$\sigma_{f,t}^2 = (1 - \rho)\sigma_{f,t-1}^2 + \rho[(1 - \psi)s_{t-2} - s_{t-1}]^2. \tag{3.22}$$

With suitable changes of variables it is possible to write the system as a six-dimensional system. Set

$$u_t = s_{t-1},$$

$$x_t = u_{t-1} = s_{t-2},$$

$$y_t = x_{t-1} = s_{t-3}.$$

The six dynamic variables are $(s_t, u_t, x_t, y_t, \sigma_{c,t}^2, \sigma_{f,t}^2)$. The state of the system at time $t - 1$, i.e., $(s_{t-1}, u_{t-1}, x_{t-1}, y_{t-1}, \sigma_{c,t-1}^2, \sigma_{f,t-1}^2)$, determines the state of the system at time t, i.e., $(s_t, u_t, x_t, y_t, \sigma_{c,t}^2, \sigma_{f,t}^2)$, through the following six-dimensional dynamical system:

$$s_t = [1 + \beta - \Theta_{f,t}(\psi + \beta)]s_{t-1} - (1 - \Theta_{f,t})\beta u_{t-1}, \tag{3.23}$$

$$u_t = s_{t-1}, \tag{3.24}$$

$$x_t = u_{t-1}, \tag{3.25}$$

$$y_t = x_{t-1}, \tag{3.26}$$

$$\sigma_{c,t}^2 = (1 - \rho)\sigma_{c,t-1}^2 + \rho[(1 + \beta)x_{t-1} - \beta y_{t-1} - s_{t-1}]^2, \tag{3.27}$$

$$\sigma_{f,t}^2 = (1 - \rho)\sigma_{f,t-1}^2 + \rho[(1 - \psi)x_{t-1} - s_{t-1}]^2, \tag{3.28}$$

where

$$\Theta_{f,t} = \frac{w_{f,t}/\sigma_{f,t}^2}{w_{f,t}/\sigma_{f,t}^2 + w_{c,t}/\sigma_{c,t}^2} \tag{3.29}$$

and

$$w_{f,t} = \frac{\exp[\gamma(\pi_{f,t} - \mu\sigma_{f,t}^2)]}{\exp[\gamma(\pi_{c,t} - \mu\sigma_{c,t}^2)] + \exp[\gamma(\pi_{f,t} - \mu\sigma_{f,t}^2)]}, \tag{3.30}$$

$$\pi_{c,t} = (s_{t-1} - u_{t-1}) \operatorname{sgn}[u_{t-1} + \beta(u_{t-1} - x_{t-1}) - s_{t-1}], \tag{3.31}$$

$$\pi_{f,t} = (s_{t-1} - u_{t-1}) \operatorname{sgn}[(1 - \psi)u_{t-1} - s_{t-1}]. \tag{3.32}$$

Here we have set $r = r^* = 0$.

It may now be shown that the model produces two types of steady-state solution. We analyze these consecutively.

3.4.1.1   The Exchange Rate Equals the Fundamental Value

We normalize the fundamental to be 0. Thus, this solution implies that $s_t = 0$. As a result, the variance terms go to 0. This also means that, in the steady state, the risk-adjusted weights of the fundamentalists and chartists are of the form

$$\Theta_{f,t} = \frac{\infty}{\infty} \quad \text{and} \quad \Theta_{c,t} = \frac{\infty}{\infty}.$$

These weights can be rewritten as follows:

$$\Theta_{f,t} = \frac{w_{f,t}}{w_{f,t} + w_{c,t}(\sigma_{f,t}^2/\sigma_{c,t}^2)} \tag{3.33}$$

and

$$\Theta_{c,t} = \frac{w_{c,t}(\sigma_{f,t}^2/\sigma_{c,t}^2)}{w_{f,t} + w_{c,t}(\sigma_{f,t}^2/\sigma_{c,t}^2)}. \tag{3.34}$$

One can show by numerical methods that in the steady state the ratio $\sigma_{f,t}^2/\sigma_{c,t}^2$ converges to 1.[5] We show this ratio in an appendix (see Figure 3.8), where we plot it as a function of time. This implies that in the steady state $\Theta_{f,t} = w_{f,t}$ and $\Theta_{c,t} = w_{c,t}$. (Note that $w_{f,t} + w_{c,t} = 1$.)

The steady state of the system is now obtained by setting

$$(s_{t-1}, u_{t-1}, x_{t-1}, y_{t-1}, \sigma_{f,t-1}^2, \sigma_{c,t-1}^2) = (s_t, u_t, x_t, y_t, \sigma_{f,t}^2, \sigma_{c,t}^2)$$
$$= (\bar{s}, \bar{u}, \bar{x}, \bar{y}, \bar{\sigma}_f^2, \bar{\sigma}_c^2)$$

in the dynamical system (3.23)–(3.28).

There is a unique steady state where

$$\bar{s}, \bar{u}, \bar{x}, \bar{y} = 0, \qquad \bar{\sigma}_f^2, \bar{\sigma}_c^2 = 0.$$

Notice also that, in the steady state,

$$\bar{w}_c = \tfrac{1}{2}, \qquad \bar{w}_f = \tfrac{1}{2}, \qquad \bar{\pi}_c = 0, \qquad \bar{\pi}_f = 0,$$

i.e., the steady state is characterized by the exchange rate being at its fundamental level, by zero profits and zero risk, and by fundamentalist and technical trader fractions equal to $\tfrac{1}{2}$.

3.4.1.2 The Exchange Rate Equals a Nonfundamental Value

The model allows for a second type of steady-state solution. This is a solution in which the exchange rate is constant and permanently different from its (constant) fundamental value. In other words, the model allows for a constant nonzero exchange rate in the steady state.

The existence of such an equilibrium can be shown as follows. We use (3.15) and set $s_t = s_{t-1} = s_{t-2} = \bar{s}$, so that

$$-\Theta_{f,t}\psi\bar{s} = 0.$$

---

[5] It does not appear to be possible to show this by analytical methods.

It can now easily be seen that, if $\Theta_{f,t} = 0$, any constant exchange rate will satisfy this equation. From the definition of $\Theta_{f,t}$, we find that a sufficient condition for $\Theta_{f,t}$ to be 0 is that $\sigma_{f,t}^2 = \bar{\sigma}_f^2 > 0$ and $\sigma_{c,t}^2 = \bar{\sigma}_c^2 = 0$. Note that in this case $\Theta_{c,t} = 1$ and $\bar{\sigma}_f^2 = \psi^2 \bar{s}^2$. In other words, in the steady state there exist fixed-point equilibria with the following characteristics: the exchange rate deviates from the fundamental by a constant amount; thus, fundamentalist forecasting rules lead to a constant error and therefore the risk-adjusted share of fundamentalist rules is zero. The latter is necessary, otherwise agents would still be using the rule so that their forecast of a reversion to the fundamental would move the exchange rate.

Note that in this model the nonfundamental equilibrium (the bubble equilibrium) is a true fixed point, i.e., it remains constant. This contrasts with the bubble equilibria obtained in the previous chapter, where we found that true fixed-point bubble equilibria could only be obtained asymptotically. Here, any value of the exchange rate (different from zero) can be a bubble equilibrium. This is certainly a powerful result. It means that any exchange rate that we observe may potentially be a bubble equilibrium. This feature also explains why the attraction of the fundamental equilibria in the stochastic simulations of the model is weaker than in the simple model of Chapter 2. Recall that in that model we found that the nonfundamental equilibria are not really fixed points, but that these "quasi-equilibria" are very weakly attracted to the fundamental.

3.4.2   Numerical Analysis

The strong nonlinearities make the analysis of the model's global stability impossible. Therefore, we use similar simulation techniques to those presented in Chapter 2. We use the same parameter values. We give the coefficient of risk aversion a value of 1, but in the next chapter we will analyze how this coefficient may be made to change and how such changes affect the results. (See Table 3.1 in Section 3.10, which gives the numerical values of the model parameters and the lags involved.) The dynamical model used in the numerical analysis is the same as in the previous section, except for the fact that we return to the specification of the technical traders' rule as given by (3.9).

We first present three-dimensional bifurcation diagrams that relate the equilibrium exchange rate (vertical axis) to the initial conditions (x-axis) and the parameter β (y-axis) in Figure 3.2. These bifurcation diagrams are explained in greater detail in the previous chapter. We contrast the diagrams obtained in this chapter ("mean-variance" model) with those obtained in Chapter 2. We present two such diagrams for each model, assuming a low and a high value of γ. The most striking aspect of this comparison is that the mean-variance model used in the present chapter leads to a shrinking of the area of fundamental equilibria, and a concomitant increase in the space of bubble equilibria. The reason why this happens can be understood from the analysis of the steady state. We found that, in the risky environment we

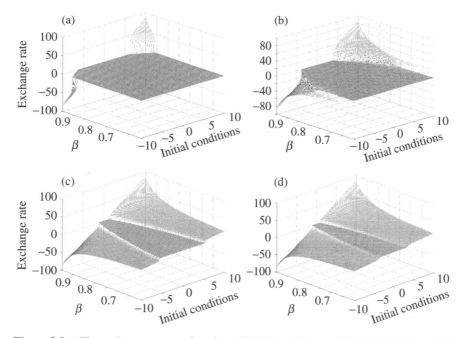

Figure 3.2. The exchange rate as a function of initial conditions and β for (a), (c) the model in Chapter 2 and (b), (d) the mean-variance model. Parts (a) and (b) show results for $\psi = 0.2$ and $\gamma = 1$, and parts (c) and (d) show results for $\psi = 0.2$ and $\gamma = 5$.

model here, any nonzero exchange rate can be a bubble equilibrium. This contrasts with the model of the previous chapter, where bubble equilibria only exist asymptotically. In addition, in the Chapter 2 model these bubble "equilibria" are not really fixed points: once they are reached, there is a very slow movement back to the fundamental equilibrium. All this implies that, in the present mean-variance model, relatively low disturbances can bring us into a bubble equilibrium. These results also enable us to better understand the stochastic simulations in which we found that the exchange rate is disconnected from its underlying fundamental for longer periods in the mean-variance model than in the simple model of Chapter 2.

There is a second difference worth noting. This has to do with the boundary between the bubble and the fundamental equilibrium. We find that, in the mean-variance model of this chapter, the boundary shows more complexity than that obtained in the Chapter 2 model. This may not be visible from Figure 3.2. It can be seen more clearly from the basins of attraction, which we present in Figure 3.3. These were obtained in the same way as in the previous chapter. From a comparison of the mean-variance model with the model of Chapter 2, we see from Figure 3.3 that the basin of attraction around the fundamental equilibrium shrinks in the mean-variance model. In addition, the border between these basins of attraction shows "roughness" in the mean-variance model, while such roughness is absent in the

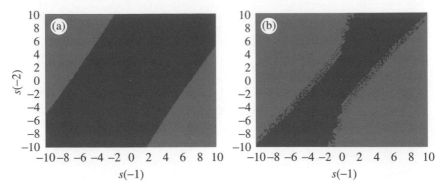

Figure 3.3. (a) Model from Chapter 1 and (b) mean-variance model.
Both parts show the basin of attraction with $\psi = 0.2$, $\beta = 0.9$, and $\gamma = 1$.

model of Chapter 2. We will return to an analysis of this border, and we will argue that it has a fractal nature. This will also be shown to create informational problems for the agents who want to make forecasts.

The main reason why we find such differences between the two models has to do with risk. In the mean-variance model of this chapter, risk plays a greater role than it does in the simple model. In particular, in the mean-variance model the weight given to chartists and fundamentalists in the determination of the market exchange rate also depends on the risks involved. This implies that when, during the bubble phase, the fundamentalists make large forecasting errors, the weight of these forecasts in the determination of the market rate is reduced. As a result, the mean-reverting force of fundamentalist forecasting rules is reduced, thereby reinforcing the bubble. Thus, relatively small shocks can lead to a departure from the fundamental and a movement towards a bubble equilibrium.

3.5 Informational Issues

We have identified a complex border between the fundamental and the bubble equilibria. Such complexity introduces informational problems, which we now explore.

We have used a model in which the informational assumption is that agents cannot comprehend and process the full complexity of the environment they face, and therefore use an informational strategy that consists in trying simple forecasting rules, subjecting these *ex post* to a fitness criterion. The rational-expectations theorists would probably object that, if the underlying model is a simple one, there is no reason why rational agents operating in this model would not use the information embodied in the model. We find, however, that, despite its simplicity, the model creates an extraordinarily complex informational environment, which makes it reasonable for agents to use the kind of forecasting strategies we have

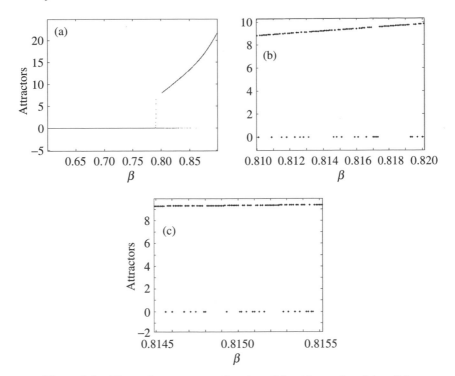

Figure 3.4. The exchange rate as a function of β, with $\gamma = 1$ and $\psi = 0.2$.

assumed here. In other words, despite its simplicity, our model creates an informational environment that is too complex for an individual agent to understand and to process. To see this, let us return to Figure 3.2(b), showing the mean-variance model, and concentrate on the parameter values that lie close to the boundary between fundamental and bubble equilibria. Suppose rational agents in need of forecasting use the information provided by the underlying model. They have estimated β to be 0.815 with a standard error of 0.005 (a remarkable econometric feat). Suppose then that the initial condition happens to be $+5$. One is tempted to think that this should be sufficient information to predict with reasonable certainty whether the exchange rate will be attracted by a fundamental or by a bubble equilibrium. In order to check whether this is the case, we take a "slice" of part (b) of Figure 3.2 at the initial condition equal to $+5$. We show this in Figure 3.4(a).

We observe that, with a value of β around 0.815, we can have a fundamental or a bubble equilibrium. In order to see this more clearly, we enlarge the figure, so that we obtain the fixed attractors for values of β between 0.81 and 0.82. The result is given in Figure 3.4(b). Thus, even with such a sharp estimate of β, agents will be uncertain whether a fundamental or bubble equilibrium will prevail. We find that

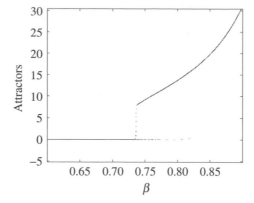

Figure 3.5.   The exchange rate as a function of β,
with $\gamma = 1$, $\psi = 0.2$, and initial shock $= +7$.

there are 22 fundamental and 78 bubble equilibria within the estimated range of
β values.

Now suppose that a new econometric technique allows these agents to reduce
the standard error by a factor of 10, so that they now estimate β to be located
between 0.8145 and 0.8155. It would now appear from Figure 3.4(b) that agents
can increase the precision with which they can predict the probability of a bubble
equilibrium. This conclusion would be incorrect, however. We show this by enlarg-
ing Figure 3.4(b) around the parameter value of $\beta = 0.815$. The result is shown
in Figure 3.4(c). We observe that the higher precision of the estimate of β has not
increased the precision with which agents can predict whether a fundamental or
a bubble equilibrium will prevail. Within that narrower range of estimated β values, we now find 23 bubble equilibria (out of 100). Successive further enlargements
around 0.815 show that this proportion remains approximately constant. This result
has to do with the fractal nature of the boundary between the fundamental and bubble equilibria. Every successive enlargement will reveal the same structure. The
agents would need infinite precision to be able to predict whether, with a given
initial condition, a particular parameter value will lead to a bubble equilibrium.

This problem is compounded by the fact that the "border values" of β depend on
the initial shock. We show this by "cutting another slice" from Figure 3.2(b) at the
initial condition equal to $+7$. We show the result in Figure 3.5. We find that, with
this new initial condition, the border values of β are located around 0.75, with a
similarly complex feature.

We conclude that agents need infinite precision in their knowledge of the initial
conditions and the parameter β (and also, in fact, the other parameters of the model)
to be able to predict whether the exchange rate will move to a fundamental or a
bubble equilibrium. In other words, infinitesimally small errors in computing the

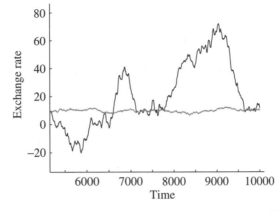

Figure 3.6. Market and fundamental exchange rates, with $\psi = 0.2$, $\beta = 0.9$, and $\gamma = 5$.

initial conditions or in estimating β (and the other parameters) lead to very large errors in the prediction of the exchange rate.

The informational problem identified here, of course, only holds in the border areas around the basins of attraction between different types of equilibrium. Although these border areas can be relatively large, given that they depend on the different parameters of the model and the different initial conditions, there are nonborder areas that allow for precise prediction. What the model thus implies is that, in a stochastic environment, agents who estimate the underlying structure will sometimes be able to make accurate predictions, while at other times they will make very large prediction errors. In other words, the forecast errors are likely to be nonnormally distributed (to exhibit fat tails).

Thus, even in the very simple model we developed here, individual agents face enormous informational problems. This helps us to understand why agents will often not attempt to use all the information provided by the underlying structural model.

3.6 Some Preliminary Remarks on Empirical Predictions of the Model

The model presented in this chapter and Chapter 2 makes a number of predictions about the dynamics of the exchange rate movements. Here we briefly discuss these and show the nature of these predictions in a qualitative way. In Chapter 8 we will analyze the empirical implications of the model in much more detail and with more statistical rigor.

One can group the empirical predictions made by the model into three categories:

(1) the disconnection of the exchange rate from its fundamental;

(2) the excess volatility of the exchange rate; and

(3) the nonnormality of the changes in the market exchange rate.

3.6.1 Market Exchange Rates Are Disconnected from Their Fundamentals

We illustrated the disconnect phenomenon of the simulated exchange rate in Figure 3.1. We obtain this result for a broad range of parameter values. We show another example of a simulation of the market and fundamental exchange rates in Figure 3.6. We observe that for most of the time the exchange rate is disconnected from its fundamental value. This phenomenon has also been observed in many empirical studies. In Chapter 1 we referred to the recent study of Ehrmann and Fratzscher (2005) (see Figure 1.3). The latter shows daily observations of the USD/DM (euro) exchange rate from 1993 to 2003, together with an index of the cumulated unexpected changes in a series of fundamental variables (e.g., growth in GDP, inflation, unemployment, etc.). Figure 3.6 strikingly resembles Figure 1.3 in a qualitative sense. Thus, our model predicts a feature that is also found in reality, i.e., that most of the movements in real-life exchange rates are unrelated to news that occurs in the fundamental economic variables.

3.6.2 Excess Volatility and Nonnormality

Our model also predicts that the exchange rate tends to be subjected to larger short-term volatility than the underlying fundamental, and that the changes in the exchange rate are not normally distributed. We illustrate these features in Figure 3.7, which is very similar to Figure 2.4. Part (b) shows the (normally distributed) changes in the fundamental exchange rate, while part (a) shows the changes in the simulated market exchange rate. We observe that the market exchange rate shows significantly higher short-term volatility. In addition, there are peaks in these changes that are absent from the normally distributed changes in the fundamental. Thus, our model transforms normally distributed changes in the fundamentals into exchange rate movements that are considerably more volatile and that exhibit statistical features that appear to be different from the normal distribution.

3.7 Rational and Behavioral Bubbles

The model presented here and in Chapter 2 provides a theoretical underpinning for the emergence of bubbles and their subsequent disappearance. It can be useful to contrast this aspect of our model with the rational-expectations model, which also provides a theory of bubbles and crashes.

Rational-expectations models typically produce "saddle-path" solutions, i.e., there is one path that leads to the unique fundamental equilibrium, and an infinity of unstable paths that lead the exchange rate (the asset price) to either $+\infty$ or $-\infty$.[6] Thus, rational-expectations models provide a potential theoretical underpinning for bubbles. These are then movements of the exchange rate (asset price) along an

---

[6] See, for example, Blanchard and Fischer (1989) for a technical analysis of solutions in rational-expectations models.

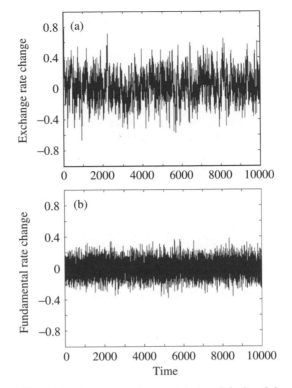

Figure 3.7. (a) Exchange rate change with $\psi = 0.2$, $\beta = 0.9$, $\gamma = 1$.
(b) Fundamental rate change.

explosive path. Such a path is one of the infinitely many unstable solutions obtained in a rational-expectations model where agents are fully and perfectly informed.

In models with perfectly and fully informed agents (perfect foresight models), however, a bubble with a crash cannot exist because, when the timing of the crash is known (and by definition this is known in a perfect foresight model), agents will anticipate this and, by backward induction, prevent the bubble from happening. The insight of Blanchard (1979) and Blanchard and Watson (1982) was to show that a bubble followed by a crash is possible in a stochastic rational-expectations model. The crash occurs in such a model because agents attach some positive probability of a future crash. As a result, at some point a probable event inevitably becomes reality and a crash occurs. Agents, however, cannot predict when this will happen. The uncertainty about the exact time of the crash is necessary to make a "rational bubble" possible.

The problem with this "rational bubble" theory is that it gives no good explanation of why crashes occur.[7] The only reason why these occur is that they are assumed to

---

[7]The Blanchard–Watson rational bubble model can also be criticized for the fact that it predicts the occurrence of bubbles whose features are not found in empirical evidence. For example, it predicts that

occur. The assumption that crashes must occur sounds reasonable, since we have not observed an everlasting bubble. It is, however, imposed in an ad hoc way, from outside the model.[8]

Other models have been developed in which rational and irrational agents interact (De Long et al. 1990; Shleifer and Vishny 1997; Abreu and Brunnermeier 2003). In these models, bubbles arise because of a failure of arbitrage by the rational agents. These models also assume that crashes occur for exogenous reasons.

Another implication of the "rational bubble" model is that the exchange rate (asset price) is always on a bubble path. The reason is that the fundamental solution has a knife-edge property (saddle path). This means that the slightest deviation from the fundamental path brings the exchange rate onto an unstable path. In a stochastic environment, these slight deviations are inevitable. Thus, the "rational bubble" theory predicts that the exchange rate will permanently be on a bubble path.

In our model, a bubble is an equilibrium (a fixed-point attractor) to which the exchange rate is attracted if exogenous shocks bring it within the basin of attraction of the bubble equilibrium. At the same time, the fundamental equilibrium is locally stable. This makes the "behavioral" bubble fundamentally different from the "rational bubble." First, in our behavioral model, one needs a sufficiently large shock away from the fundamental to move the exchange rate towards a bubble attractor. Thus, in "normal" times, the exchange rate is driven by its fundamental value. This contrasts with the "rational bubble" theory, in which the fundamental equilibrium is unstable, so that the exchange rate is always on an unstable bubble path. Second, the forces that lead to a bubble are the same as the forces that lead to a crash. In the previous chapter, we showed that large shocks in the fundamental increase the probability of the occurrence of a bubble. Once in a bubble equilibrium, a sufficiently large shock in the fundamental leads to a crash. In this sense our model provides for a theory of both the occurrence of a bubble and its subsequent crash. Third, the timing of the bubble and of the crash is uncertain. This uncertainty is not imposed exogenously, but comes from the structure of the model. For we have shown that the basins of attraction around the fundamental and the bubble equilibrium have a fractal nature. As a result, the exact timing of the bubble and of the crash is dependent on "trivial events."

---

the bubbles are exponentially distributed, whereas the empirical evidence suggests that there are fat tails in the distribution of bubbles (see Mandelbrot 1997; Lux and Sornette 2002). In addition, the rational bubble model predicts that there is symmetry between bubble and crash phases, i.e., that after the crash the asset price returns to its fundamental value. Again, this does seem to square with the empirical evidence (see Sornette 2003).

[8] There is an important literature analyzing the conditions under which rational bubbles occur in general equilibrium models. In general, the conditions for such bubbles to occur are tighter in these models than in partial equilibrium models because of some finiteness condition (e.g., a finite number of individuals (see Tirole 1982)). Typically, these models have not been concerned with an explicit modeling of the crash.

The view of a bubble as an equilibrium concept is reminiscent of the notion of "sunspots," which is also an equilibrium concept in rational-expectations models (see Blanchard and Fischer 1989, p. 255; Azariadis and Guesnerie 1984). Sunspot equilibria arise because some agents believe that an arbitrary variable (number of sunspots) influences the asset price. As a result, rational agents who know this attach some probability that a sunspot equilibrium will be reached. In our model, a bubble equilibrium exists because some agents use extrapolative forecasting rules which, under certain conditions, can crowd out agents who believe in the existence of a fundamental value of the exchange rate. Thus, a bubble equilibrium is possible not because some agents are irrational and believe that sunspots affect the exchange rate, but because these agents are agnostic about the existence of fundamentals (including sunspots), and therefore rely only on the past exchange rate movements as the source of their information.

3.8 Conclusion

In this chapter we added more structure to the underlying exchange rate model. We did this by introducing risk in the portfolio decision of individual agents. This has enriched the dynamics of the model, and has strengthened our previous finding that the exchange rate can be attracted by fundamental and nonfundamental equilibria in an unpredictable way. In addition, adding risk to the model has complicated the informational problem that individual agents face. In particular, we found that investing in better econometric tools in order to understand the underlying structure may not pay off, in that it does not always increase the precision with which agents can predict the occurrence of bubbles.

The other conclusions arrived at in Chapter 2 can be maintained. In particular, the more complex model of the present chapter generates a dynamics in which the exchange rate is disconnected from its fundamental value much of the time, and in which normally distributed shocks in the fundamental variable appear to be transformed in nonnormally distributed exchange rate changes.

In the next chapter we study some additional features of the model derived here. In particular, we explore the issues of risk and risk perception.

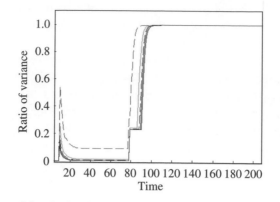

Figure 3.8.   Ratio of variances for fundamentalists and chartists
with $\psi = 0.2$, $\beta = 0.9$, and $\gamma = 1$.

3.9   Appendix: The Variance Ratio $\sigma^2_{f,t}/\sigma^2_{c,t}$ in the Steady State

In Figure 3.8 we show the ratio of the variance of the fundamentalists to the variance of the chartists $\sigma^2_{f,t}$ and $\sigma^2_{c,t}$, as it converges to its steady-state value. We simulated the model for different parameter configurations and different initial values of the exchange rate. In each case we found that the variance ratio converged to 1 as the system approached the steady state. In Section 3.2 we described in more detail how these simulations are set up.

Table 3.1. Numerical values of parameters.

Parameters	Values	Sensitivity analysis
ψ	0.2	No
ρ	0.5	No
β	0.9	Yes
γ	5	Yes
μ	1	No
r and r^*	0	No

3.10 Appendix: Numerical Values of the Parameters Used in the Base Simulation

In Table 3.1 we present the numerical values of the model. In the first column we list the model parameters, and in the second column we present the numerical values in the base simulations. The last column indicates whether or not we have performed a sensitivity analysis on these numerical values. If not, we use the same numerical value in all simulations.

Limits to Arbitrage

4.1 Introduction

In the previous two chapters, we developed a model that produces two types of equilibrium: fundamental and nonfundamental. The nonfundamental equilibrium is reached because a series of stochastic disturbances in one direction makes extrapolative (chartist) forecasting rules profitable, thereby leading fundamentalists to abandon their forecasting rules and to embrace extrapolative rules. The paradox is that, while such rallies in the exchange rate develop, the fundamentalists' forecasting rules tell agents that there are profits to be made in the future by taking a fundamentalist position. And yet fundamentalists do not act on this information. Thus, fundamentally the occurrence of bubbles and subsequent crashes is made possible because agents fail to arbitrage. In this chapter we develop this theme further and we analyze the sources of these arbitrage failures.[1]

In the first part of this chapter we stress the importance of risk aversion as a reason why agents in our model fail to arbitrage and we show how changes in the degree of risk aversion can fundamentally alter the dynamics of bubbles and crashes.

In the second part we introduce a new element in the analysis, the existence of transaction costs in the goods market. We will show how these transaction costs also lead to arbitrage failures.

4.2 Risk Aversion and Limits to Arbitrage

Up to now we have treated the degree of risk aversion, μ, as a fixed parameter. In fact, in all the simulations performed up to now we have set $\mu = 1$. Is there reason to believe that risk aversion may not be constant? The answer is that most probably the degree of risk aversion is very much affected by how agents perceive risk and that this perception changes over time. Thus, there are periods in which agents

---

[1] The concept of arbitrage failures is well-known in the behavioral finance literature (see Shleifer 2000). One could quarrel about semantics here. In particular, the term "arbitrage" is often used for buying and selling activities that do not involve risk. This contrasts with speculation that also involves buying and selling where agents take risk. Thus, in a way it would be better to talk about "failures to speculate." We will stick to the term "failures to arbitrage" because this has become the more familiar term in the literature.

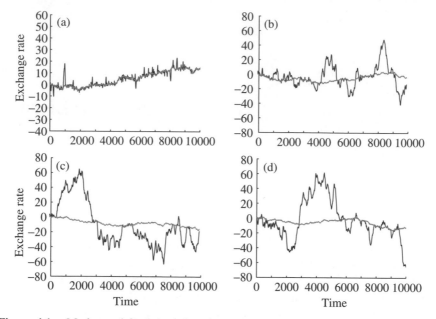

Figure 4.1. Market and fundamental exchange rates with $\psi = 0.2$, $\beta = 0.9$, $\gamma = 5$, $\rho = 0.5$, and (a) $\mu = 0.1$, (b) $\mu = 0.5$, (c) $\mu = 0.75$, (d) $\mu = 1$. Gray line, exchange rate; black line, fundamental rate.

have a high awareness of risk. It is as if their risk aversion increases. During other periods agents' perception of risk declines. It is as if their risk aversion declines.[2] In this section we analyze how changes in risk aversion affect the working of the model.

It should be noted that we want to analyze changes in perceptions of risk that occur without any underlying objective changes in risk. Clearly, if risk perception were tightly linked to objective changes in risk, the mean-variance model would be well suited to deal with this. In that case, the conditional variance of the underlying asset price would reflect whatever changes may occur in measurable risk. The model would capture these changes perfectly. There is, however, a lot of psychological evidence indicating that agents' perception of risk may have little to do with objective risk (see Tversky and Kahneman 1981; Thaler 1994). We will analyze these changes in perception here, by allowing μ to change exogenously. In the next chapter we will make these changes endogenous by linking them to the degree with which the exchange rate deviates from its fundamental.

We first present simulations in the time domain on assuming different values of the coefficient of risk aversion, μ. We show examples of such a simulation in Figure 4.1. We use the mean-variance model developed in Chapter 3. We find

---

[2] Lee et al. (1991) provide interesting evidence of changing risk perceptions using data on the discounts of closed-end funds.

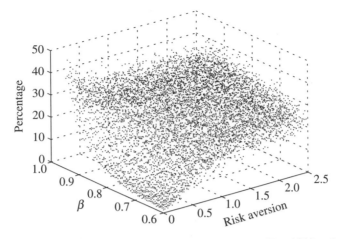

Figure 4.2. Percentage of the time in which bubbles occur: $T = 1000$ and $\gamma = 5$.

that when risk aversion is sufficiently low the exchange rate remains in the close neighborhood of the fundamental most of the time. As μ increases, however, the deviations from the fundamental are larger and more sustained. With a risk aversion μ close to or exceeding 0.5, we find that the exchange rate is often disconnected from its fundamental for long periods of time, suggesting that it is attracted by nonfundamental (bubble) equilibria.

In order to further analyze the different dynamics produced by changing degrees of risk aversion, we apply similar techniques to those in previous chapters. We first simulate the model stochastically for different values of the degree of risk aversion μ. We compute the percentage of time for which the exchange rate is involved in a bubble. (In Chapter 2 we described in greater detail how such simulations were implemented.) We show the results in Figure 4.2. The vertical axis shows the percentage of time for which the exchange rate is involved in a bubble. We see that this percentage depends both on the degree of risk aversion and the chartists' extrapolation parameter, β. Let us concentrate on risk aversion here. We observe from Figure 4.2 that an increase in the degree of risk aversion increases the probability of the occurrence of bubbles. Thus, what we observed in the time domain is confirmed here. This means that, as agents' perception of risk increases (keeping objective risk unchanged), the probability of bubbles also increases. Before trying to understand this, it will also be useful to analyze the deterministic component of the model. We argued in the previous chapters that such an analysis allows us to understand the structure of the model and the nature of the equilibria produced in the model. In Figure 4.3, we present a three-dimensional bifurcation diagram which is constructed in the same way as those presented in the previous chapters, i.e., we plot the equilibrium exchange rate on the vertical axis, for different initial conditions (x-axis) and for different values of the coefficient of risk aversion, μ (y-axis).

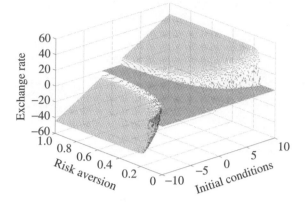

Figure 4.3.   The exchange rate as a function of initial conditions and
risk aversion with $\psi = 0.2$, $\beta = 0.9$, $\gamma = 5$, and $\rho = 0.5$.

We find that when the degree of risk aversion is low (typically less than 0.2) the
model produces only fundamental equilibria. (Remember that we have normalized
the fundamental to be 0. As a result, exchange rate equilibria that are zero are fundamental equilibria.) As μ increases, the space of fundamental equilibria shrinks
and the space of nonfundamental equilibria increases. Note also that the border
between the two spaces is not smooth, but is characterized by discontinuities. We
encountered this phenomenon when we analyzed the sensitivity of the solutions to
other parameters of the model.

How can this result be interpreted? Let us focus first on the fundamentalists to
answer this question and suppose that the exchange rate moves upward, away from
its fundamental, as a result of some shock. Fundamentalists will then expect to
make profits by betting on a future decline in the exchange rate. At the same time,
however, they observe that their past forecast errors are high. If their degree of
risk aversion is low, they will attach a low weight to these forecast errors. As a
result, they will be willing to exploit the ensuing profit opportunities and to remain
fundamentalists. Thus, they will push the exchange rate back to its fundamental
value. If, however, their risk aversion is high, they will attach a high weight to the
forecast errors they are making during a bubble. In other words, their perception
of the risk will be high. As a result, they may not be willing to exploit the profit
opportunity, and instead they may switch to chartist rules. It follows that the mean-
reverting force exerted by fundamentalists is weak, allowing bubbles to arise. Thus,
nonfundamental equilibria arise because of a failure of arbitrage by fundamentalists.
The source of this arbitrage failure then lies in the fact that fundamentalists do not
want to take risks.

Let us now turn to the chartists. During the bubble phase, the chartists make
small forecasting errors, so they perceive risk to be low. Thus, if they are very risk
averse, the weight attached to this favorable risk development is high, leading to an

increase in the utility of chartist rules and a surge in their attractiveness. When risk aversion is low, this force of attraction towards chartism is correspondingly lower.

Thus, quite surprisingly risk aversion has opposing effects on the utility of fundamentalist and chartist rules during a bubble. When risk aversion is high, the weight attached to the high forecasting errors that are made with fundamentalist rules is high, and so is the weight attached to the low forecasting errors made by chartist rules. As a result, chartism becomes attractive during a bubble, while fundamentalism becomes unattractive. The failure of arbitrage by fundamentalists is reinforced, and as a result the mean-reverting dynamics in the market is weakened. This also means that, in a world where agents perceive risks to be high, nonfundamental equilibria will be more frequent. Thus, there is a self-fulfilling element here: because agents perceive the world to be risky, they fail to arbitrage, which leads to bubbles, thereby increasing the riskiness of the world.

4.3 Transaction Costs and Limits to Arbitrage

Transaction costs in international trade continue to be substantial. There is a perception today that, thanks to globalization, transaction costs in international trade have become very small. Certainly, transport costs have declined. There are, however, other large sources of transaction costs. These arise because borders continue to act as major obstacles to trade. Several recent empirical studies report the continued existence of large price differentials for the same traded goods across borders. The well-known study of Engel and Rogers (1995) comes to the conclusion that the existence of a border between the United States and Canada has the effect of adding a distance of more than 2000 miles between twin cities on both sides of the border. McCallum (1995) finds that trade between Canadian provinces is about ten times higher than their trade with American states, after correction for distances. In another study, Haskel and Wolf (2001) find that the IKEA furniture stores apply price differentials of 20–40% for exactly the same products sold in different countries. Similar price differentials have been found for many other products. In Table 4.1 we provide additional evidence. We show the price dispersion of a sample of identical products in the European Union. We observe that price differentials of up to 40% occur in both the foodstuff and electronic product categories.

These price differentials suggest that producers apply "pricing to market," i.e., they adjust their prices to local market conditions. Such pricing strategies, however, can only be applied successfully if transaction costs prevent arbitrage. Thus, the large observed price differentials suggest that transaction costs for traded goods are large and of the order of 20–40%. These transaction costs are not only the costs of transportation, but also the costs arising from different legislations and regulations across countries. For example, different health and safety regulations add to the costs of goods arbitrage across countries. The existence of transaction costs has led

Table 4.1.   Inter-country price dispersion for selected products (excluding VAT), 2000.

Supermarket product	Price dispersion (%)
Evian mineral water	43
Rexona deodorant	21
Sensodyne toothpaste	21
Mars bars (single)	21
Mars bars (multipack)	22
Coca Cola	21
Pedigree Pal dog food	10
Plenitude face care	21
Colgate toothpaste	14
Bonne Maman marmalade	19

Electronic products	Price dispersion (%)
Philips audio system	28
Sony audio system	38
Canon camcorder	32
Panasonic portable CD player	40
Philips portable CD player	56
Pioneer CD player	34
Sony CD player	28
Phillips TV (14 in.)	41
Sony TV (14 in.)	33
Panasonic TV (28 in.)	25
Philips TV (28 in.)	61
JVC VCR	30
Panasonic VCR	22
Sony VCR	44

Source: European Commission, *Price dispersion in the internal market* and *Price differentials for supermarket goods in the EU*. Both documents can be downloaded from www.europa.eu.int. Note: price dispersion is defined as the percentage difference between the most expensive and the cheapest item.

Obstfeld and Rogoff (2000) to argue that transaction costs are key to understanding the major puzzles in international economics.[3]

The continued existence of large transaction costs in the goods markets has important implications. In general, transaction costs produce a band of inaction in the goods market. Let us take an example. Suppose that the cost of transaction of goods across the border is a uniform 20%. This means that price differentials for the same good in two countries will have to exceed 20% in order to make it worthwhile for agents to engage in arbitrage. Conversely, price differentials that are lower than

---

[3] The importance of transaction costs in exchange rate modeling has been stressed by Dumas (1992), Sercu et al. (1995), and Obstfeld and Rogoff (2000). The importance of transaction costs in the goods market has also been confirmed empirically (Taylor et al. 2001; Kilian and Taylor 2003).

20% will not lead to arbitrage. As a result, these price differentials can continue to exist indefinitely. There is, in other words, a band of inaction within which the forces of arbitrage do not operate.

The existence of a band of inaction in the goods market has important implications for the modeling of the exchange rate. We discuss these in the next sections.

4.3.1 The Model with Transaction Costs

Remember that the fundamentalists make a forecast of the exchange rate based on their knowledge of its fundamental value. Thus, when the exchange rate exceeds its fundamental value, fundamentalists expect it to decline in the future so as to return to its fundamental value. This is because of the existence of a mechanism in the goods market that will bring the exchange rate back to its fundamental value. In a world with transaction costs, things are different. In such a world, fundamentalists know that there is a band of inaction in the goods market. Thus, when the exchange rate deviates from its fundamental value by less than the transaction costs, fundamentalists know that there is no mechanism in the goods market that will bring the exchange rate back to its fundamental value. Only when the deviation of the exchange rate from its fundamental value exceeds the transaction costs will such a mechanism exist, and only in that case will the fundamentalists expect that the future exchange rate will be driven back towards its fundamental value. In other words, when the exchange rate deviates from the fundamental by less than the transaction-cost band, fundamentalists do not expect profit opportunities to arise in the future because they know that the mean-reverting forces that bring back the exchange rate to its fundamental are not operative. As a result, they will then not engage in arbitrage.

We implement this idea more formally in the following way.

When $|s_{t-1} - s_{t-1}^*| > C$, fundamentalists make the following forecasts:

$$E_t^f(\Delta s_{t+1}) = -\psi(s_{t-1} - s_{t-1}^*), \tag{4.1}$$

where C is the transaction cost in the goods market, which we assume to be constant. Equation (4.1) is the forecasting rule we have used in the previous chapter.[4]

However, when the exchange rate deviations from the fundamental value are smaller than the transaction costs in the goods markets, fundamentalists know that there is no mechanism that drives the exchange rate towards its equilibrium value. As a result, they expect the changes in the exchange rate to follow a white-noise process and the best they can do is to forecast no change. Thus,

$$\text{when } |s_t - s_t^*| \leqslant C, \quad E_t^f(\Delta s_{t+1}) = 0.$$

---

[4] Note that since $\psi < 1$, market inefficiencies other than transaction costs continue to play a role when the exchange rate moves outside the transaction-cost band. As a result, these inefficiencies prevent the exchange rate from adjusting instantaneously.

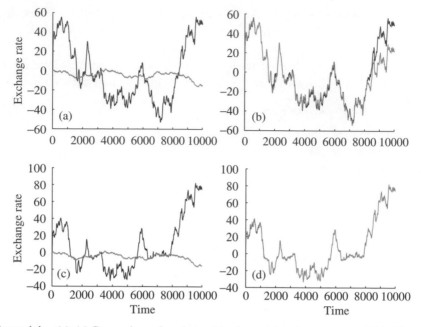

Figure 4.4. (a), (c) Comparison of market and fundamental exchange rates and (b), (d) comparison of exchange rates showing the sensitivity to initial conditions. In (a) and (b) $C = 5$, and in (c) and (d) $C = 0$; in all parts $\psi = 0.2$, $\beta = 0.9$, and $\gamma = 2$. In (a) and (c) the black line denotes exchange rate and the gray line denotes fundamental rate. In (b) and (d) the black line denotes "without shock" results and the gray line denotes "with shock" results.

4.3.2 Stochastic Simulations and Sensitivity to Initial Conditions

We now analyze the model in its stochastic environment. As before, we assume that the fundamental exchange rate is driven by a random-walk process. We compare results of the model with and without transaction costs. We show an example of a stochastic simulation in Figure 4.4. Parts (a) and (b) show the exchange rate in the time domain in the presence of transaction costs. Parts (c) and (d) show the exchange rate in the absence of transaction costs. The difference between the two models is quite striking. Let us first concentrate on a comparison of parts (a) and (c), which show the market exchange rate and the fundamental rate. When transaction costs exist (here we set $C = 5$, but we will analyze other values later), we see that the fundamental exchange rate exerts very little attraction on the market exchange rate. The exchange rate wanders around the fundamental exchange rate without staying in its neighborhood for longer than a few periods. When transaction costs are absent, we observe a different dynamic. There are now longer periods during which the exchange rate stays very close to its fundamental value. These periods alternate with others during which the exchange rate is attracted by bubble equilibria. Thus, when transaction costs are absent, the exchange rate switches between fundamental and bubble regimes. We identified this phenomenon in the previous chapters. This regime switching does not seem to occur with the same frequency when transaction costs are present, because the attractive power of the fundamental is absent in a close neighborhood around it. Note also that the transaction-cost band does not exert a strong power of attraction, i.e., we do not observe that the exchange rate stays within the transaction-cost band around the fundamental for long periods of time. Finally, when comparing parts (a) and (c), it appears that the existence of transaction costs does not produce larger deviations from the fundamental. These deviations, however, become more frequent when transaction costs exist.

A second difference in the dynamics of the exchange rate in a model with and without transaction costs relates to "sensitivity to initial conditions." Comparing parts (b) and (d), we find that sensitivity to initial conditions is significant when transaction costs exist, while it is relatively weak when transaction costs are zero. In fact, in part (d) we show a simulation where there is no sensitivity to initial conditions in the model without transaction costs (the lines with and without shock coincide exactly). In Chapter 3, we documented that sensitivity to initial conditions does occasionally occur in a model without transaction costs. This, however, is relatively rare. When transaction costs are nonzero, sensitivity to initial conditions is pervasive.

Sensitivity to initial conditions is a measure of the complexity of a system. In this sense it can be concluded that the addition of transaction costs adds to the complexity of the model.

4.3.3 Analysis of the Deterministic Version of the Model

The analysis of the deterministic version of the model will enable us to better understand the previous results. We proceed in the same way as in the previous chapters, although we do not perform a steady-state analysis here. Such an analysis is made difficult because of the additional discontinuity introduced by transaction costs. We solve the model numerically and we plot the solutions for the exchange rate as a function of the initial conditions and different parameters of the model. We obtain similar bifurcation diagrams as in the previous chapters. We show such bifurcation diagrams in Figure 4.5(a),(b). In part (a) we have set the transaction costs, $C = 5$. In part (b) we have set $C = 0$. A comparison of the two then allows us to find out how the introduction of transaction costs affects the nature of the equilibria. Two results stand out. First, the bifurcation diagram in the presence of transaction costs shows many more discontinuities than that without transaction costs. This is not really surprising. The transaction-cost band adds a discontinuity in the model. Second, and more surprisingly, we find that, in the presence of transaction costs, the area of fundamental equilibria is smaller and the zone of bubble equilibria is larger than in the absence of transaction costs. Note that in the presence of transaction costs we call all the exchange rate solutions that are located within the

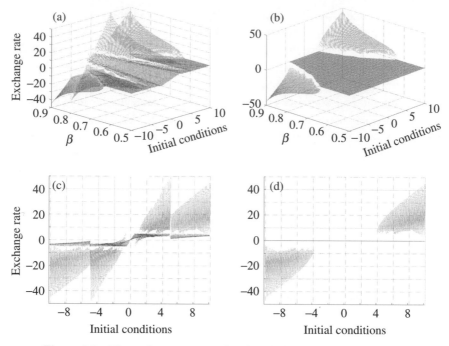

Figure 4.5. The exchange rate as a function of the initial conditions and β with $\psi = 0.2$, $\gamma = 1$, and (a), (c) $C = 5$, and (b), (d) $C = 0$.

transaction-cost band "fundamental equilibria." This is because points within the transaction-cost band do not induce fundamentalists to forecast a change. From the fundamentalist point of view all these points are fundamentals. Exchange rate solutions (attractors) located outside the transaction-cost band are nonfundamental (bubble) equilibria.

The increased area of nonfundamental equilibria in the presence of transaction costs is also made very clear from parts (c) and (d). These show the projection of the exchange rate solutions from the three-dimensional space of parts (a) and (b) into two-dimensional spaces, where the initial conditions are plotted on the horizontal axis. We clearly see that in the presence of transaction costs the number of non-fundamental equilibria has increased relative to the case without transaction costs. More specifically, we find that, in the presence of transaction costs, small shocks in the initial exchange rate drive the exchange rate towards a nonfundamental equi-librium, while in the absence of transaction costs we need much larger shocks in the initial exchange rate to move to a nonfundamental equilibrium. It is even more surprising to find that, in the presence of transaction costs, initial shocks that are smaller than the transaction band can lead to a nonfundamental equilibrium. To give an example, when $\beta = 0.9$, an initial shock of $+2$ leads to a nonfundamental equilibrium in the presence of a transaction cost of 5. In the absence of transaction

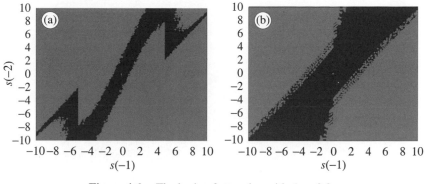

Figure 4.6. The basin of attraction with $\psi = 0.2$,
$\beta = 0.9$, $\gamma = 1$, and (a) $C = 5$, and (b) $C = 0$.

costs, an initial shock of $+2$ leads to a fundamental equilibrium. It should also be noted that, in the presence of transaction costs, the distance (deviation) between nonfundamental and fundamental equilibria is not higher than in the absence of transaction costs. However, smaller initial shocks will drive the exchange rate into a nonfundamental equilibrium when transaction costs exist.

How can one explain this surprising result? Within the transaction-cost band there is no mean reversion. Thus, a small initial shock, which, in the absence of the band, would have set in motion a force pulling back the exchange rate to its fundamental value, is now absent. As a result, when transaction costs exist, even small initial shocks can create sufficient chartist momentum to "propel" the exchange rate outside the band towards a nonfundamental equilibrium. Once outside the transaction-cost band, the propelling forces of the chartists have accumulated sufficient momentum to overcome the mean-reversion forces exerted by the fundamentalists. The latter "arrive too late" because they are triggered only when the exchange rate has left the transaction-cost band. Note that the phenomenon whereby the exchange rate is "propelled" outside the transaction-cost band occurs only when the extrapolation parameter β is sufficiently large.

In contrast, in the absence of the transaction-cost band, the mean-reverting forces start working immediately, even for very small initial shocks in the exchange rate. Thus, one needs much larger initial shocks to create sufficient chartist momentum to overcome the "gravitational force" exerted by the fundamentalists.

Another way to illustrate this result is to compute the basins of attractions around the fundamental and the nonfundamental equilibria. We explained in Chapter 3 how this is done. In Figure 4.6 we show the result. Part (a) shows the basins of attraction in the presence of transaction costs, while part (b) shows these basins when transaction costs are absent. Note that the black area is the collection of initial values of the exchange rate attracted to the fundamental equilibrium, while the gray area is the collection of the initial exchange rates that is attracted by the nonfundamental

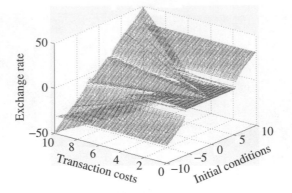

Figure 4.7. The exchange rate as a function of the initial conditions and transaction costs, with $\psi = 0.2$, $\beta = 0.8$, and $\gamma = 1$.

equilibria. Note also that, while in the absence of transaction costs there is only one fundamental equilibrium, i.e., the point with coordinates $(0, 0)$, in the presence of transaction costs, all exchange rate solutions within the transaction-cost band are fundamental equilibria. It can be seen that the single fundamental equilibrium has a stronger attractive force in the absence of transaction costs than the whole collection of fundamental equilibria obtained in the presence of transaction costs.

We conclude that the transaction-cost band works not as an attracting (gravitational) force but as a repulsing one. This is, in a way, quite surprising. We tend to imagine a band of inaction such as our transaction-cost band as a stabilizing force. This is not the case here because its existence weakens the mean-reverting (stabilizing) forces exerted by agents who use fundamentalist rules. As a result, the extrapolative forecasting rules used by chartists are given more leeway to exert their destabilizing effects.

This feature of the model allows us to understand the results obtained in the stochastic simulations. There we found that the exchange rate does not seem to be attracted to the fundamental value. It tends to move around it in unpredictable ways, and remains disconnected for longer periods than in the model without transaction costs. Thus, the existence of transaction costs and the ensuing failure to arbitrage adds an additional dimension to the phenomenon of disconnection of the exchange rate from its fundamental.

4.3.4 Sensitivity Analysis with Respect to Transaction Costs

The importance of transaction costs can also be illustrated by analyzing the sensitivity of the exchange rate solutions to different values of the transaction cost parameter. We do this by constructing a bifurcation diagram in the same way as in the previous section. We now set the transaction costs (C) on the y-axis (see Figure 4.7). On the vertical axis we plot the exchange rate solutions corresponding to these different values of C (and the different initial conditions on the x-axis). We

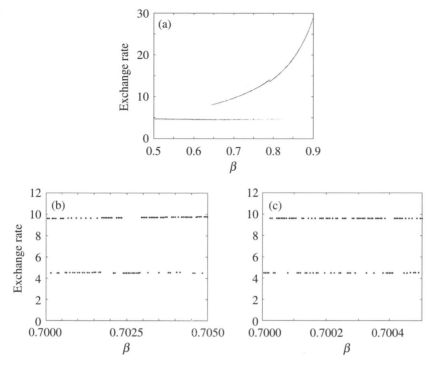

Figure 4.8. The exchange rate as a function of β with $\psi = 0.2$, $\gamma = 1$, and $C = 5$.

observe the following. For small values of transaction costs we obtain a relatively large zone of fundamental equilibria (represented by the horizontal plane parallel to the x-axis). As transaction costs increase, this zone of fundamental equilibria tends to disappear. We also obtain many more discontinuities in the space of bubble equilibria. This illustrates in a different way the increase in complexity associated with transaction costs.

4.3.5 Complexity and Information

In this section we analyze the question of how the additional complexity introduced by the existence of transaction costs affects the informational problems of agents making forecasts using the model. We start by performing a similar experiment to that in Chapter 3, when we discussed informational problems (see Section 3.5). We "cut a slice" from Figure 4.5 at the initial condition +3. We show this in Figure 4.8, which plots the solutions of the exchange rate as a function of β, given the initial condition +3. We find that for small values of β the exchange rate solution is a fundamental equilibrium located within the transaction-cost band. For large values of β the exchange rate solution is a bubble equilibrium located outside the transaction-cost band. As in Chapter 3, we find

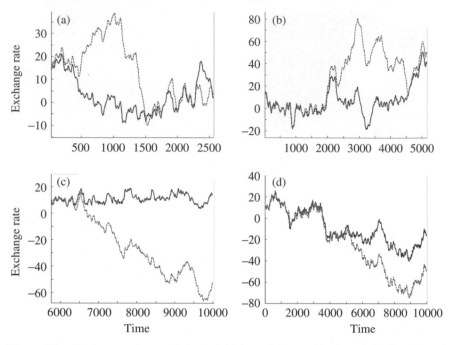

Figure 4.9. Exchange rate sensitivity to initial conditions, with $\psi = 0.2$, $C = 5$, and (a) $\gamma = 1$, (b) $\gamma = 1.5$, (c) $\gamma = 2$, and (d) $\gamma = 5$. In (a) and (b) the black line denotes $\beta = 0.9$ and the gray line denotes $\beta = 0.91$; in (c) and (d) the black line denotes $\beta = 0.8$ and the gray line denotes $\beta = 0.81$.

that there is a border region between these two types of equilibrium. This border region is characterized by the fact that small changes in β lead to switches from one type of equilibrium to the other. We also found this feature in Chapter 3, where transaction costs were absent. The difference is that this border region is much larger when transaction costs exist. It now stretches between 0.65 and 0.83. Thus, the informational problems of agents in the model are increased. This is also apparent from parts (b) and (c) of Figure 4.8 which show successive enlargements of part (a). We find that an increase in the precision with which agents estimate the parameter β does not help them at all in making more precise forecasts of the nature of the equilibrium to which the exchange rate will converge.

The informational problem that agents encounter can be illustrated in another way. We simulated the model stochastically, assuming two slightly different values of β. We show the simulations in the time domain in Figure 4.9. Take part (a). It shows two exchange rate paths in the time domain, one assuming $\beta = 0.9$, and the other that $\beta = 0.91$. The two simulations use exactly the same parameters and identical values of the underlying fundamental variable. We see that after some time the two exchange rates tend to deviate from each other. The same feature is

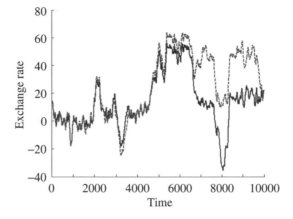

Figure 4.10. Exchange rate sensitivity to initial conditions, with $\psi = 0.2$, $C = 5$, and $\gamma = 1$. The black line denotes $\beta = 0.9$ and the dashed gray line denotes $\beta = 0.901$.

repeated in the other figure parts, with different parameter values for γ. This feature is the result of the "sensitivity to initial conditions," whereby small differences in parameter values can lead to switches in the nature of the (fundamental or bubble) regime. This also creates the impression of structural breaks in the data although no such breaks occur in the underlying model parameters.

This result illustrates the informational problems that agents have in this model. Suppose that the true value of β is 0.9. Agents would like to use this information to make better predictions. Suppose they estimate β and make a very small estimation error of 0.01, so that they set $\beta = 0.91$, a remarkable econometric achievement. Suppose that, in addition, they know all the other parameters of the model exactly and they also know the underlying value of the fundamental. With this information they forecast the exchange rate. The evidence of Figure 4.9 shows that the small estimation error in just one parameter of the model is sufficient to generate very large forecast errors.

Let us now assume that econometric advances allow our agent to estimate β with a precision that is ten times higher. Our agent-econometrician now estimates β to be 0.901, which is extremely close to the true value. Does this dramatic increase in the precision of econometric techniques lead to an equally dramatic improvement in the precision of the forecast of the exchange rate? The answer is shown in Figure 4.10. We find that the more precise knowledge of one parameter of the model allows the forecaster-econometrician to track the exchange rate for a longer time than was possible with information that is less precise. However, after some time this advantage is lost and the forecast exchange rate departs dramatically from the observed exchange rate, and forecast errors increase significantly. Thus, even with extremely precise econometric estimates, agents will start making large forecast errors when they base their forecasts on an estimate of the underlying structural model.

4.4   Conclusion

In this chapter, we argued that the reason why the exchange rate tends to deviate from its fundamental value much of the time is to be found in failures of arbitrage. We analyzed two sources for such failures. One has to do with risk aversion. When agents, in particular fundamentalists, are very risk averse, they are not willing to exploit the profit opportunities that arise from large misalignments of the exchange rate. As a result, chartists will tend to dominate, and the market will be more prone to bubble-like developments. The paradox is that, because agents are more risk averse, they create a more risky environment, in which bubbles and crashes are more likely to occur.

A second source of arbitrage failure arises from the existence of transaction costs in the goods markets. These create a band of inaction in the goods market, preventing arbitrage from occurring. As a result, when the exchange rate is located within this band there is no dynamics present that will bring the exchange rate back to its fundamental value. Fundamentalists are aware of this and, as a result, when the exchange rate is within this band, they will not expect movements towards the fundamental.

This arbitrage failure arising from transaction costs in the goods markets creates a rich dynamics, in which the disconnect phenomenon is reinforced. In addition, the existence of transaction costs adds an additional element of complexity which manifests itself in a stronger sensitivity to initial conditions compared with the model without transaction costs. Furthermore, the addition of transaction costs intensifies the information problem of agents who want to understand the underlying structure of the model. As we will argue in Chapter 7 (see Section 7.6), this feature has important implications for the predictability of the effects of news in the fundamentals.

5

Changes in the Perception of Risk

5.1 Introduction

In the previous chapter we found that an underlying reason for the coexistence of fundamental and nonfundamental equilibria is to be found in arbitrage failures. These arbitrage failures arise because of risk aversion and transaction costs. In this chapter we ask whether there are forces in the market that work in the other direction and that tend to strengthen the attractive force of fundamental equilibria. We will identify such a force in this chapter.[1] This attractive force will be shown to arise because risk perception is not constant, but reacts to changing market circumstances. We will model changing risk perceptions in several ways. First, we will assume that perception of risk is related to the size of the misalignment of the exchange rate. Second, in another modeling approach, we will invoke prospect theory and analyze how the insights from this theory affect the model. We will show that these different modeling approaches lead to very similar results.

5.2 Risk Perception and Misalignment

Bubbles occur because, even though fundamentalists know that the currency may be misaligned, they find it too risky to take a fundamentalist position. As a result, as the bubble develops and the use of fundamentalist rules leads to increasingly large losses, fewer and fewer agents want to use such forecasting rules. In a way the fundamentalists in our model lose their confidence in the soundness of a fundamental analysis during the bubble phase. The more the exchange rate departs from its fundamental, the less confident the fundamentalists become about the use of fundamentalist forecasting.

This feature of the model is unattractive because it disregards the fact that the essence of the fundamentalist forecasting rule is its long-term nature, i.e., as the bubble develops and the exchange rate increasingly deviates from its fundamental, fundamentalists who take a long view are aware that the probability of a future return of the exchange rate to its fundamental value increases. The more the exchange

---

[1] In Chapter 6 we will analyze another force that comes from the fact that the supply of net foreign assets is endogenous.

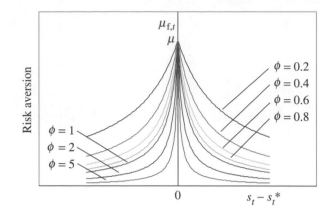

Figure 5.1.   Risk aversion and misalignment.

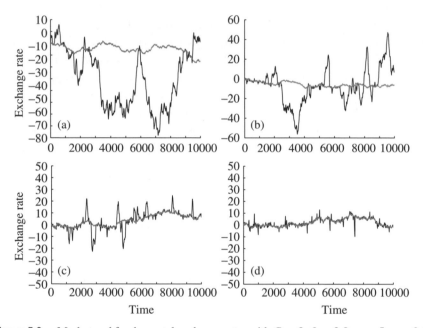

Figure 5.2.   Market and fundamental exchange rates with $C = 0$, $\beta = 0.9$, $\gamma = 5$, $\rho = 0.5$, and (a) $\phi = 0$, (b) $\phi = 0.1$, (c) $\phi = 0.2$, and (d) $\phi = 0.5$. Black line, exchange rate; gray line, fundamental rate.

rate deviates from the fundamental, the higher the probability of a future return to the fundamental. It looks reasonable, therefore, to assume that, as the bubble develops, agents will find it increasingly less risky to use such a fundamentalist forecasting rule, even if the forecast errors they made in the recent past have been high. We implement this idea as follows. We will assume that, as the misalignment increases, fundamentalists' perception of the risk involved in using a fundamentalist

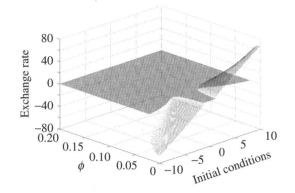

Figure 5.3.   The exchange rate as a function of initial conditions and ϕ, with $\psi = 0.2$, $C = 0$, $\beta = 0.9$, $\gamma = 5$, and $\rho = 0.5$.

forecasting rule declines.[2] In other words, as the degree of misalignment increases, fundamentalists' risk aversion declines. We specify this relationship between misalignment and risk aversion as follows:

$$\mu_{\mathrm{f},t} = \frac{\mu}{1 + \phi|s_t - s_t^*|}, \tag{5.1}$$

where $\mu_{\mathrm{f},t}$ is the degree of risk aversion, which is now assumed to be time dependent and to decline when the degree of misalignment, $|s_t - s_t^*|$, increases. Thus, when $s_t = s_t^*$, the degree of risk aversion is equal to μ, which is the constant risk-aversion parameter used in the previous chapters. When the misalignment becomes very large, $\mu_{\mathrm{f},t} \to 0$. We show the relation between the degree of risk aversion of fundamentalists, $\mu_{\mathrm{f},t}$, and the degree of misalignment, $|s_t - s_t^*|$, graphically in Figure 5.1 for different values of the parameter ϕ.[3] As misalignment increases (whether positive or negative), the degree of risk aversion of fundamentalists declines. This can be interpreted to mean that, as the exchange rate increasingly deviates from its fundamental, the fundamentalists perceive the risk of taking a fundamentalist position to decline. The speed with which risk aversion declines depends on the value of ϕ. With a small value of ϕ risk aversion declines slowly when misalignment increases; with a high value, risk aversion declines very fast.

We now introduce equation (5.1) into our model and solve it for different values of the parameter ϕ. We show stochastic simulations for increasing values of ϕ in Figure 5.2. We find that, as ϕ increases, the deviations from the fundamental become less pronounced and increasingly short-lived. Thus, in a world where fundamentalists' risk perception is very sensitive to the degree of misalignment, bubbles will not easily arise.

---

[2] See De Grauwe et al. (1993) for such an approach.
[3] Note that the exact shape of the curve depends on ϕ.

An analysis of the deterministic part of the model allows us to understand how the parameter ϕ affects the dynamics of the system. As in the previous chapters, we compute a three-dimensional bifurcation diagram (see Figure 5.3). On the x-axis we have, as before, the initial values of the exchange rate, and on the y-axis we set out the numerical values of ϕ and on the z-axis the equilibrium values of the exchange rate (the attractors). We find that, for small values of ϕ, the model generates two types of equilibrium: fundamental and nonfundamental. As ϕ increases, however, the zone of nonfundamental equilibria shrinks. There is a critical value of ϕ for which all nonfundamental equilibria disappear. The exchange rate is then always attracted by the fundamental equilibrium. The exact numerical value of this critical ϕ depends on the other parameters of the model.

5.3   Risk Perception and Losses: Prospect Theory

When we modeled the switching rules, we implicitly relied on the mean-variance framework. This assumes that agents evaluate the utility of their forecasting rules based on the return and on the risk associated with these rules, whereby agents are assumed to give a constant weight (risk aversion) to the risk. This framework has a long tradition in economics and forms the backbone of modern finance theory. There is an increasing body of scientific evidence, however, showing that agents do not behave towards risk in the way postulated by the mean-variance framework. Many "anomalies" have been found in the behavior of agents towards risk (see Kahneman (2002) for a survey of this literature, and our discussion in Chapter 1; see also Thaler (1994) and Shleifer (2000)). It has been found that this behavior is not consistent with the mean-variance theory.

An implication of the mean-variance model is that there is symmetry in the utility agents attach to expected gains and losses. There is, however, a large literature inspired by psychological analysis, showing that agents typically do not evaluate expected gains and losses symmetrically. Kahneman and Tversky (1973) have done pathbreaking work in this area, showing the existence of such an asymmetry experimentally and analyzing its implication. A well-known experiment consisted in giving subjects the following choices. First, subjects are asked to choose between two outcomes: a certain outcome, A, and an uncertain one, B. Outcome A is a sure cash payment of \$900; outcome B is a cash payment of \$1,000 which has a probability of 0.9 and a cash payment of \$0 with probability of 0.1. The expected value of A and B is equal (+\$900). Since outcome B is risky, risk-averse individuals should, according to the theory, choose A. And this is indeed what most subjects choose.

Then, Kahneman and Tversky presented the same subjects with a similar choice, this time involving expected losses. Subjects were presented with two outcomes: a certain outcome, C, and an uncertain one D. Outcome C is a sure loss of \$900; outcome D is a loss of \$1,000 that occurs with probability 0.9, and a loss of \$0 realized with probability 0.1. Again the expected value of these two outcomes is equal (−$900). Since outcome D is riskier than outcome C, risk-averse individuals should choose C. In fact, most subjects confronted with this choice select the risky outcome, D, even though, when confronted with the choice between A and B, these same subjects select the sure outcome A. Similar experiments were performed by other researchers with similar results. It appears therefore that agents do not treat expected gains and losses in a symmetrical way as the mean-variance theory tells us agents should do. Instead, it appears that agents become less risk averse as their losses become larger. Thus, in the example given here, when agents expect to make a loss of $900, they are willing to take a bet with the same expected value that will give them a slight chance of avoiding the loss, knowing that they have a much larger chance of making an even larger loss of $1,000.

This, and other evidence about the asymmetry in the utility agents attach to expected gains and losses, has led Kahneman and Tversky to develop what they call the "prospect theory" of risk (Kahneman and Tversky 1973; Brunnermeier 2004). In this section we apply just one insight of this theory to our model, i.e., that when agents have recently made large losses, they are willing to take larger risks.[4] In other words, as their losses mount, agents become less risk averse. What are the implications of this insight?

Up to now we have assumed that the risk aversion of fundamentalists and chartists is independent of the losses they make. We now depart from this symmetry assumption. The way we implement this idea is to make the degree of risk aversion a function of the losses that agents have made in the past. We write

$$\mu_{f,t} = \frac{\mu}{1 + \phi' |\pi_{f,t}^*|}, \tag{5.2}$$

$$\mu_{c,t} = \frac{\mu}{1 + \phi' |\pi_{c,t}^*|}, \tag{5.3}$$

where $\pi_{f,t}^*$ and $\pi_{c,t}^*$ are weighted averages of past profits, i.e.,

$$\pi_{f,t}^* = (1 - \rho) \sum_{i=0}^{\infty} (\rho^i \pi_{f,t-i}),$$

$$\pi_{c,t}^* = (1 - \rho) \sum_{i=0}^{\infty} (\rho^i \pi_{c,t-i}),$$

and where ϕ' measures the extent to which losses affect agents' risk aversion. When $\pi_{f,t-1}$ and $\pi_{c,t-1}$ are positive, we set $\phi' = 0$. In that case we are in the situation analyzed earlier, i.e., the degree of risk aversion is constant. When, however, agents make losses, i.e., $\pi_{f,t-1}$ and $\pi_{c,t-1}$ are negative, we set $\phi' > 0$. In this case agents'

---

[4] Another implication of prospect theory is that agents attach a different utility to gains and losses. In general, the utility loss attached to losses is larger than the utility gain of gains.

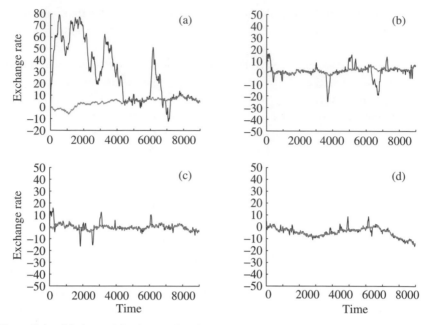

Figure 5.4. Market and fundamental exchange rates with $C = 0$, $\beta = 0.9$, $\gamma = 1$, $\rho = 0.5$, and (a) $\phi' = 0.5$, (b) $\phi' = 1$, (c) $\phi' = 2$, and (d) $\phi' = 5$. Black line, exchange rate; gray line, fundamental rate.

risk aversion declines with the size of the losses. Thus, when fundamentalists make large losses on their forecasts, they become less risk averse. This implies that, when a bubble develops and fundamentalists make large losses, they will be willing to take more risk and to take larger positions against the developing bubble. Similarly, chartists will be willing to take more risk when their losses mount.

We now introduce equations (5.2) and (5.3) into our model. We are primarily interested to see how this asymmetry affects the main results of our model. We first present stochastic simulations for different values of ϕ'. These results (Figure 5.4) show that, as ϕ' increases, the exchange rate becomes increasingly attracted by the fundamental exchange rate. For example, when $\phi' = 5$ the exchange rate stays very close to its fundamental, and the dynamics of bubbles and crashes almost never occur.

The next step in the analysis consisted in analyzing the deterministic part of the model. As before, we do this by presenting a three-dimensional bifurcation diagram which shows the equilibrium exchange rate on the vertical axis, the initial values of the exchange rate on the x-axis and the numerical values of the parameter ϕ' on the y-axis (see Figure 5.6). We obtain a result that is very similar to that in Section 5.2, where we allowed the degree of risk aversion to vary with the size of the degree of misalignment. We find that, as the parameter ϕ' increases, the area of fundamental equilibria becomes larger. (This result is found for all parameter

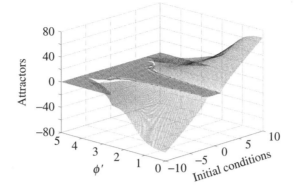

Figure 5.5. The exchange rate as a function of ϕ' and the initial conditions, with $\psi = 0.2$, $\beta = 0.9$, and $\gamma = 1$.

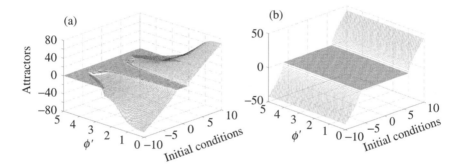

Figure 5.6. The exchange rate as a function of ϕ' and the initial conditions, with $\psi = 0.2$, $\beta = 0.9$, and $\gamma = 1$: (a) only fundamentalists and (b) only chartists.

configurations.) Thus, when losses increase and agents' risk aversion declines, the scope for the emergence of bubble equilibria is reduced. The interpretation is very similar to that in the previous section. When the exchange rate is moving towards a bubble equilibrium, fundamentalists make increasing losses. They now react to these losses by becoming less risk averse. As a result, they are more willing to take a "contrarian view" and speculate against the continuation of the bubble. In other words, they are more willing to exploit the future profit opportunities and to arbitrage. This increases the mean-reverting forces in the market and makes a bubble less likely. This effect increases with the size of the parameter ϕ'.

This is a quite remarkable result. It implies that a greater willingness of fundamentalists to take risks makes bubbles less likely. If these fundamentalists behave like prospect theory tells us they do, they will be willing to take more risk when a bubble emerges (and thus when their losses accumulate), thereby reducing the probability of the emergence of bubbles. Thus, if the world is as described by the prospect theory, arbitrage failures will be less pronounced, leading to fewer

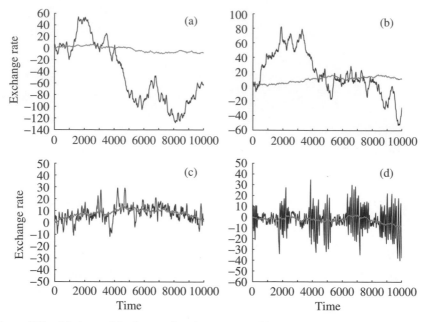

Figure 5.7. Market and fundamental exchange rates with $C = 5$, $\beta = 0.9$, $\gamma = 5$, $\rho = 0.5$, and (a) $\phi = 0$, (b) $\phi = 0.1$, (c) $\phi = 0.2$, and (d) $\phi = 0.4$. Black line, exchange rate; gray line, fundamental rate.

bubbles and crashes, than in a model based on the standard mean-variance utility maximization.

What about chartists? Does their willingness to take on more risk when their losses accumulate affect the results? We answer this by simulating the model, first assuming that only the fundamentalists take on more risk and, second, that only chartists do this. We show bifurcation diagrams under these two assumptions in Figure 5.6. Part (a) shows the diagram when only fundamentalists take more risk as their losses increase (while chartists keep their risk aversion constant); part (b) assumes the reverse. We observe that part (a) is almost identical to Figure 5.5, which assumed that both chartists and fundamentalists take on more risk when their losses increase. Figure 5.6(b) shows that the size of ϕ' has no influence on the equilibria. Thus, it appears that the fundamentalists' risk taking drives the results, and not that of the chartists. This has much to do with the fact that, during bubbles, fundamentalist losses tend to accumulate. Chartists then typically make profits. It is therefore crucial that fundamentalists be willing to take on more risk when a bubble emerges, in order to kill it.

These results reveal an interesting paradox. This is that, by taking on more risk, fundamentalists in fact reduce the scope for the exchange rate to move towards bubble equilibria. In so doing, they reduce the risk in the market. In other words,

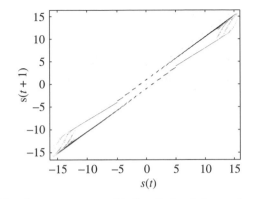

Figure 5.8. Strange attractor with $C = 5$, $\beta = 0.9$, $\gamma = 5$, and $\phi = 1$.

the unwillingness to take risks increases the probability that a particular exchange rate movement will develop into a bubble.

5.4 Changing Risk Perception and Transaction Costs

In this section we introduce transaction costs into the analysis. Remember, the existence of transaction costs leads to a failure of arbitrage, because they introduce a band of inaction within which goods arbitrage does not operate. As a result, fundamentalists do not expect the exchange rate to be pushed towards its fundamental when the exchange rate is located in this band.

We introduce transaction costs into the model where fundamentalists allow their risk perception to vary with the degree of misalignment (the model of Section 5.2). The results with the model in which we introduced prospect theory (the model of Section 5.3) are very similar and are not shown here.

We simulated the model by assuming transaction costs to be positive ($C = 5$). In Figure 5.7 we show the results in the time domain for different values of ϕ. We observe that, for small values of ϕ, we obtain movements that are consistent with the existence of fundamental and nonfundamental attractors. With sufficiently large values of ϕ, nonfundamental attractors seem to disappear (as we found before in Section 5.2; see Figure 5.2). However, the movements around the fundamental become extremely volatile. We will show later (in Chapter 10) that these movements are characteristic of a chaotic attractor. We present here some preliminary evidence by showing the exchange rate in the phase space, i.e., we set s_t and s_{t-1} on the horizontal and the vertical axes. If the exchange rate converges to a fixed point (either a fundamental equilibrium or a nonfundamental one), this will show up in the phase space by the fact that the exchange rate converges to one stable point. When ϕ is sufficiently large, we do not observe such a convergence to a fixed point (see Figure 5.8). We observe that the exchange rate converges to a "strange attractor" (or "chaotic attractor") which is located around the fundamental (which

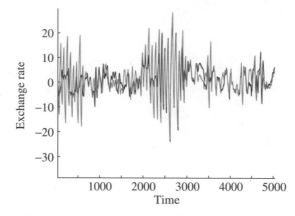

Figure 5.9. Sensitivity to initial conditions, with $C = 5$, $\beta = 0.9$, $\gamma = 5$, and $\phi = 1$. Black line, without shock; gray line, with shock.

is normalized to zero here).[5] The strange attractor describes the movements of the exchange rate from one period to the other. The number of points in such an attractor is infinite. This implies that the cyclical movements around the fundamental never repeat themselves: each cycle is unique. In this sense, one says that the dynamics of the exchange rate is "aperiodic." In Chapter 10 we will go into more detail, when we discuss techniques about how to identify chaotic dynamics. Here it suffices to say that chaotic dynamics occurs in nonlinear models producing cyclical movements in a variable (here the exchange rate) which never repeat themselves.

The existence of a chaotic attractor creates a strong sensitivity to initial conditions. We show this in Figure 5.9, where we simulate the model with and without a small shock in the initial conditions. Note that, as before, the stochastic realization of the fundamental is identical in the two simulations. We observe that it is now possible that a small difference in the initial conditions leads to a situation in which not only the level of the exchange rate but also the variance can differ. We see that a small change in the initial conditions can lead the exchange rate into periods of high turbulence, while this turbulence is absent in the base simulation. Thus, sensitivity to initial conditions applies to both the level and the variance of the exchange rate.

A question that we will have to analyze is whether the existence of attractors that create high turbulence (chaotic attractors), like those we have detected in Figures 5.8 and 5.9, have an empirical basis. We will do this in Chapter 8.

One implication of a model that combines transaction costs and endogenous risk perception is that it creates periods of relative tranquillity followed by periods of high turbulence. The switch from low to high turbulence occurs in a very unpredictable way, as the sensitivity analysis of Figure 5.9 shows. When the exchange

---

[5] Note that the simulation of the chaotic attractor in Figure 5.8 is a deterministic simulation, i.e., we have eliminated the stochastics driving the fundamental. The latter was set equal to 0. The nice thing is that the cyclical movements around the fundamental are created in a deterministic environment.

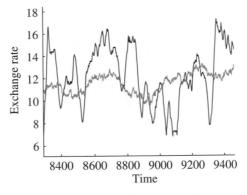

Figure 5.10. Market and fundamental exchange rates with $C = 5$, $\beta = 0.9$, $\gamma = 5$, $\rho = 0.5$, and $\phi = 0.4$ Black line, exchange rate; gray line, fundamental rate.

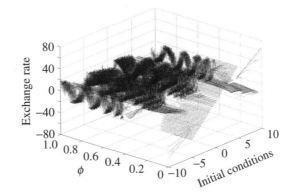

Figure 5.11. The exchange rate as a function of ϕ and the initial conditions, with $C = 5$, $\beta = 0.9$, $\gamma = 5$, and $\rho = 0.5$.

rate is in a tranquil period it tends to move around the fundamental within the transaction-cost band. We show this pattern in Figure 5.10, which plots the exchange rate during a period when it is not involved in a strange attractor. We also see that in tranquil periods the exchange rate often stays for long periods on one side of the fundamental and then experiences a sudden movement towards the other side of the fundamental.

Finally, we also produce three-dimensional bifurcation diagrams in which we present the exchange rate as a function of the initial conditions (x-axis) and the parameter ϕ (y-axis). This is done in Figures 5.11 and 5.12 for two different values of the transaction cost ($C = 5$ and $C = 20$). These figures should be compared with Figure 5.5, which shows the same bifurcation diagram when transaction costs are zero. The contrast is very stark. In Figure 5.5 we found that for sufficiently high values of ϕ the exchange rate always returns to its fundamental value, i.e., we always obtain fundamental equilibria. In Figures 5.11 and 5.12, however, the

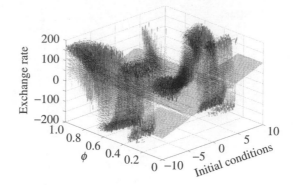

Figure 5.12. The exchange rate as a function of ϕ and the initial conditions, with $C = 40$, $\beta = 0.9$, $\gamma = 5$, and $\rho = 0.5$.

model produces fundamental equilibria (fixed points) and chaotic attractors for large values of ϕ.[6] Whether the exchange rate will be attracted by a fundamental equilibrium or a chaotic attractor then depends on the initial conditions. This can be seen in Figures 5.11 and 5.12 by the fact that, for some initial conditions, the exchange rate stays on the plane of fundamental equilibria, while for others the exchange rate is caught in a band which has many points. These bands correspond to the chaotic attractors we identified earlier. This feature, whereby the exchange rate is attracted by either the fundamental equilibrium or a chaotic attractor, explains why, in a stochastic simulation, the exchange rate switches from tranquil periods (when attracted by the fundamental) to turbulent periods (when moving in a chaotic attractor).

From the preceding analysis, one can also draw some conclusions about the role of transaction costs in the model. In Chapter 4, when we assumed constant risk aversion ($\phi = 0$), we found that the existence of transaction costs has the effect of reducing the attractive power of the fundamental equilibrium, because transaction costs create a band of inaction within which the forces of arbitrage do not operate. As a result, when the exchange rate moves within this band, fundamentalists see no reason to arbitrage and to move the exchange rate back to its fundamental value. When we assume, as we do here, that risk aversion declines with the degree of misalignment ($\phi > 0$), and when this effect is strong enough, the existence of transaction costs creates very different dynamics. In particular, the combination of a strong sensitivity of risk aversion to misalignment (a high ϕ) and transaction costs eliminates the bubble equilibria. Instead, it creates two different dynamic regimes. One is characterized by the fact that the exchange rate is attracted by equilibria within the transaction-cost band; the other is one where the exchange rate is attracted by a chaotic attractor.

---

[6] Note that, when ϕ is small, i.e., typically less than 0.4, we obtain fundamental and nonfundamental equilibria (fixed points) confirming our earlier results.

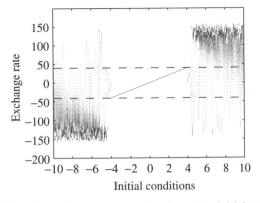

Figure 5.13. The exchange rate as a function of the initial conditions, with $C = 40$, $\psi = 0.2$, $\beta = 0.9$, $\gamma = 5$, and $\phi = 1$.

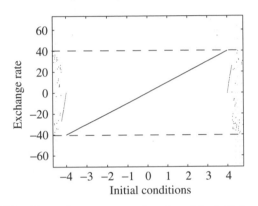

Figure 5.14. The exchange rate as a function of the initial conditions, with $C = 40$, $\psi = 0.2$, $\beta = 0.9$, $\gamma = 5$, and $\phi = 1$.

The existence of two dynamic regimes can be seen from Figure 5.12. We see that, for small initial shocks, the exchange rate settles on a plane that is the collection of fundamental equilibria.[7] This feature can be shown more clearly in Figure 5.13, which takes a "slice" of Figure 5.12 at the value of $\phi = 1$. We see that, for relatively small initial shocks (noise), the exchange rate remains within the transaction-cost band. We also observe discontinuities within this band. We make this clear by zooming in on Figure 5.13, the result of which is shown in Figure 5.14. There are small shocks in the initial conditions that bring the exchange rate to a very different attractor within the transaction-cost band. In a stochastic environment, this feature creates the possibility of cyclical movements within the transaction-cost band. In addition, it generates strong sensitivity to initial conditions. We show an example of this phenomenon in Figure 5.15, which presents a stochastic simulation with

---

[7] Note that all points within the transaction-cost band are fundamental equilibria. See our discussion in Chapter 4.

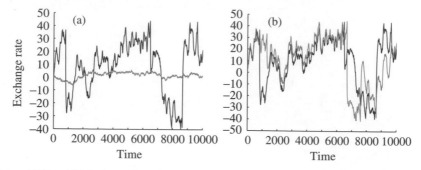

Figure 5.15. (a) Market and fundamental exchange rates and (b) sensitivity to initial conditions. In both parts, $C = 40$, $\beta = 0.9$, $\gamma = 5$, $\rho = 0.5$, and $\phi = 1$. Black line, without shock; gray line, with shock.

the same parameter configuration as in Figure 5.14. The underlying assumption in Figure 5.15 is that the stochastic shocks are small relative to the transaction-cost band. As a result, the exchange rate remains attracted by the fixed-point equilibria inside the transaction-cost band. The result of all this is that the exchange rate exhibits cyclical movements and strong sensitivity to initial conditions. An interesting aspect of this regime is that it is qualitatively very similar to the regime of bubbles and crashes obtained with constant risk aversion.

The second dynamic regime is obtained for sufficiently large initial shocks (noise), as can be seen in Figure 5.12. In this case, we obtain a chaotic dynamics characterized by large short-term turbulence in the exchange rate.

5.5 Conclusion

It is now well established that risk perceptions are not constant. Their changes add an additional source of volatility to markets. In this chapter we dropped the assumption, used until now, that risk aversion is a constant parameter. Instead, we allowed risk aversion to be influenced by market conditions. We did this in two ways. In a first approach we allowed risk aversion to change with the degree of misalignment. The underlying idea was that, as the exchange rate increasingly deviates from its fundamental, the fundamentalists become increasingly confident that the exchange rate will have to return to its fundamental value. This assumption has the effect of making the fundamentalists less afraid to take a position when bubbles emerge. In other words, their risk perception of using a fundamentalist forecasting rule declines when the exchange rate deviates from its fundamental. In a second approach, we used notions borrowed from prospect theory. One implication of that theory is that agents are willing to take more risks when they have accumulated large losses. In the context of our model, this means that, when fundamentalists make large losses when a bubble develops, they are willing to take more risks.

We applied these two insights to our model and found that they led to very similar results. In both cases the risk perception of fundamentalists declines as the exchange rate increasingly deviates from its fundamental. This has the effect of stabilizing the market and eliminating bubbles. However, we also found that, when combined with transaction costs, the endogeneity of risk perception generates a very complex exchange rate behavior, characterized by sensitivity to initial conditions of both the level and the volatility of the exchange rate. In addition, we detected that, during tranquil periods, the exchange rate will tend to move around the fundamental within the confines of the transaction-cost bands. (We argued in Chapter 4 that this transaction-cost band may be relatively large.) Finally, we also found that tranquil periods alternate with periods of high turbulence. The latter are periods during which the exchange rate is attracted by a chaotic attractor.

6

Modeling the Supply of Foreign Assets and the Current Account

6.1 Introduction

In the previous chapters, we used a model in which fundamental and bubble equilibria coexist. In a stochastic environment this feature leads to frequent switching between two regimes: fundamental and bubble. As a result, the exchange rate is disconnected from the fundamentals much of the time. These results were obtained in a model where the real sector of the economy is exogenous. This implies that the exchange rate does not affect the real sector. Thus, there is no feedback of exchange rate changes into goods prices, output, export, and import. In reality, however, it is likely that exchange rate movements affect real variables. In particular, during a bubble the exchange rate becomes increasingly undervalued. This is likely to stimulate exports and discourage imports.

The issue that arises now is whether these feedback mechanisms affect our basic results. Let us return to the mechanism we have just described. An increase in the exchange rate leads to more exports and fewer imports and thus to an improvement of the current account. The latter improvement, however, means that the supply of foreign assets to domestic wealth owners increases. But such an increase in the supply of the foreign asset must have some effect on its price, because domestic agents will have to hold these additions to the foreign assets in their portfolio. Since we have fixed the interest rates, the exchange rate will have to change. In general, as we will see, such an increase in the supply of foreign assets will tend to reduce their price.[1]

The mechanism above implies that we have a potential mean-reverting process in the exchange rate. That is to say, when the exchange rate increases, say, during a bubble, the ensuing increase in the supply of the foreign asset will tend to reduce the exchange rate again. Thus, even if there are no longer any agents using

---

[1] The treatment of the current account as an exogenous variable follows from the partial equilibrium nature of our model. In a general equilibrium setup, in which agents decide about spending, production, and asset allocation simultaneously, a current account surplus could be the result of a desire to hold foreign assets. In that case it would not be sensible to call a current account surplus an increase in the supply of net foreign assets.

fundamentalist forecasting rules, there is still a mean-reverting mechanism in the economy that can push back the exchange rate towards its fundamental value.

Our model allows us to study this mechanism. Remember that, up to now, we have kept the supply of foreign assets fixed. The mechanism just described suggests that the supply of foreign assets is not fixed and that it will react to movements of the exchange rate. Our purpose in this chapter is to find out how the dynamics of the exchange rate is affected by this feedback mechanism.

How can we model the interaction between exchange rate movements and the supply of foreign assets? A first step in the analysis is to postulate that there is a stable relationship between the equilibrium supply of the foreign asset and the fundamental exchange rate, i.e.,

$$Z_t^* = \epsilon s_t^*, \tag{6.1}$$

where Z_t^* is the equilibrium supply of foreign assets. Thus, we take the view that there is a one-to-one relationship between the fundamental exchange rate and the equilibrium supply of foreign assets. The intensity of the effect of changes in the fundamental exchange rate on the equilibrium supply of net foreign assets is measured by the parameter ϵ, which we will call the "elasticity."

The next step is to model the dynamics of the changes in the supply of foreign assets. We will specify the following mechanism

$$Z_t - Z_t^* = \rho_z(Z_{t-1} - Z_{t-1}^*) + (1 - \rho_z)\epsilon(s_t - s_{t-1}^*). \tag{6.2}$$

This equation says that, when the exchange rate is above its fundamental value, the supply of foreign assets is also above its equilibrium value. The reason why this is so was explained earlier: when the exchange rate is above its fundamental value, the supply of foreign assets increases, pushing it above its fundamental value. This process, however, has some inertia. As a result, the adjustment of the supply is gradual. We express this in equation (6.2) by introducing a gradual adjustment mechanism, where the parameter ρ_z regulates the speed of adjustment of the supply of foreign assets. When $\rho_z = 0$, the adjustment is instantaneous; higher values of ρ_z imply slower speeds of adjustment.

We now have the tools with which to analyze the implications of the endogenous asset supply mechanism. The full model is described in an appendix (see Section 6.7). In comparison to the model of the previous chapter, we now have a model with seven dynamic variables, including Z_t. The appendix also provides an analysis of the steady state.

6.2 Stochastic Simulations of the Model

In this section we present some simulations of the model in a stochastic environment. We simulated the model for different values of the parameter ϵ (the "elasticity"), and we show the results in Figure 6.1. Parts (a)–(d) assume increasing values

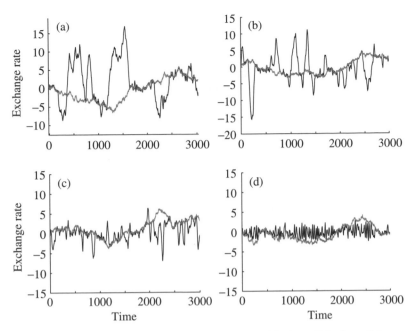

Figure 6.1. Market and fundamental exchange rates with $\psi = 0.2$, $\beta = 0.9$, $\gamma = 5$, $\rho = 0.5$, and (a) $\epsilon = 0.01$, (b) $\epsilon = 0.02$, (c) $\epsilon = 0.1$, and (d) $\epsilon = 0.5$. Black line, exchange rate; gray line, fundamental rate.

of the elasticity parameter. We observe that, for low elasticities, the exchange rate follows pretty much the same dynamics as that found in the absence of an endogenous asset supply mechanism, i.e., the exchange rate is regularly attracted towards a bubble equilibrium but then returns to its fundamental value. As the elasticity is increased, the bubbles become more short-lived (compare part (b) with part (a)). Further increases in the elasticity eliminate the bubbles. We move into a regime in which the exchange rate is attracted towards the fundamental equilibrium all the time. However, the short-term volatility around the fundamental tends to increase. At the same time, the amplitude of the movements around the fundamental tends to decline as the elasticity is increased. Thus, the strength of the asset supply mechanism has the effect of tying down the exchange rate to its fundamental value. At the same time, this mechanism creates additional short-term volatility around the fundamental. The nature of this short-term volatility is important. We will return to this issue later. First, we analyze the deterministic part of the model in the next section.

6.3 Deterministic Analysis of the Model

The first thing we want to establish is whether the endogenous nature of the supply of foreign assets affects the coexistence of fundamental and nonfundamental equilibria. In order to do this we analyze the deterministic part of the model. We solve

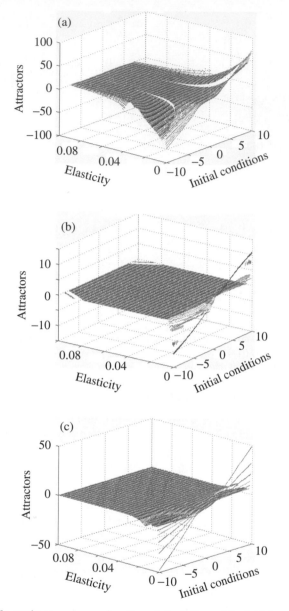

Figure 6.2. The exchange rate as a function of elasticity and the initial conditions, with $\psi = 0.2$, $\beta = 0.9$, and (a) $\gamma = 1$, $\rho_z = 0.9$, (b) $\gamma = 5$, $\rho_z = 0.6$, and (c) $\gamma = 1$, $\rho_z = 0.1$.

the model and analyze the sensitivity of the solutions to changes in the parameters ϵ and ρ_z in the asset supply function (6.2). We obtain three-dimensional bifurcation diagrams like those we used in the previous chapters (see Figure 6.2). Each panel in Figure 6.2 shows the solution for the exchange rate (the attractor) for different

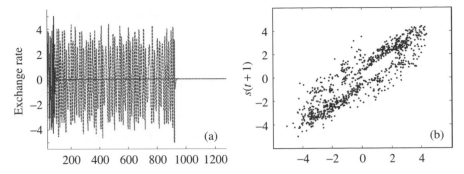

Figure 6.3. (a) Exchange rate sensitivity to initial conditions ($\epsilon = 0.5$, black line, without shock; gray line, with shock) and (b) strange attractor ($\epsilon = 0.5$). For both parts, $\psi = 0.2$, $\beta = 0.9$, and $\gamma = 5$.

initial shocks to the exchange rate (x-axis) and different values of the parameter ϵ ("elasticity"). Each assumes a different speed of adjustment ρ_z. The results lend themselves to the following interpretation. Take part (a) first. This assumes a slow speed of adjustment. We find that, for small values of the ϵ, the two types of solution, fundamental and bubble solutions, coexist. As ϵ increases, however, the zone of fundamental solutions increases. We find something similar in parts (b) and (c), which assume increasing speeds of adjustment: as ϵ increases, the zone of fundamental solutions increases. Note also the importance of the speed of adjustment. A high speed of adjustment (low ρ_z) has the effect of increasing the zone of fundamental equilibria.

From the preceding analysis we conclude that the existence of a feedback mechanism whereby the current account, and thus the supply of foreign assets, reacts to exchange rate changes affects the nature of the equilibria. The stronger and the faster the supply of foreign assets reacts to the exchange rate, the less likely it is that bubble equilibria will occur. This is not really surprising. The asset supply mechanism that we modeled introduces a mean-reverting process. If this mean-reverting process is sufficiently strong, it strengthens the hands of the fundamentalists who use a mean-reverting forecasting rule. As a result, the probability that chartist rules will tend to dominate and generate bubbles is reduced.

There are other features of the dynamics that are worth analyzing. One is that the fundamental equilibria we find for sufficiently large values of ϵ hide the fact that, during the transition toward the fundamental equilibrium, the exchange rate can go through a period of turbulence. We show an example of such a turbulent transition towards the fundamental equilibrium in Figure 6.3. We see that after an initial shock in the exchange rate there is a period of high turbulence, after which the exchange rate settles toward its fundamental value. The duration of this turbulence depends on the initial conditions. In fact, in part (a) we show two different exchange rates in the time domain, one with an initial shock of $+3$, and the other with an initial shock of $+3.1$. We observe that, despite the small difference in initial conditions, the duration of turbulence is very different.

It should be mentioned that we do not obtain periods of turbulence for all initial shocks. There are many initial conditions that lead the exchange rate to its fundamental value very quickly. We show a few examples in Section 6.8.

The period of turbulence toward the fundamental equilibrium may seem surprising. The most surprising aspect of this turbulence is that the exchange rate movements during this period appear to be stochastic, despite the fact that the simulations are deterministic. This feature is produced by the chaotic dynamics underlying it. We encountered chaotic attractors in the previous chapter. They reappear here, although in a different form, i.e., as temporary attractors. In Chapter 10 we will analyze chaotic dynamics in more detail. We will also use techniques that enable us to identify chaotic dynamics in a more precise way than in this chapter. As shown in Chapter 5, chaotic dynamics can also be recognized by the existence of a "strange attractor." We show this "strange attractor" in Figure 6.3(b). This presents the exchange rate in period t on the horizontal axis and in period $t + 1$ on the vertical axis (the phase space). Thus, during the period of transition, the exchange rate is caught by a strange attractor that determines its movements. As shown earlier, after some time the exchange rate leaves the strange attractor and settles into a fundamental equilibrium (a fixed point in the phase space).

Where does the temporary turbulence come from? An easy answer is that it is the result of a mathematical characteristic of the model, especially its nonlinear nature. There must be some economic reason, however, for the occurrence of such turbulence. The underlying economics can be explained as follows. When the feedback mechanism from the asset supply is very strong (large elasticity) the mean reversion gives a strong direction to the market. This makes the fundamental forecasting rule very valuable, so this rule will be used a lot. As a result, the exchange rate is driven very quickly to its fundamental value after a shock. Now take the other extreme, and assume that the asset supply feedback mechanism is very weak or even totally absent. We know that, in this case, for sufficiently large initial shocks to the exchange rate, the system moves to a bubble equilibrium. The turbulence observed for an intermediate strength feedback mechanism can now be interpreted as a searching mechanism of the kind of equilibrium to which the exchange rate converges. When the elasticity has an intermediate value, the mean reversion inherent in the asset supply mechanism is too weak to ensure that a sufficient number of agents will use a fundamentalist rule that will guide the exchange rate to its fundamental value. At the same time, there are sufficiently many agents using fundamentalist rules to prevent the exchange rate from being attracted to a bubble equilibrium. It is as if the market cannot make up its mind where the exchange rate will go. This hesitation then leads to cyclical movements in the exchange rate, which can even become aperiodic.

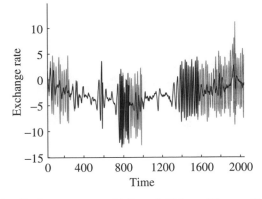

Figure 6.4. Exchange rate sensitivity to initial conditions, with $\psi = 0.2$, $\beta = 0.9$, $\gamma = 5$, and $\epsilon = 0.5$. Black line, without shock; gray line, with shock.

The existence of strange attractors to which the exchange rate is attracted during the transition toward the fundamental equilibrium is not without significance in a stochastic environment. To analyze this we return to the stochastic model in the next section.

6.4 Sensitivity to Initial Conditions and Informational Issues

The short-term volatility created by the asset supply mechanism is characterized by sensitivity to initial conditions. This means that a very small change in the initial conditions leads to a change in the future path of the exchange rate. We show the nature of this sensitivity to initial conditions in the stochastic simulation in Figure 6.4. We have simulated two exchange rates. The first is simulated under exactly the same conditions as in Figure 6.1(d). The second is obtained by assuming that the initial shock in the exchange rate is 0.1 (instead of 0, for the exchange rate without shock). Apart from this difference in initial conditions, the two simulations are identical (i.e., the same parameters and identical stochastics of the fundamental exchange rate). We observe that, after some time, the two exchange rate paths start to diverge. We also observe, as in the previous chapter, that both the level and the variance of the exchange rate are sensitive to initial conditions.

This feature of sensitivity to initial conditions creates great complexity in the short-term volatility of the exchange rate. It also has important informational implications that are similar to those in the previous chapter. This is because this feature of sensitivity to initial conditions also applies to the parameter values of the model. To show this, we performed the following experiment. We simulated the model with two different values of the elasticity: $\epsilon = 0.5$ and $\epsilon = 0.51$. All the other parameters were assumed to be the same. In addition, we assumed exactly the same stochastics for the underlying fundamental and the same initial conditions in the two simulations. The results are shown in Figure 6.5. We find that a small

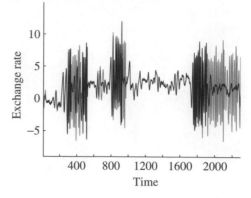

Figure 6.5.   Exchange rate sensitivity to initial conditions, with $\psi = 0.2$, $\beta = 0.9$, and $\gamma = 5$. Black line, $\epsilon = 0.5$; gray line, $\epsilon = 0.51$.

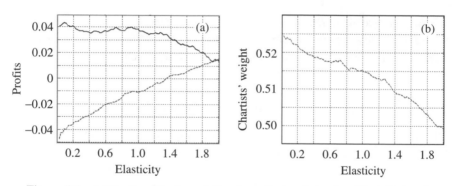

Figure 6.6.   (a) Profits of fundamentalists (gray line) and chartists (black line) and (b) weight of chartists. For both parts, $\psi = 0.2$, $\beta = 0.9$, and $\gamma = 1$.

change in the elasticity produces a similar sensitivity to initial conditions: after some time the two exchange rates start to follow their own short-term dynamics.

The informational implication of this sensitivity to initial conditions can be described as follows. Suppose fundamentalists want to use information about the elasticity parameter to forecast the exchange rate better. Assume that the true parameter is 0.5, and suppose fundamentalists have estimated the parameter to be 0.51. If the fundamentalists use this estimated value, we know from Figure 6.5 that this very small estimation error will, after some time, lead to very large prediction errors. In order to avoid these errors, the fundamentalists would need to be able to estimate the parameter with much greater precision than is actually possible. In other words, the payoff of using estimates of the parameter values is likely to be small, so agents may not find it attractive to do this.[2]

---

[2] Note that there is a burgeoning literature analyzing statistical learning and the conditions in which such learning converges to a rational-expectations equilibrium (see Evans and Honkapohja 2001).

6.5 Profitability of Chartist and Fundamentalist Rules

The existence of an endogenous supply of foreign assets has important implications for the dynamics of the exchange rate. As we have documented in the previous section, it adds a mean-reverting process to the model and therefore strengthens the position of the fundamentalists who follow a mean-reverting forecasting rule. An implication of this result is that the existence of a mean-reverting supply mechanism should increase the profits of those agents who follow mean-reverting forecasting rules. We checked whether this is the outcome of the model by performing the following experiment. We simulated the model and computed the average profits made by chartists and fundamentalists for different values of the elasticity parameter. The averages were computed over 5000 periods. We show the results in Figure 6.6(a). The values of the elasticity parameter are set out on the horizontal axis. The average one-period profits of chartists and fundamentalists are shown on the vertical axis. Our intuition is confirmed, i.e., when the elasticity increases, fundamentalists make more profits (make fewer losses), while the reverse is true for the chartists. The effect of these changes in relative profitability can be seen in Figure 6.6(b). This shows that, as the elasticity increases, the share of the chartists declines (the share of the fundamentalists increases).

6.6 Conclusion

Exchange rate movements affect the current account. The latter then, in turn, changes the net supply of foreign assets and feeds back on the exchange rate. We modeled this mechanism in this chapter. The effect of making the supply of net foreign assets endogenous is that it can eliminate bubble equilibria. This will happen if the exchange rate changes have a sufficiently large and fast-acting effect on the current account. In this case we also found that the profitability of fundamentalist rules is strongly increased, thereby also increasing the popularity of these rules in forecasting the exchange rate.

What is the empirical evidence of the sensitivity of the current account? The consensus today is that this sensitivity is rather weak (see Krugman 1987; Frankel and Rose 1994; Obstfeld and Rogoff 2000). In the short run, i.e., over periods extending to several quarters, there is very little evidence that the exchange rate affects the current account. This has a lot to do with the fact that firms tend to "price to market," i.e., they do not easily allow the price of their exports in the foreign markets to be affected by exchange rate movements, certainly when these exchange rate movements are perceived to be temporary. As a result of this pricing to market, trade flows do not react much to (short-term) exchange rate movements. Trade flows appear to be disconnected from short-term exchange rate movements. Thus, the disconnect puzzle has two dimensions. It relates to the fact that trade flows are not very responsive to exchange rate changes, and it also means that the exchange rate is disconnected from its underlying fundamental. This dimension of the disconnect phenomenon was analyzed in detail in previous chapters.

The existence of a disconnect phenomenon whereby the current account is only weakly sensitive to the exchange rate implies that the feedback mechanism analyzed in this chapter is a weak force, so it will most often not prevent bubbles and crashes in the exchange rate from emerging.

6.7   Appendix: The Steady State of the Model

The seven dynamic variables are $(s_t, u_t, x_t, y_t, \sigma_{c,t}^2, \sigma_{f,t}^2, Z_t)$. The state of the system at time $t - 1$, i.e.,

$$(s_{t-1}, u_{t-1}, x_{t-1}, y_{t-1}, \sigma_{c,t-1}^2, \sigma_{f,t-1}^2, Z_{t-1}),$$

determines the state of the system at time t, i.e., $(s_t, u_t, x_t, y_t, \sigma_{c,t}^2, \sigma_{f,t}^2, Z_t)$ through the following seven-dimensional dynamical system:

$$s_t = [1 + \beta - \Theta_{f,t}(\psi + \beta)]s_{t-1} - (1 - \Theta_{f,t})\beta u_{t-1}, \tag{6.3}$$

$$u_t = s_{t-1}, \tag{6.4}$$

$$x_t = u_{t-1}, \tag{6.5}$$

$$y_t = x_{t-1}, \tag{6.6}$$

$$\sigma_{c,t}^2 = (1 - \rho)\sigma_{c,t-1}^2 + \rho[(1 + \beta)x_{t-1} - \beta y_{t-1} - s_{t-1}]^2, \tag{6.7}$$

$$\sigma_{f,t}^2 = (1 - \rho)\sigma_{f,t-1}^2 + \rho[(1 - \psi)x_{t-1} - s_{t-1}]^2, \tag{6.8}$$

$$Z_t = \rho_z Z_{t-1} + (1 - \rho_z)\epsilon s_t, \tag{6.9}$$

where

$$\Theta_{f,t} = \frac{w_{f,t}/\sigma_{f,t}^2}{w_{f,t}/\sigma_{f,t}^2 + w_{c,t}/\sigma_{c,t}^2} \tag{6.10}$$

and

$$w_{f,t} = \frac{\exp[\gamma(\pi_{f,t} - \mu\sigma_{f,t}^2)]}{\exp[\gamma(\pi_{c,t} - \mu\sigma_{c,t}^2)] + \exp[\gamma(\pi_{f,t} - \mu\sigma_{f,t}^2)]}, \tag{6.11}$$

$$\pi_{c,t} = (s_{t-1} - u_{t-1})\,\mathrm{sgn}[x_{t-1} + \beta(x_{t-1} - y_{t-1}) - u_{t-1}], \tag{6.12}$$

$$\pi_{f,t} = (s_{t-1} - u_{t-1})\,\mathrm{sgn}[(1 - \psi)x_{t-1} - u_{t-1}]. \tag{6.13}$$

Note that, as in the previous chapters, we have normalized the fundamental variable s_t^* to zero and we have assumed that the chartist extrapolation rule has one lag.

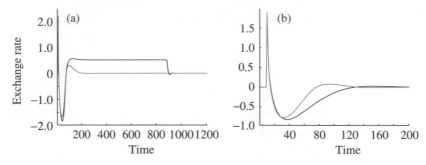

Figure 6.7. Exchange rate sensitivity to initial conditions, with $\psi = 0.2$, $\beta = 0.9$, $\gamma = 5$, and $\epsilon = 0.5$: (a) $s(9) = 2.5$ (black line) and 2.6 (gray line); (b) $s(9) = 2.0$ (black line) and 2.1 (gray line).

6.8   Appendix: Transitional Dynamics

In this appendix we show a few examples of movements of the exchange rate after the initial shock (see Figure 6.7). These are examples where the transition is periodic, in contrast with the chaotic transition shown in the main text. The difference between the two is that in a periodic transition there are a finite number of points in the phase space (e.g., if the exchange rate follows a four-period cycle, there are four points in the phase space). In chaotic dynamics the strange attractor has infinitely many points.

We also made a sensitivity analysis to discover for which parameter combinations one obtains chaotic dynamics during the transition. In order to do so we performed a simulation analysis as in Figure 6.2. Instead of simulating the model until the exchange rate settles to its equilibrium value (either a fundamental or a bubble equilibrium), we now stop the simulation after 200 periods, when the exchange rate has not always settled. We show the result in Figure 6.8. The way this simulation was performed is as follows. After the initial shocks in the exchange rate (shown on the x-axis) the exchange rate is simulated for 200 periods. We then collect the last 50 values of the exchange rate. If we obtain the same value, this means that the exchange rate has converged to a fixed point during that period. If we collect 50 different values for the exchange rate this means that the exchange rate is involved in a periodic movement of 50 periods or more. There can also be periodic movements with fewer periods. Part (a) shows the results in three dimensions. On the x-axis we present the initial shocks in the exchange rate; on the y-axis we have the value of the elasticity (ϵ-parameter), and on the vertical axis we find the exchange rate during the last 50 periods of simulation runs of 200 periods. We find that, for small values of the elasticity, the exchange rate is moving around the bubble equilibria in a periodic way, where the number of periods is typically less than 50. A second finding is that, for larger values of the elasticity, the exchange rate is caught in periodic movements exceeding 50 periods. We show this more

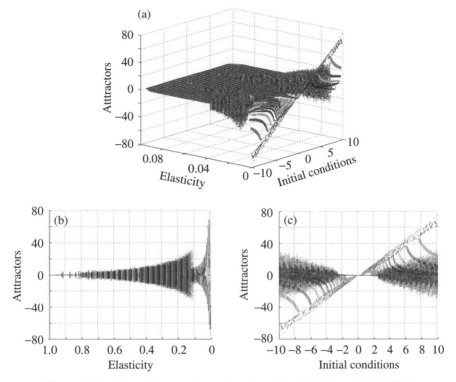

Figure 6.8. The exchange rate as a function of the elasticity and the initial conditions, with $\psi = 0.2$, $\beta = 0.9$, $\gamma = 4$, and $\rho_z = 0.6$.

clearly in parts (b) and (c), which present the same data as in (a), except that (b) is a projection of (a) in the two-dimensional (y, z)-space, while part (c) is a projection in the (x, z)-space. Part (b) shows that there is a range of elasticity values for which the periodicity of the cycles exceeds 50 (i.e., we find 50 different exchange rates during the last 50 periods of the simulation runs). This, of course, does not prove that the dynamics is chaotic, but it suggests that it could be the case. We return to an analysis of chaotic dynamics in Chapter 10. When the elasticity parameter continues to increase, the chaotic dynamics disappears. From part (c) we learn that chaotic dynamics becomes more likely when the size of the initial shocks is large.

7

Risk Appetite in an Evolutionary Perspective

7.1 Introduction

In this chapter we extend the model further by allowing the parameter ϕ to be time dependent. Remember that this parameter regulates the degree with which fundamentalists change their risk perception when market conditions change. Thus, in a way, this parameter can be interpreted as reflecting risk appetite. When ϕ is large, fundamentalists have a lot of risk appetite; when ϕ is small they have little appetite for risk (their risk aversion is high).

7.2 The Extended Model

We extend the model and allow ϕ to be time dependent. We postulate that ϕ changes randomly according to

$$\phi_t = \phi_{t-1} + \epsilon_t, \tag{7.1}$$

where ϵ_t is a random variable driven by an evolutionary process to be defined later. We also impose that $\phi_t \geqslant 0$. This is equivalent to assuming that the coefficient of risk aversion μ_t cannot become negative.

The time-varying parameter ϕ_t can be interpreted as a time-varying risk appetite. This can be seen from equation (5.1), which we repeat here. An increase in ϕ_t has the effect of reducing the time-varying coefficient of risk aversion, $\mu_{f,t}$, for any given degree of misalignment $|s_t - s_t^*|$:

$$\mu_{f,t} = \frac{\mu}{1 + \phi_t |s_t - s_t^*|}. \tag{7.2}$$

Thus, an increase in risk appetite (ϕ_t) leads fundamentalists to react more strongly to increasing deviations of the exchange rate from its fundamental. In equation (7.1), we assume that in each period there is a random change ("mutation") in the parameter ϕ_t. In other words, we assume that risk appetite changes stochastically.

We now make the additional assumption that the risk appetite, defined in (7.1), is subject to an evolutionary dynamics, i.e., we assume that changing risk appetites that improve profits are preserved according to the following evolutionary rule: agents keep the new value of ϕ_t if their profits are higher than in the previous period; if profits are equal to or lower than in the previous period, they drop the new value

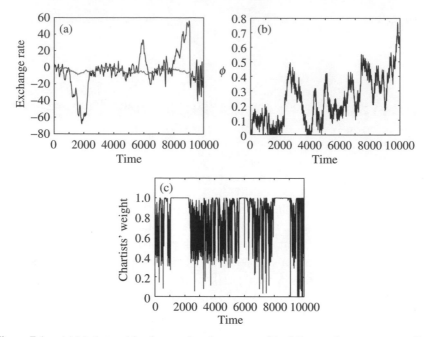

Figure 7.1. (a) Market and fundamental exchange rates (black line, exchange rate; gray line, fundamental rate), (b) risk appetite, ϕ, and (c) weight of chartists. All parts have $\psi = 0.2$, $C = 5$, $\beta = 0.9$, $\gamma = 5$, $\rho = 0$, and $\mu = 1$.

of ϕ_t and revert to the old value. Thus, we model the selection of ϕ according to a genetic algorithm. In other words, when agents increase risk appetite, they will maintain this new appetite if their profits increase. Conversely, if the increased risk appetite is associated with fewer profits, agents revert to their old appetite.[1]

We show the result of a stochastic simulation of this synthesis model in Figure 7.1. In part (a) we present the exchange rate and its fundamental in the time domain; in part (b) we show the values of ϕ_t in the time domain, and in part (c) we exhibit the chartists' weight in the time domain. We find that the exchange rate appears to oscillate between two regimes. We will call the first one "regime I." This is obtained when risk appetite is low (the coefficient ϕ_t is low) and fundamentalists are not willing to take risky positions. We then have a regime of bubbles and crashes. Note that in such a regime the weight of the chartists is close to 1. At other times, however, agents' risk appetite is high (ϕ_t is high), so that agents are willing to take risky positions. In that case the exchange rate fluctuates within the transaction-cost band. We call this regime "regime II." We note from Figure 7.1(b) that risk appetite is subject to strong cyclical movements, whereby periods of high and low risk appetite alternate in an unpredictable fashion.

---

[1] Similar assumptions of an evolutionary dynamics have been made by Lux and Schorstein (2005), Kirman and Teyssière (2002), Sargent (1993), and Dawid (1999).

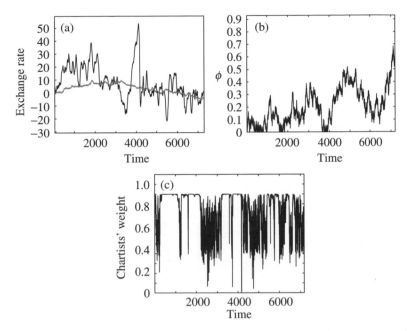

Figure 7.2. (a) Market and fundamental exchange rates (black line, exchange rate; gray line, fundamental rate), (b) risk appetite, ϕ, and (c) weight of chartists. All parts have $\psi = 0.2$, $C = 5$, $\beta = 0.9$, $\gamma = 5$, $\rho = 0$, and $\mu = 1$.

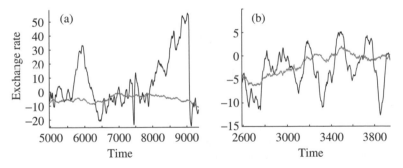

Figure 7.3. Market and fundamental exchange rates with $\psi = 0.2$, $C = 5$, $\beta = 0.9$, $\mu = 1$, $\gamma = 1$, and $\rho = 0$. Black line, exchange rate; gray line, fundamental rate.

We also note that in Figure 7.1 the two regimes are clearly distinguishable. This is, however, not always the case. In Figure 7.2 we show a stochastic simulation using exactly the same parameter configuration as in Figure 7.1. The transition from one regime into the other, however, is much less clear-cut. This has to do with the fact that in this simulation there are less pronounced cyclical movements in risk appetite.

In Figure 7.3 we show a blow-up of the two regimes generated by the model: part (a) shows regime I and part (b) shows regime II. Apart from the difference

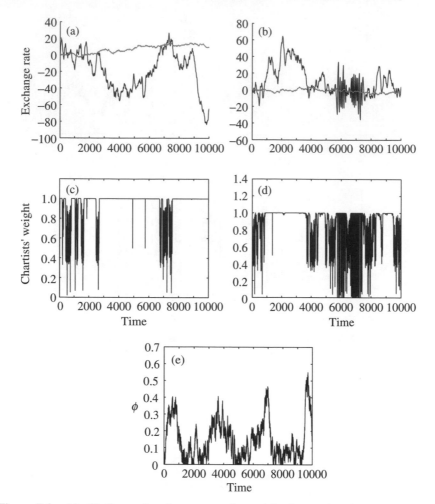

Figure 7.4. (a), (b) Comparison between market and fundamental exchange rates (gray lines, fundamental rate; black lines, exchange rate). (c), (d) Comparison between chartists' weights. Parts (a) and (c) show results when $\phi = 0$, (b)–(d) show results for time-dependent ϕ, (e) Risk appetite, ϕ. All parts have $C = 5$, $\psi = 0.2$, $\beta = 0.9$, $\gamma = 5$, $\rho = 0$, and $\mu = 1$.

in scale, the two regimes produce protracted disconnection of the exchange rate from its fundamental. The dynamics of these disconnections are very similar. The difference is in the scale. When regime I prevails we have very long and sustained deviations from the fundamental, while when regime II prevails we obtain smaller and less protracted deviations. We will then also observe that the exchange rate remains closer to the fundamental than in the first regime. The first regime is obtained when risk appetite is low and agents fail to arbitrage, while the second regime prevails when risk appetite is high. Our extended model describes how one can move from one regime to the other.

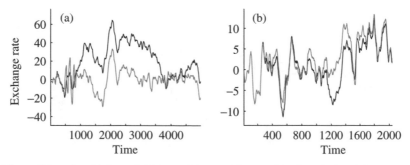

Figure 7.5. Sensitivity to initial conditions, with $\psi = 0.2$, $C = 5$, $\beta = 0.9$, $\gamma = 5$, $\rho = 0$, and $\mu = 1$. Black line, without shock; gray line, with shock.

7.3 The Nature of Risk Appetite

The synthesis model developed in this chapter is characterized by the fact that risk appetite is endogenously determined. As a result, the parameter of risk aversion is also endogenous. It is useful to contrast the features of this model with the features of the model where we assume that $\phi_t = 0$ (which implies that risk aversion is constant). In order to do so, we simulate the two versions of the model, assuming the same values of the other parameters of the model. We show the results in Figure 7.4. The model that assumes $\phi_t = 0$ produces long and protracted deviations of the market rate from the fundamental. In the model with variable risk appetite, ϕ_t, these deviations are reduced. The mechanism that produces this is the endogenous movements in risk appetite. These can be described as follows. When risk appetite is low, departures from the fundamental become more likely. Random increases in risk appetite occur, however. Typically, these random increases will tend to be self-validating during the bubble phase because they lead fundamentalists to exploit the emerging profit opportunities and to increase their profits.

7.4 Sensitivity to Initial Conditions

Sensitivity to initial conditions was shown to be important in the model developed in the previous chapters. This is also the case in the present version of the model. We simulated the model twice, assuming exactly the same stochastics were driving the fundamental variable and the genetic algorithm. The only difference between the simulations was the difference in initial conditions. We imposed the same initial values of zero on the lagged exchange rates, except for the period immediately preceding the start of the simulation, where we assumed that, in the second simulation, this initial value was 0.001. We show the results in Figure 7.5. We first concentrate on part (a). This shows an extreme sensitivity to initial conditions. In particular, we observe that a trivially small initial shock can lead the exchange rate into different regimes. In this case, we see that a small difference in initial conditions leads

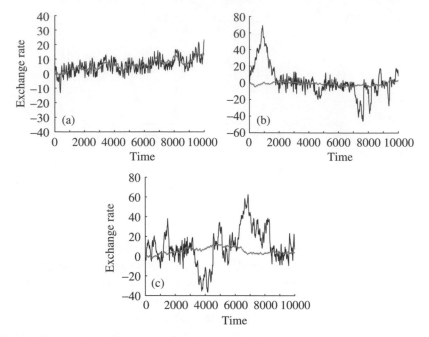

Figure 7.6. Market and fundamental exchange rates with $\psi = 0.2, C = 5, \beta = 0.9, \mu = 1$, and (a) $\gamma = 1, \rho = 0.5$, (b) $\gamma = 5, \rho = 0$, (c) $\gamma = 10, \rho = 0$. Gray lines denote fundamental rate; black lines denote exchange rate.

the exchange rate into either regime I, characterized by a bubble and a crash, or regime II, where bubbles and crashes are absent. Thus, trivially small shocks can fundamentally alter the time path of the exchange rate.

Figure 7.5(b) shows the case when the two exchange rates remain in the same regime (regime II). Even in that case, the small difference in initial conditions produces quite different time patterns in the exchange rate movements.

7.5   Sensitivity Analysis

In this section we present the results of a sensitivity analysis. We first allow the parameter γ to change. Remember, this parameter measures the sensitivity of the switching rules with respect to the relative profitability. We find the results are very similar to those in previous chapters, i.e., increases in γ lead to an increased likelihood of bubbles and crashes (see Figure 7.6). When γ is small (here $\gamma = 1$), the exchange rate remains in what we have called "regime II," i.e., it moves around in the neighborhood of the transaction-cost band. With increasing γ, the exchange rate switches between the two regimes in an unpredictable manner.

There is an interesting paradox in the previous results. The size of γ can be interpreted as a measure of how rational agents are. When γ is small there is a strong departure from rationality, in that agents do not greatly adjust their behavior when relative profitability changes. Conversely, when γ is large, agents come closer to rational behavior, in that they allow their behavior to adjust to changing relative profitability. In the limit when $\gamma = \infty$, all agents will always select the most profitable rule. We find, however, that when agents come closer to rational behavior the exchange rate tends to be most disconnected from the underlying fundamental and to be involved in frequent bubbles and crashes. Conversely, when agents' behavior departs the most from rationality, the exchange rate reflects the underlying fundamentals more closely.

7.6 The Effect of News

Above, and in the previous chapters, we have shown how the interactions between agents using different forecasting rules create a dynamics in which the exchange rate wanders around its fundamental value, and in which periods of tranquillity and turbulence alternate in an unpredictable fashion. There are two reasons why we obtain these results. First, the model has different equilibria (fundamental and nonfundamental). Second, unexpected shocks in the fundamental (news) lead to switches from one equilibrium to the other. Thus, the news in the fundamental variables is important in generating switches from one regime to another. In the remainder of this chapter, we analyze in more detail how news in the fundamentals is transmitted into the exchange rate.

We analyzed the question of the effect of news in the fundamentals by performing an impulse response analysis. In order to do so, we first performed a cointegration test on the simulated exchange rate and the fundamental exchange rate. We found that, over sufficiently long time periods (10 000 periods), these two variables are cointegrated. This confirms what we have shown in previous chapters, i.e., that the exchange rate always tends to return to its fundamental value, even if this may take a very long time. We then estimated an error-correction model and used the results to compute the impulse response functions. We repeated this many times using different realizations of the random-walk process driving the fundamental exchange rate. Each time, however, we used exactly the same parameters of the model ($\beta = 0.9$, $\gamma = 5$, $\rho = 0.5$, $\mu = 1$). We show the resulting impulse response functions in Figure 7.7 for a number of different simulations of the model. We concentrate on the lower gray lines first. These lines represent the response of the exchange rate to a one-standard-deviation unexpected shock ("news") in the fundamental. The most striking aspect of the results is the following. The long-term effects of the same positive news in the fundamentals are very different in the different simulations. Thus, it is very difficult to predict what the effect of the same news in the fundamentals is on the exchange rate. In other words, there appears to be an indeterminacy in the effect of the same news. Sometimes this news raises the exchange rate; at other times it has no visible effect. There are even times during which the sign of the effect is changed.

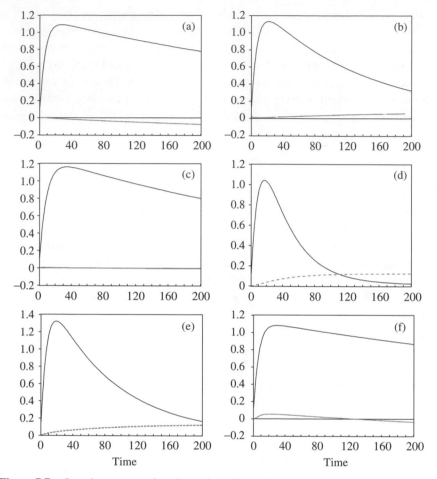

Figure 7.7.   Impulse response functions when $C = 5$, $\beta = 0.9$, $\gamma = 5$, and $\rho = 0.5$. Upper (black) line, response of S to a one-standard-deviation innovation in S; lower (gray) line, response of S to a one-standard-deviation innovation in S^*.

Figure 7.7 also shows the dynamic response of the exchange rate to a shock in its own past (the upper (black) line). We observe that the response of the exchange rate to a shock in its own past can be very different from one simulation to the other, despite the fact that the model used to generate the simulations is the same. In some cases we find a quick return of the exchange rate to its initial value. In other cases we find that the return is exceedingly slow.[2] This result is related to the sensitivity

---

[2] Note also that the effect of a fundamental shock appears to be much smaller than the effect of a one-standard-deviation disturbance in the exchange rate. This difference has to do with the fact that the volatility of the fundamental is much lower than the volatility in the exchange rate. Thus, a one-standard-deviation shock in the fundamental is a much lower number than a one-standard-deviation shock in the exchange rate.

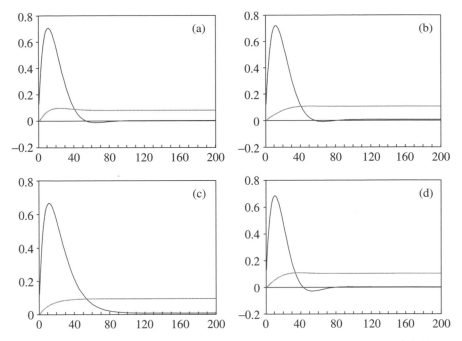

Figure 7.8. Impulse response functions when $C = 5$, $\beta = 0.9$, $\gamma = 1$, and $\rho = 0.5$. Upper (black) line, response of S to a one-standard-deviation innovation; lower (gray) line, response of S to a one-standard-deviation innovation in S^*.

to initial conditions that we documented earlier. Thus, the same shocks applied in a different stochastic environment have very different effects on the exchange rate.

These results have interesting implications. The most important one is that the impulse response functions seem to come from different underlying models. The same shocks in the fundamentals have very different effects, and the exchange rate follows very different dynamic paths after the initial shocks. Yet the underlying model structure is the same in all these simulations. In other words, if we consider these impulse response functions to have been computed during different sample periods, we would be tempted to conclude that the underlying model that generates the variables must have changed. Yet no such change occurs.

It should be stressed that these surprising results are not obtained for all parameter values of the model. More specifically, when the parameter γ is small, we obtain results that come closer to what linear models produce. We show an example in Figure 7.8, where we assume that $\gamma = 1$. We now find that the impulse response functions obtained from different simulations of the same model are very similar. It can be observed that the long-term effect of the news in the fundamentals is always the same. A one-standard-deviation shock in the fundamental (which was set at 0.1) leads to an increase in the exchange rate by 0.1 in all these different simulations. In addition, the dynamics of the response of the exchange rate is very similar in

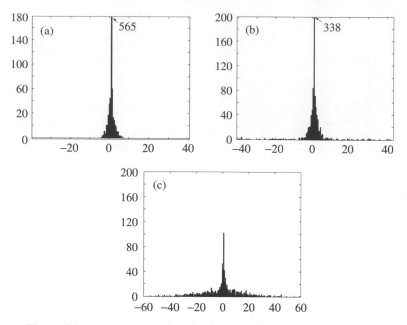

Figure 7.9. Frequency distribution effect of news with $C = 5$, $\beta = 0.9$,
$\rho = 0.5$, $\phi = 0$, and (a) $\gamma = 0.5$, (b) $\gamma = 1$, and (c) $\gamma = 5$.

the different simulations. Thus, in a world where agents do not respond greatly to changing profitabilities of forecasting rules, the indeterminacy in the response to news that was visible in Figure 7.7 disappears. This result is related to the fact that, when γ is small, the model produces only fundamental equilibria (see Chapters 2 and 3, where we have shown this). As a result, when stochastic shocks occur, the exchange rate is always reattracted to the fundamental equilibrium. There is no indeterminacy in the effect of news in the fundamentals. The long-term effect of news in the fundamentals on the exchange rate can easily be predicted. This result is also implicit from Figure 7.6, where we show that, for small values of γ, the exchange rate tends to fluctuate around the fundamental.

In order to obtain additional insight into the nature of the effects of news, we simulated the model 1000 times and computed the final effect of news in the fundamentals on the exchange rate. As before, we introduced a one-standard-deviation shock in the fundamental. In Figure 7.9 we show the frequency distribution of these effects. We concentrate on Figure 7.9(a), where we set $\gamma = 0.5$. We observe that, for this small value of γ, the response of the exchange rate to the news is more than half of the simulations (56%), an increase in the exchange rate by one standard deviation. In other words in more than half of the simulations the change in the exchange rate perfectly reflects the news. As γ increases, however, the changes in the exchange rate reflect less and less the news in the fundamentals. When $\gamma = 5$, the change in the exchange rate reflects the news in only 10% of the simulations.

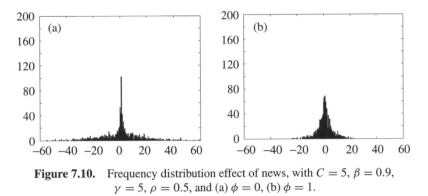

Figure 7.10. Frequency distribution effect of news, with $C = 5$, $\beta = 0.9$, $\gamma = 5$, $\rho = 0.5$, and (a) $\phi = 0$, (b) $\phi = 1$.

Most of these exchange rate changes subsequent to the news do not reflect the news very well. We see that when $\gamma = 5$ the distribution of the effects of news on the exchange rate has fat tails, indicating that quite often these exchange rate changes are completely dissociated from the news in the fundamentals.

Finally, we also analyzed the sensitivity of these results to the parameter ϕ, which we have called "risk appetite." We selected two values of ϕ ($\phi = 0$ and $\phi = 1$) and we show the results in Figure 7.10. When risk appetite is low we find the same strong disconnection of the changes in the exchange rate from the news in the fundamentals. With a positive risk appetite, the distribution is significantly less heavy tailed and is more concentrated around 1 (one standard deviation).

These results confirm our previous conclusion. For parameter values that create a regime in which fundamental and nonfundamental attractors coexist (large γ and small ϕ), the news in the fundamentals has no predictable effect on the exchange rate. In this regime, the exchange rate changes reflect poorly the news in the fundamentals. Conversely, in a regime in which the exchange rate is attracted to the fundamental most of the time (small γ and large ϕ), the same news in the fundamentals has a more predictable effect on the exchange rate.

Another way to interpret these results is as follows. If the market is involved in a bubble dynamics, the news in the fundamentals may not affect the exchange rate at all; it may even move it in the wrong direction. Conversely, if the market is involved in a fundamental regime (i.e., the exchange rate is attracted by the fundamental equilibrium), the same news in the fundamentals will affect the exchange rate in a more predictable manner. Thus, the way news in the fundamentals affects the exchange rate depends on market conditions.

7.7 Conclusion

In this chapter we elaborated further on the model derived in the previous chapters. More specifically, we allowed for changing "risk appetites," i.e., we assumed that there is a random component in the degree of risk aversion. These changes in risk appetite have the effect of creating switches in regimes, whereby the exchange rate moves from a regime where the exchange rate closely follows the fundamental to a regime where the exchange rate is caught up in a bubbles-and-crashes dynamic.

We also analyzed how news in the fundamentals is transmitted into the exchange rate. Our main finding here is that news in the fundamentals has an unpredictable effect on the exchange rate. Sometimes news has a strong effect on the exchange rate; at other times the same news has no effect whatsoever. In addition, it is essentially unpredictable when news will have an effect and when it will not. The fundamental reason for this indeterminacy is that there is no unique equilibrium to which the exchange rate will converge. For example, when the exchange rate is involved in a bubble at the moment the news reaches the market, the news may not affect the exchange rate at all, while at more tranquil times the same news will strongly affect the exchange rate. This result is also related to the fact that, when the exchange rate is involved in a bubble (i.e., a movement towards a nonfundamental equilibrium), the chartists tend to dominate the market. As a result, fundamental information is not given much weight, so that news in the fundamentals does not influence exchange rate forecasting.

Thus, our model predicts that news in the fundamentals has unpredictable effects on the exchange rate. This is also observed in reality. For example, there is a lot of evidence suggesting that news in fundamentals, like inflation differentials, the current account, and economic growth, has unpredictable effects on the euro/USD exchange rate (see De Grauwe 2000). There have been periods during which news in the U.S. current account had no effect whatsoever on the euro/USD rate. At other times, the same news about the U.S. current account had very strong effects on the exchange rate. Similar phenomena have been observed with other fundamental variables. Our model allows us to understand why the unpredictability of the effects of news is the rule rather than the exception.

8

The Empirical Evidence

8.1 Introduction

In this chapter, we present the stylized facts and empirical regularities observed in the foreign exchange markets. We then analyze how well our model reproduces these regularities. We calibrate the model so that it replicates the observed statistical properties of exchange rate movements. In order to do so, we select a parameter configuration that mimics these properties most closely. However, we also present the results of a sensitivity analysis analyzing the statistical properties of the model under different parameter configurations. Although we restrict our analysis to the foreign exchange markets, it is important to note that the statistical properties are common across price changes in various types of financial market (see Mandelbrot 1963; Lux and Marchesi 2000; Gaunersdorfer and Hommes 2000). We discuss these statistical properties in the following sections.

A note on the nature of the time periods is in order here. Our model is not explicit about the units of time. The way we have specified the chartist behavior makes it plausible to identify a time unit to be a day, so that the returns relate to daily returns. We will therefore confront the simulations of our model with daily observations of real-life exchange rates.

8.2 The Distribution of Returns: A Tale of Fat Tails and Excess Kurtosis

In the early 1960s, Mandelbrot (1963) pointed out the insufficiency of the normal distribution for modeling the distribution of asset returns and their heavy tail feature. Since then the non-Gaussian character of the distribution of price changes has been observed in many other asset markets, including the exchange market (see Lux and Marchesi 2000; Gaunersdorfer and Hommes 2000; de Vries 2000; Werner and Upper 2004). The distribution of exchange rate returns is typically characterized by excess kurtosis, i.e., it shows more mass concentrated around the mean. Thus, one way to quantify the deviation from the normal distribution is by computing the kurtosis index as a measure of the peakedness of the distribution. The kurtosis is defined as

$$\text{kurtosis} = \frac{\mu_4}{\sigma^4}, \tag{8.1}$$

Table 8.1. Kurtosis and Hill index USD/DM and JPY/DM over the period 1975–98.

		Median Hill index		
Exchange rate	Kurtosis	2.5% tail	5% tail	10% tail
USD/DM	12.1	4.0	3.6	3.1
JPY/DM	19.6	3.7	3.6	2.9

where μ_4 is the fourth central moment of the distribution. The kurtosis of Gaussian changes is equal to 3. Exchange rate changes have a kurtosis typically exceeding 3 (see Huisman et al. 2002).

The distribution of exchange rate returns also deviates from the normal distribution in another respect. It exhibits heavy tails. A measure of the fatness of tails is the Hill index. This is a more sophisticated measure of the fatness of tails than the kurtosis index and is defined as follows. We first take the absolute values of the returns and order these according to size, i.e., $\text{ret}_1 \leqslant \text{ret}_2 \leqslant \cdots \leqslant \text{ret}_n$. The Hill index is then

$$\text{Hill index} = \frac{1}{m}\left[\sum_{t=1}^{m}(\text{ret}_{n+1-t} - \text{ret}_{n-m})\right], \qquad (8.2)$$

where m is the number of extreme observations in the tail. The choice of size of the tail is a little arbitrary. We will therefore show the Hill index for different values of cut-off points of the tail.

Empirical evidence shows that the Hill index for exchange rate returns typically ranges between 2 and 5 (see Koedijk et al. 1992; Huisman et al. 2002).[1] In Table 8.1 we show the kurtosis and the Hill index of both the USD/DM and JPY/DM exchange rate returns for the period 1975–98. We computed the Hill index for different cut-off points of the tails (2.5%, 5%, 10%) and for four different subsamples of the original series. We then took the median value of these four series. We find that these exchange rates exhibit excess kurtosis and fat tails during the sample period. This implies that, most of the time, the exchange rate movements are relatively small but that occasionally periods of turbulence occur with relatively large changes in the exchange rate.

Another phenomenon that has been observed is that the kurtosis is reduced under time aggregation (see Lux 1998). We checked this finding for the same exchange rates. In Table 8.2, we show the results for USD/DM and JPY/DM exchange rates, and we confirm that the kurtosis declines under time aggregation.

The next step in the analysis is to check whether these empirical features are also shared by our simulated exchange rate changes. Note that in the empirical literature the returns are usually defined as the first differences of the logarithms of

---

[1] The larger the Hill index, the thinner the tails of the distribution.

Table 8.2. Kurtosis and time aggregation USD/DM and JPY/DM over period 1975–98.

Exchange rate	5-period returns	10-period returns	20-period returns
USD/DM	7.4	5.3	3.4
JPY/DM	14.9	5.7	2.7

Table 8.3. Kurtosis and Hill index.

Parameter values	Kurtosis	Median Hill index		
		2.5% tail	5% tail	10% tail
$C = 5,\ \beta = 0.9,\ \gamma = 0.5,\ \phi = 1$	5.65	4.92	4.98	3.98
$C = 5,\ \beta = 0.9,\ \gamma = 1,\quad \phi = 1$	4.39	4.06	4.46	3.90
$C = 5,\ \beta = 0.9,\ \gamma = 5,\quad \phi = 1$	6.30	4.42	3.00	2.40
$C = 5,\ \beta = 0.8,\ \gamma = 0.5,\ \phi = 1$	8.33	4.39	4.19	3.80
$C = 5,\ \beta = 0.8,\ \gamma = 1,\quad \phi = 1$	7.92	4.15	4.37	3.73
$C = 5,\ \beta = 0.8,\ \gamma = 5,\quad \phi = 1$	11.08	3.63	3.90	3.54

the exchange rate. Since, in our theoretical model, the exchange rate is not defined in logarithms, we will define the returns to be the first differences in the levels of the exchange rate. We proceed as follows. We simulate the model for a broad range of parameter values, using normally distributed random disturbances in the fundamental (with a mean of 0 and a standard deviation of 1). We compute the median Hill index of the simulated exchange rate returns for four different subsamples of 2000 observations. In addition, as before, we considered three different cut-off points of the tails (2.5%, 5%, and 10%). We show the results of the kurtosis and of the Hill index in Table 8.3.[2] We find that for a broad range of parameter values the kurtosis exceeds 3 and the Hill index indicates the presence of fat tails.

In Figure 8.1 we show the probability density of the USD/DM exchange rate (part (a)), of our simulated exchange rates (part (b)), and in the prospect model (part (c)). In Figure 8.1(d) we plot the probability density of normally distributed returns. First, we observe that the empirical distribution differs from the normal distribution. Indeed, the distribution of the USD/DM shows excess kurtosis and fat tails. Second, the empirical distribution strikingly resembles the distribution of our simulated exchange rate returns.[3]

Finally, we check if the kurtosis of our simulated exchange rate returns declines under time aggregation. In order to do so, we chose different time aggregation

---

[2] We have also simulated the model in which we introduce the assumptions of prospect theory (see Chapter 5). We show the results in an appendix (see Table 8.14 in Section 8.9). In general using prospect theory does not mimic the empirical regularities very well.

[3] We find very similar results in other exchange markets.

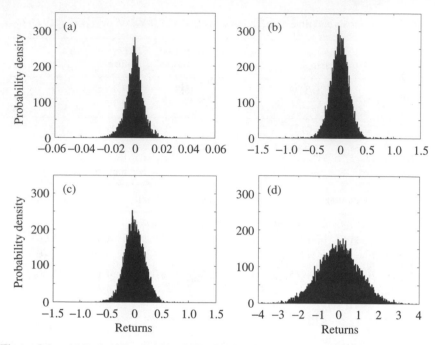

Figure 8.1. (a) Probability density of USD/DM during the period 1975–93. (b) Probability distribution, simulated returns, misalignment model. (c) Probability distribution, simulated returns, prospect model. (d) Probability density, normal distribution. In parts (b) and (c), $c = 5, \beta = 0.9, \gamma = 1, \phi = 1, \rho = 0$.

Table 8.4. Kurtosis and time aggregation.

Parameter values	1-period returns	10-period returns	25-period returns	50-period returns
$C = 5, \ \beta = 0.9, \ \gamma = 0.5, \ \phi = 1$	5.65	5.96	3.17	3.08
$C = 5, \ \beta = 0.9, \ \gamma = 1, \quad \phi = 1$	4.39	4.11	3.67	3.45
$C = 5, \ \beta = 0.9, \ \gamma = 5, \quad \phi = 1$	6.30	2.77	2.15	2.19
$C = 5, \ \beta = 0.8, \ \gamma = 0.5, \ \phi = 1$	8.33	8.52	3.14	3.43
$C = 5, \ \beta = 0.8, \ \gamma = 1, \quad \phi = 1$	7.92	7.39	3.28	3.30
$C = 5, \ \beta = 0.8, \ \gamma = 5, \quad \phi = 1$	11.08	10.14	3.46	3.05

periods and we computed the kurtosis of the time-aggregated exchange rate returns. We found that the kurtosis declines under time aggregation. In Table 8.4 we show the results for some parameter value sets.[4]

The previous results suggest that the speculative dynamics of the model transform normally distributed noise in the exchange rate into exchange rate movements with

---

[4]Another empirical regularity of the distribution of exchange returns is its symmetry. We computed the skewness, and we could not reject the fact that the distribution is symmetric.

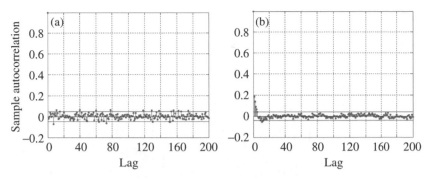

Figure 8.2.   (a) Autocorrelation function of USD/DM (1975–98). (b) Autocorrelation function of simulated returns, with $C = 0$, $\beta = 0.8$, $\phi = 1$, $\gamma = 0.5$.

tails that are significantly fatter than the normal distribution and with more density around the mean. Thus, this model mimics an important empirical regularity, i.e., that exchange rate movements are characterized by tranquil periods (occurring most of the time) and turbulent periods (occurring infrequently). This phenomenon has also been called the *intermittency phenomenon* (see Lux 1998). It should be noted that similar models with heterogeneous agents applied to the stock markets have been equally successful in replicating fat tails and excess kurtosis (see Lux and Marchesi 1999, 2000; Kirman and Teyssière 2002; Gaunersdorfer and Hommes 2000).

8.3 Dependence Properties of Returns

8.3.1 *Absence of Linear Autocorrelation*

It is well-known that exchange rate returns do not exhibit significant autocorrelation. The absence of significant linear correlations in returns is often cited as support for the "efficient-market hypothesis" (see Fama 1991).[5] We define the autocorrelation function (ACF) as the correlations of the returns with different lags. In Figure 8.2(a), we show the ACF for the daily returns of the USD/DM exchange rate over the sample period 1975–98.[6] The absence of linear autocorrelation implies that the ACF rapidly decays to zero.

In order to check whether our model mimics the empirical evidence, we computed the ACF of the simulated returns. In Figure 8.2 we represent an example of the ACF of the simulated data. We find that, except for a few initial lags, our raw returns are not autocorrelated. We find similar results for other parameter configurations, in particular for those used in Tables 8.3 and 8.4.

---

[5] Note that the absence of autocorrelation in the returns is a necessary condition for the efficient market to hold. It is not a sufficient condition, however.

[6] We find very similar results in other foreign exchange markets.

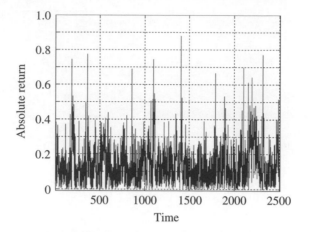

Figure 8.3.   Absolute exchange rate returns.

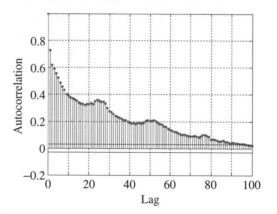

Figure 8.4.   Autocorrelation function of absolute returns,
with $C = 5$, $\beta = 0.9$, $\gamma = 3$, and $\phi = 1$.

8.3.2   *Volatility Clustering*

In contrast to the "raw returns" we analyzed in the previous section, the absolute
returns and squared returns show significant positive autocorrelation, i.e., they show
persistence. This phenomenon has been observed in most asset markets. Since the
absolute returns and the squared returns are measures of variability of the exchange
rate changes, their autocorrelation implies that there is volatility clustering, i.e.,
large changes are more likely to be followed by large changes, and small changes
by small changes. In other words, there is time dependency in the volatility of
exchange rate returns. Volatility clustering has been widely observed in exchange
rate changes (Kirman and Teyssière 2002; Lux and Marchesi 2000).[7]

---

[7] For some theoretical insights see Gaunersdorfer et al. (2003).

Table 8.5. LM test for autocorrelation in residuals (sample size = 5000).

Parameter values	LM test	p value	R^2
$C = 0$, $\beta = 0.9$, $\gamma = 10$, $\phi = 1$	9.7	0.008	0.002
$C = 5$, $\beta = 0.9$, $\gamma = 10$, $\phi = 1$	13.2	0.001	0.003
$C = 5$, $\beta = 0.9$, $\gamma = 1$, $\phi = 0$	11.1	0.003	0.003
$C = 5$, $\beta = 0.8$, $\gamma = 10$, $\phi = 1$	6.9	0.032	0.002

In order to check if our model is capable of reproducing the observed statistical property of volatility clustering, we first computed the absolute value of the simulated returns and plotted them in Figure 8.3. This figure creates the visual impression of volatility clustering. In the second step we computed the ACF of the absolute returns of the simulated exchange rate returns for a broad range of parameter values. In Figure 8.4 we show an example of the ACF for a certain set of parameters. At first glance, Figure 8.4 suggests that the ACF dies out slowly, i.e., that the volatility in the exchange rate returns has a long memory. In order to confirm whether this visual impression is correct, we proceed as follows. We first estimate an autoregressive, moving-average (ARMA) model on the absolute returns and we find that an ARMA(2, 1) performs best. We then tested for serial correlation in the residuals by computing the Breusch–Godfrey LM statistic. In Table 8.5 we show the results obtained for some parameter configurations. We conclude that for a wide range of parameter sets we reject the null hypothesis of no serial correlation in the error term.

In order to test for GARCH effects in the exchange rate returns, we specified a GARCH(2, 1) model:[8]

$$\left.\begin{aligned} \Delta s_t &= a + \varepsilon_t, \\ \sigma_t^2 &= b + \alpha \epsilon_{t-1}^2 + \delta_1 \sigma_{t-1}^2 + \delta_2 \sigma_{t-2}^2, \end{aligned}\right\} \tag{8.3}$$

where ε_t is the error term, a is a constant, and σ_t^2 is the conditional variance of the returns. We first performed an ARCH test for heteroskedasticity (see Table 8.6). We then estimated (8.3) using the simulated exchange rate returns, and present the results in Table 8.7 for different parameter values.

We observe that the GARCH coefficients, α, δ_1, and δ_2, are significantly different from 0, implying that there is volatility clustering in the exchange rate returns. In addition, we find that, for values of β between 0.8 and 0.9, the sum of α, δ_1, and δ_2, which is a measure of the degree of the inertia of the volatility, is close to 1. This implies that the effect of volatility shocks dies out slowly, i.e., there is persistence in volatility. Thus, our model is capable of reproducing a widely observed phenomenon of clustering and persistence in volatility.

---

[8] We also used a GARCH(1, 1) specification with similar results.

Table 8.6. ARCH test for heteroskedasticity in residuals (sample size = 5000).

Parameter values	ARCH test	p value	R^2
$C = 5$, $\beta = 0.9$, $\gamma = 1$, $\phi = 0.5$	64.2	0.000	0.01
$C = 0$, $\beta = 0.9$, $\gamma = 10$, $\phi = 1$	121.7	0.000	0.03
$C = 5$, $\beta = 0.9$, $\gamma = 10$, $\phi = 1$	18.2	0.000	0.004
$C = 5$, $\beta = 0.9$, $\gamma = 1$, $\phi = 0$	12.3	0.002	0.003
$C = 5$, $\beta = 0.8$, $\gamma = 10$, $\phi = 1$	151.7	0.000	0.03

Table 8.7. Estimation of GARCH model.
(Parameter values $C = 5$, $\beta = 0.9$, $\phi = 1$, γ as given.)

	$\gamma = 0.5$		$\gamma = 1$	
	Coefficient	T-statistic	Coefficient	T-statistic
a	0.003	1.3	−0.007	−3.9
b	0.004	11.3	0.001	12.4
α	0.36	14.5	0.38	14.2
δ_1	0.45	6.0	0.41	5.7
δ_2	0.08	1.3	0.12	2.3

8.3.3 Leverage Effect

Another empirical regularity observed in financial markets is the so-called *U-shaped volatility*, i.e., the relationship between the exchange rate changes and future volatility is not linear and has a U-shape. It implies that small exchange rate changes trigger little future volatility while large changes in the exchange rate lead to high future volatility. The empirical evidence about this fact is strong (see Franses and van Dijk 2000) and it is clearly at odds with the theoretical underpinning of the traditional macro-models which fail to explain it. In this section we investigate whether our model is capable of reproducing this empirical fact. In order to do so, we computed the volatility of exchange rate changes for different size windows. We chose three size-windows: 5, 10, and 20 periods. Then we plotted the volatilities (absolute returns) against the exchange rate changes. We obtained a U-shaped relationship for a broad range of parameter values. In Figure 8.5 we show the results for one selected parameter configuration, i.e., $c = 5$, $\beta = 0.9$, $\gamma = 1$, $\phi = 1$, and a window size of five periods. In Figure 8.6 we show the results for the USD/DM exchange rate.

From Figure 8.5 we can see that the mass is concentrated around 0 and that there are relatively few outliers. Thus, it might be argued that this U-shaped relationship is due to these few outliers. In other words, the U-shaped relationship might not hold for a narrow range of values, i.e., where the mass concentrates. In order to check this, we selected a narrower range of exchange rate changes, i.e., between

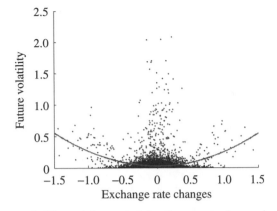

Figure 8.5. Future volatility and five periods' exchange rate changes in the misalignment model, with $C = 5$, $\beta = 0.9$, $\gamma = 1$, $\phi = 1$, $\rho = 0.6$. Points denote exchange rate changes, line shows fitted.

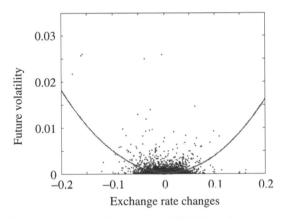

Figure 8.6. Future volatility and five periods' US/DM exchange rate changes over the period 1975–98. Points denote exchange rate changes, line shows fitted.

-0.6 and 0.6, and we estimated the relationship between the changes and the future volatility. We show the results in Figure 8.7.

We observe that the U-shaped relationship between exchange rate changes and volatility also holds for a narrower range of exchange rate changes. We conclude that the U-shaped relationship is not due to a few outliers, but is an intrinsic feature of exchange rates and their volatility.

To get a better insight into such a visual analysis, we estimate an ordinary least squares (OLS) regression of the second-order polynomial, which is the simplest U-shape function, of the conditional volatility:[9]

$$v_{t+1} = c_0 + c_1 \Delta s_t + c_2 (\Delta s_t)^2. \tag{8.4}$$

---

[9] We also estimate an OLS regression of fourth order. The results are qualitatively the same.

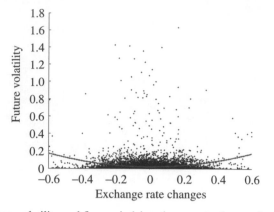

Figure 8.7. Future volatility and five periods' exchange rate changes in the misalignment model, with $C = 5$, $\beta = 0.8$, $\gamma = 1$, $\phi = 1$, and $\rho = 0.6$. Points denote exchange rate changes, line shows fitted.

Table 8.8. OLS estimation results of equation (8.4).
(The numbers in parentheses are t-statistics.)

Parameter values	c_0	c_1	c_2
$c = 5$, $\beta = 0.9$, $\gamma = 1$, $\phi = 1$, $\rho = 0.6$	0.01 (68.0)	0.00 (0.15)	0.02 (7.21)
$c = 5$, $\beta = 0.8$, $\gamma = 1$, $\phi = 1$, $\rho = 0.6$	0.02 (67.9)	0.00 (0.21)	0.02 (9.80)
$c = 5$, $\beta = 0.9$, $\gamma = 3$, $\phi = 1$, $\rho = 0.6$	0.01 (68.4)	0.00 (0.32)	0.02 (13.45)
$c = 5$, $\beta = 0.9$, $\gamma = 3$, $\phi = 3$, $\rho = 0.6$	0.01 (57.6)	0.00 (1.30)	0.01 (20.22)

The results of estimating equation (8.4) on the simulated returns for different parameter values of the model are shown in Table 8.8.

In all our estimations we find that the quadratic term is positive and highly significant. This implies that our model reproduces the same U-shaped relationship between the current exchange rate changes and its future volatility. As pointed out earlier, this phenomenon has also been observed in reality.

An explanation for this U-shaped relationship can be found in our model. Large changes in the exchange rate increase the probability of a shift to a new equilibrium. Such a shift in regime is accompanied by increased turbulence of the exchange rate. Note also that the leverage effect discussed in this section is also related to the phenomenon of volatility clustering discussed in the previous section. Our model predicts that when large changes occur in the exchange rate, volatility in the future will tend to increase and this volatility is likely to be clustered.

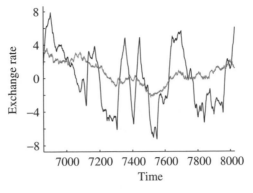

Figure 8.8. Market and fundamental exchange rates, with $C = 5$, $\beta = 0.9$, $\gamma = 5$, $\phi = 1$, $\psi = 0.2$, and $\rho = 0.5$. Gray line denotes fundamental rate; black line denotes exchange rate.

8.4 The Disconnect Puzzle

In this section we analyze the foremost empirical puzzle, which has been called the "disconnect" puzzle (see Obstfeld and Rogoff 2000), i.e., the exchange rate appears to be disconnected from its underlying fundamentals for most of the time.[10] It was first analyzed by Williamson (1985), who called it the "misalignment problem." This puzzle was also implicit in the celebrated Meese and Rogoff studies of the early 1980s, documenting that there is no stable relationship between exchange rate movements and the news in the fundamental variables (Meese and Rogoff 1983). Goodhart (1989) and Goodhart and Figlioli (1991) found that most of the changes in the exchange rates occur when there is no observable news in the fundamental economic variables. This finding contradicted the theoretical models (based on the efficient-market hypothesis), which imply that the exchange rate can only move when there is news in the fundamentals.

Our model is capable of mimicking this empirical regularity. In previous chapters we have documented this feature of our model by visual inspection of time series simulations. In Figure 8.8 we show another example of how our model predicts that the market rate can deviate from the fundamental value substantially, and in a persistent way.

In this section we perform a more precise analysis of the disconnect puzzle. We do this by applying a cointegration analysis to the simulated exchange rate and its fundamental using the same parameter values as in Figure 8.8 for a sample of 9000 periods (Johansen 1991). We found that there is a cointegration relationship between the exchange rate and its fundamental. Note that in our setting there is

---

[10] In its original formulation the disconnect puzzle has two dimensions. One says that the exchange rate is disconnected from its fundamental. The second dimension relates to the fact that real variables (for example, the trade account) do not react to the changes in the exchange rate. In this chapter we analyze only the first dimension. The disconnect puzzle is also related to the excess volatility phenomenon inherent in a flexible exchange rate system. This phenomenon was documented by Flood and Rose (1995).

Table 8.9. Error-correction model. (The numbers in parentheses are t-statistics.)

Error correction		Δs_{t-i}				Δs^*_{t-i}			
ν	δ	λ_1	λ_2	λ_3	λ_4	ω_1	ω_2	ω_3	ω_4
-0.003	0.92	0.32	0.20	0.13	0.08	0.03	0.02	0.01	0.01
(-5.9)	(4.9)	(22.8)	(13.7)	(8.7)	(5.9)	(1.9)	(1.0)	(0.6)	(0.1)

only one fundamental variable. This implies that no bias from omitted variables can occur.

In the next step we specify an error correction (EC) model in the following way:

$$\Delta s_t = \nu(s_{t-1} - \delta s^*_{t-1}) + \sum_{i=1}^{n} \lambda_i \Delta s_{t-i} + \sum_{i=1}^{n} \omega_i \Delta s^*_{t-i}. \qquad (8.5)$$

The first term on the right-hand side is the error-correction term. We have estimated this equation for a broad range of parameter values. The result of estimating equation (8.5) for selected parameter values is presented in Table 8.10, where we have set $c = 5$, $\beta = 0.9$, $\gamma = 1$, $\phi = 1$, and number of lags $n = 4$. In Section 8.11 we show more results for different parameter sets.

We find that the error-correction coefficient (ν) is low. This suggests that the mean reversion towards the equilibrium exchange rate takes a long time. In particular, only 0.3% of the adjustment takes place each period. It should be noted that in the simulations we have assumed a speed of adjustment in the goods market equal to 0.2. This implies that, during each period, the adjustment in the goods market is 20%. Thus, the nominal exchange rate is considerably slower to adjust towards its equilibrium than is implied by the speed of adjustment in the goods market. This slow adjustment of the nominal exchange rate is due to the chartists' extrapolation behavior. This phenomenon has been observed in reality. Cheung et al. (2001) have showed empirically that most of the slow mean reversion of the real exchange rate is due to slow adjustment of the nominal exchange rate and not of the goods prices.

From Table 8.9, we also note that the changes in fundamentals have a small and insignificant impact on the change in exchange rate. In contrast, the past changes in the exchange rate play a significant role in explaining the change in exchange rate. These results are consistent with the empirical findings using the VAR approach, which suggests that the exchange rate is driven by its own past (see De Boeck 2000).[11]

---

[11] We also performed a cointegration analysis for shorter sample periods (1000 periods). We find that, in some sample periods, the exchange rate and its fundamental are cointegrated, and in others we do not find cointegration. This is in line with the empirical evidence, indicating that in some periods the exchange rate seems to be disconnected from its fundamental, while in other periods it tightly follows the fundamentals.

Table 8.10. Error-correction bubble model. (The numbers in parentheses are *t*-statistics.)

Error correction		Δs_{t-i}				Δs^*_{t-i}			
ν	δ	λ_1	λ_2	λ_3	λ_4	ω_1	ω_2	ω_3	ω_4
−0.001	1.03	0.40	0.23	0.14	0.09	0.01	0.01	0.00	0.01
(−6.7)	(3.9)	(38.3)	(21.0)	(12.2)	(8.4)	(1.7)	(1.5)	(0.8)	(1.1)

We obtain similar results for a large range of parameter sets. Unsurprisingly, we also obtain these results in a bubble-and-crash regime, when we set $\phi = 0$ (see Table 8.10). In fact, this is the case where the market exchange rate is most disconnected by its fundamental. During a bubble, the size of the misalignment is large and the deviation from the fundamentals is persistent. This implies that the parameter ν is very small, which indicates that the speed with which the market exchange rate reverts to its fundamental is very slow. However, a crash will occur and the exchange rate movements will mirror changes in fundamentals more closely. Thus, in the very long run, the exchange rate and the fundamental rate are cointegrated. As in the previous case, the changes in exchange rate are explained by its own past changes rather than the changes in fundamentals. In Table 8.10 we present the EC analysis in a typical bubble-and-crash regime. We set $c = 5$, $\beta = 0.9$, $\gamma = 1$, $\phi = 0$, and the number of lags $n = 4$. In an appendix (see Section 8.11) we present more results.

Thus, our model generates an empirical regularity (the "disconnect" puzzle) that has also been observed in reality. We can summarize the features of this puzzle as follows. First, over the long run, the exchange rate and its fundamentals are cointegrated. However, the speed with which the exchange rate reverts to its equilibrium value is slow. Second, in the short run, the exchange rate and its fundamentals are "disconnected," i.e., they do not appear to be cointegrated. Our model mimics closely these empirical regularities.

8.5 Transaction Costs: Do They Matter?

We analyzed the roles of transaction costs in Chapter 5. The main features can be summarized as follows. When regime I prevails, i.e., when the exchange rate is involved in a bubble-and-crash dynamics, the existence of transaction costs will work as a repulsive force, tending to "propel" the exchange rate outside the transaction-cost band. When, however, regime II prevails, i.e., when the exchange rate is attracted to the fundamental equilibrium, the transaction-cost band sets a limit to the movements of the exchange rate.[12]

---

[12] In Chapter 5 we saw that if the noise is high relative to the transaction-cost band, the dynamics can be characterized by chaos.

Table 8.11.   Intercountry price dispersion, 2000.

Supermarket products	Price dispersion (%)
Evian mineral water	43
Mars bars (multipack)	22
Mars bars (single)	21
Colgate toothpaste	14
Coca-Cola	21
Electronic products	**Price dispersion (%)**
Canon camcorder	32
Philips portable CD player	56
Philips television	61
Sony video recorder	44

Source: De Grauwe (2003). Price dispersion is defined as the percentage difference between the most expensive and the cheapest items.

As we have seen, regime I will occur when risk appetite of economic agents is low, so that arbitrage failures occur. In the second regime, agents are more willing to take risks. As a result, bubbles and crashes do not materialize. When transaction costs are taken into account, this regime, however, also predicts that the exchange rate will fluctuate around its fundamental. An implication of this regime is that the exchange rate remains within the transaction-cost band most of the time (see Figure 8.8). Thus, the explanation of the misalignment puzzle in this particular regime relies very much on the existence of a relatively wide band of transaction costs compared to the variability of the underlying fundamentals. Is this a reasonable explanation for the existence of misalignments? Our claim is that it is, at least for the currencies of the industrial countries like the United States, Japan, and the EU countries. There are two pieces of evidence that substantiate this claim.

First, transaction costs in international trade continue to be substantial. Several recent empirical studies report the continued existence of large price differentials for the same traded goods across borders (see Haskel and Wolf 2001; Engel and Rogers 1995). In Table 8.11, we show the price dispersion of a sample of exactly the same products in the European Union (De Grauwe 2003). We observe that price differentials of up to 40% occur in the categories of both foodstuff and electronic products. This indicates that producers apply "pricing to market." Such pricing strategies, however, can only be applied successfully if transaction costs prevent arbitrage. Thus, the large observed price differentials suggest that transaction costs for traded goods are large and of the order of 20–40%. In addition, for many services, which are nontraded goods, transaction costs are even higher (see Obstfeld and Rogoff (2000), who argue that transaction costs are key to understanding the major puzzles in international economics).

Table 8.12. Transaction costs and speed of adjustment.

	$\beta = 0.9,\ \gamma = 1,\ \phi = 1$		$\beta = 0.8,\ \gamma = 5,\ \phi = 1$	
C	ν	Time outside transaction-cost band (%)	ν	Time outside transaction-cost band (%)
0.5	−0.07	34	−0.04	12
1.0	−0.04	17	−0.03	8
2.5	−0.01	4	−0.02	3
3.0	−0.01	3	−0.01	2
5.0	−0.004	2	−0.005	1

Table 8.13. Skewness as a measure of asymmetry.

Parameter values	Skewness
$c = 2,\ \beta = 0.8,\ \gamma = 3,\ \phi = 0$	−2.1
$c = 5,\ \beta = 0.8,\ \gamma = 3,\ \phi = 0$	−2.0
$c = 3,\ \beta = 0.9,\ \gamma = 2,\ \phi = 0$	−0.4
$c = 0,\ \beta = 0.9,\ \gamma = 2,\ \phi = 0$	−0.6
$c = 0,\ \beta = 0.9,\ \gamma = 3,\ \phi = 0$	−0.3

Second, the size of the shocks in the fundamentals driving the exchange rates of the major currencies is typically small. These fundamentals include inflation differentials, and differentials in interest rates, in growth rates of the money stock, and in growth rates of output. These differentials are typically a few percentage points per year. Thus, one can conclude that the exchange rates of the major currencies move in an environment in which the shocks in the fundamentals are relatively small compared to the size of transaction costs. As a result, the exchange rates of these currencies move most of the time within a band within which few opportunities exist for goods market arbitrage. This considerably weakens the mean-reversion dynamics on which fundamentalism is based.

It is important to analyze the dynamics of the exchange rate under different combinations of transaction costs and size of shocks in fundamentals. After all, there are many countries in the world where the size of the shocks in fundamentals is very large compared to transaction costs (e.g., Latin American countries that have experienced triple-digit inflation rates and growth rates of their money stocks). The way we proceed is to simulate the model under different assumptions about the size of transaction costs, while keeping the size of the shocks unchanged. (Note that we could also vary the size of the fundamental shocks while keeping the transaction cost unchanged. This gives qualitatively the same results.) We then apply a similar error-correction model on the estimated exchange rate, as we did earlier.

We show the coefficients of the error-correction term (v) in Table 8.12 for some selected parameter values. We observe that there is an inverse relationship between the size of transaction costs and the speed of adjustment. With low transaction costs (relative to the size of fundamental shocks), the speed of adjustment is high; with high transaction costs the speed of adjustment is slow. Thus, in a world where the transaction costs are small relative to the size of the fundamental shocks, misalignments are quickly corrected. In such a world, the exchange rate is frequently pushed outside the transaction-cost band (see the first row of Table 8.12), so that the mean-reverting forces originating from goods market arbitrage are forceful.

We can summarize these previous results as follows. The nature of the disconnect puzzle depends on the relative size of transaction costs versus the size in the fundamental shocks. When transaction costs are large relative to the size of fundamental shocks, misalignment is relatively long and protracted. This is the case with the currencies of the major industrial countries. When the size of the fundamental shocks is large relative to transaction costs, misalignments, although large, are quickly corrected. The empirical evidence substantiates these results (see Michael et al. (1997) and Taylor et al. (2001), who show that when the size of the shocks to the PPP-relation is large, the speed of adjustment towards PPP is also high (see also Sarno and Taylor 2002)).

8.6 Asymmetry of Bubbles and Crashes

In this section we analyze an empirical fact which is a pervasive feature of bubbles in financial markets, i.e., bubbles start gradually and build up speed, while crashes occur suddenly. Gradual bubbles and sudden crashes are a well-known feature of many financial and currency crises (see Sornette 2003). In Figure 8.9 we present the euro/USD rate for the period 1995–2004, which is a remarkable example of a bubble in foreign exchange markets.[13] As may be seen from Figure 8.9(a), the upward movement in the euro/USD exchange rate is gradual and builds up momentum until a sudden and faster crash occurs that brings the exchange rate back to its value. We check to see if our model is capable of reproducing such a feature. Indeed, as we showed earlier, when the risk appetite ϕ is low, the model produces bubbles and crashes. We find that bubbles and crashes are often (but not always) asymmetric. It is important to note that asymmetry is a natural outcome of the model, in the sense that additional assumptions on the parameter values do not need to be superimposed in order to produce slow bubbles and sudden crashes. In Figure 8.9(b) we present a typical bubble in our simulated exchange rates where the asymmetry in bubble and crash is visible.

In order to quantify the symmetry properties of the simulated data, we use the skewness index. A bubble is characterized by slow and steady upward movements

---

[13] We discussed this bubble, together with the bubble of the 1980s, in Chapter 1.

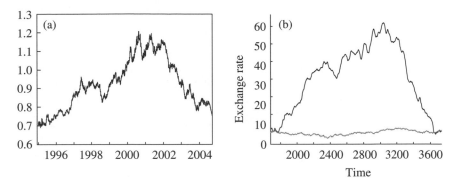

Figure 8.9. (a) Euro/USD rate for the period 1995–2004. Intervals run from March 6 to March 5 in the following year. (b) Market and fundamental exchange rates, with $C = 0$, $\psi = 0.2$, $\beta = 0.9$, $\gamma = 5$, $\phi = 0$, and $\rho = 0.5$. Gray line denotes fundamental rate; black line denotes exchange rate.

in the exchange rate, which are due to frequent relatively small positive changes, while a crash is characterized by a sudden downward movement, which is due to fewer larger negative changes. Thus, the distribution of exchange rate returns in a bubble environment is negatively skewed, i.e., it has an elongated negative tail. We also checked the skewness of the DM/USD rate, which is equal to -0.92. Table 8.13 lists the average skewness measure of changes in our simulated exchange rate for selected parameter values. The average skewness measure is the average of the skewness indices of 100 repeated simulations, each with 10 000 periods. In all our simulations, the skewness is negative, implying that bubbles build gradually up and sudden crashes occur. Thus, our model mimics this empirical fact.

8.7   Is Chartism Evolutionarily Stable?

An important issue is whether chartism survives in our model. In other words, under which conditions is chartism profitable such that it does not disappear? Note that there is a broad literature that shows that technical analysis is used widely, also by large players (see Taylor and Allen 1992; Brunnermeier 2001; Wei and Kim 1997; Cheung et al. 2004), and that the use of chartism is a constant feature of the foreign exchange markets. Thus, contrary to the prediction of Friedman (1953), chartism does not tend to disappear in the market. Our model should be able to mimic this empirical feature.

We investigate this issue by analyzing how chartism evolves under different conditions. First, we compute the average profits of chartists and fundamentalists over long periods (10 000). We then compute the average weight of chartists over the same period. We repeat this exercise for different parameter values of γ and β. We show the results in Figures 8.10 and 8.11. Figure 8.10(a) shows the average profits of chartists and fundamentalists for different values of the parameter γ.

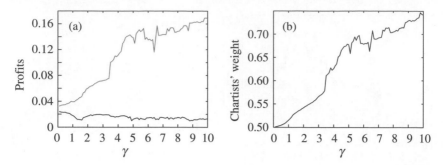

Figure 8.10. (a) Profits of chartists and fundamentalists as a function of γ. Black line, fundamentalists; gray line, chartists. (b) Weight of chartists. For both parts, $C = 0$, $\beta = 0.9$, $\phi = 0$, $\rho = 0.5$.

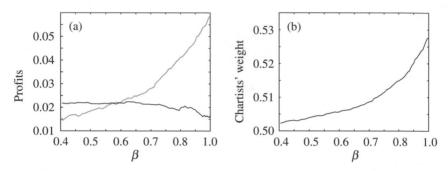

Figure 8.11. (a) Profits of chartists and fundamentalists as a function of β. Black line, fundamentalists; gray line, chartists. (b) Weight of chartists. For both parts, $C = 0$, $\gamma = 1$, $\phi = 0$, $\rho = 0.5$.

Remember that this parameter measures the intensity with which agents switch rules when relative profitabilities change. We observe that, for all values of γ, chartists make more profits than fundamentalists, and that the relative profitability of chartism increases with the size of γ. Thus, as agents switch forecasting rules more intensely, chartism becomes more profitable. This feature is due to the fact that, with high values of γ, bubbles and crashes occur more frequently, thereby making the use of extrapolative forecasting rules more profitable. The result of this is that the weight of chartists increases as γ increases (see Figure 8.10(b)).

In Figure 8.11, we show the results of a similar exercise for different values of the chartist extrapolation parameter, β. We find that, for small values of β, chartists make less money than fundamentalists. As β increases, however, the relative profitability of chartists increases. The effect of this increase in the relative profitability of chartism is that the weight of chartists increases with β (see Figure 8.11(b)). Note also that, even when β is low and chartists' profits are less than the fundamentalists' profits, the share of the chartists exceeds 50%. This is due to the fact that the risk involved in chartism is lower than in fundamentalism. This compensates for the lower return, so that the chartist's weight is always higher than 50%.

We conclude that our model mimics an important empirical regularity, i.e., that chartism is profitable,[14] and survives over the long run. In addition, the empirical evidence suggests that chartism (technical analysis) is more widely used than fundamentalism. All these empirical regularities are reproduced in our model.

From the preceding analysis, we conclude that chartism is evolutionarily stable, and that it is generally more profitable than fundamentalism. In addition, there is a positive correlation between turbulence (noise) and the share of chartism in the market. With more noise there are more chartist profits and thus more chartists. The reverse is also true: with more chartists, there is more noise and thus there are more profits for chartists. These results suggest that there is a self-fulfilling evolutionary dynamics present in the system, which can be described as follows. As the chartists increase in numbers, the noise they create makes the use of chartist rules more profitable. At the same time, the chartists have the effect of "creating smoke around the fundamentals," making fundamentalists' forecasting less profitable. Another way to interpret this result is that chartism creates noisy information that becomes the source of profitable speculation. The more chartists there are, the more such information is created and the more profitable chartist forecasting becomes. Thus, chartists create an informational environment which makes it valuable to use chartist rules.

8.8 Conclusion

In this chapter, we analyzed the extent to which our model is capable of reproducing the exchange rate puzzles that we observe in reality. The first puzzle we investigated is related to the statistical properties of the exchange rate returns. Fat tails and excess kurtosis have been detected in real-life exchange rate returns. Our model generates returns whose distribution exhibits excess kurtosis and heavy tails.

A second empirical puzzle concerns the volatility clustering and persistence of exchange rate returns. We found GARCH effects in the simulated exchange rate returns that come close to the GARCH effects observed in real-life exchange rate returns. Thus, our model produces a complex dynamics of the exchange rate, with intermittency of periods of high and low turbulence. We find that this alternation of periods of tranquillity and turbulence is itself unpredictable.

The most notorious empirical puzzle is the disconnect puzzle. The exchange rates appear to be disconnected from their underlying fundamentals most of the time. Only in the long run do they tend to return to their fundamentals. Our model closely mimics these empirical phenomena.

---

[14] There is now a large literature documenting the profitability of chartist rules (see LeBaron 1992; Dewachter 2001; Dewachter and Lyrio 2005).

Next, we discussed the empirical importance of transaction costs. We argued that transaction costs remain sizeable and that they create a band of inaction that enriches the exchange rate dynamics.

Finally, we investigated the conditions under which chartism is evolutionarily stable. We found that chartism does not disappear, i.e., in all simulations for many different parameter configurations we find that the number of chartists never goes to zero. In fact, our model predicts that chartism is used more than fundamentalism as a forecasting rule. This result is consistent with the empirical evidence of the importance of chartism in foreign exchange markets. We also detected a self-fulfilling character of chartist profitability, i.e., when more chartists enter the market they create more noise and thereby make chartists' rules more profitable, inducing more entry. Another way to interpret this result is that chartism creates noisy information that becomes the source of profitable speculation. The more chartists there are, the more such information is created and the more profitable chartists' forecasting becomes. Thus, chartists create an informational environment which makes it rational to use chartists' rules.

Table 8.14. Hill index and kurtosis in the prospect model.

		Hill index		
Parameter values	Kurtosis	2.5%	5%	10%
$C = 5,\ \beta = 0.9,\ \rho = 0.6,\ \gamma = 1,\quad \phi = 1$	3.3327	6.5703	5.9663	4.7958
$C = 5,\ \beta = 0.9,\ \rho = 0.6,\ \gamma = 1,\quad \phi = 10$	3.0127	7.0712	5.7520	4.8281
$C = 5,\ \beta = 0.8,\ \rho = 0.6,\ \gamma = 1,\quad \phi = 1$	2.9821	7.1574	6.3580	5.1538
$C = 0,\ \beta = 0.9,\ \rho = 0.6,\ \gamma = 1,\quad \phi = 1$	3.5264	6.7612	5.7000	4.2725
$C = 0,\ \beta = 0.9,\ \rho = 0.6,\ \gamma = 1,\quad \phi = 10$	3.0419	7.3976	5.9443	4.6798
$C = 5,\ \beta = 0.9,\ \rho = 0.6,\ \gamma = 10,\ \phi = 1$	3.1674	6.1373	5.2041	4.3725
$C = 0,\ \beta = 0.9,\ \rho = 0.6,\ \gamma = 10,\ \phi = 1$	3.0096	7.0952	5.6431	4.9061

8.9 Appendix: Hill Index and Kurtosis in Prospect Model

In Table 8.14 we show the results of simulating the model using the assumptions of prospect theory as explained in Chapter 5. In general we find that these assumptions do not produce excess kurtosis and fat tails.

Table 8.15.   GARCH for different values of parameters C, β, γ, and ϕ.

	$C = 0$, $\beta = 0.9$, $\gamma = 0.5$, $\phi = 10$		$C = 0$, $\beta = 0.9$, $\gamma = 5$, $\phi = 1$	
	Coefficient	T-statistic	Coefficient	T-statistic
a	−0.000	−0.5	0.000	0.5
b	0.006	11.8	0.005	11.1
α	0.66	37.7	0.40	16.6
δ_1	0.22	5.6	0.16	3.2
δ_2	0.06	2.1	0.23	6.0

	$C = 0$, $\beta = 0.9$, $\gamma = 1$, $\phi = 1$		$C = 5$, $\beta = 0.8$, $\gamma = 10$, $\phi = 1$	
	Coefficient	T-statistic	Coefficient	T-statistic
a	−0.001	−0.7	−0.002	−0.7
b	0.003	3.5	0.004	10.6
α	0.08	5.0	0.42	24.5
δ_1	0.32	1.6	0.18	6.5
δ_2	0.36	2.0	0.33	14.3

8.10   Appendix: Some More Results on Volatility Clustering

In Table 8.15 we present some more results on volatility clustering.

Table 8.16. Error-correction model: $c = 5$, $\beta = 0.9$, $\gamma = 10$, $\phi = 0.5$.

Error correction		Δs_{t-i}				Δs^*_{t-i}			
μ	δ	λ_1	λ_2	λ_3	λ_4	ω_1	ω_2	ω_3	ω_4
−0.003 02	−1.15	0.43	0.21	0.1	0.1	0.03	0.01	−0.00	−0.00
−8.4	−13.5	41.3	18.3	8.6	5.9	2.4	1.1	−0.1	−0.1

Table 8.17. Error-correction model: $C = 5$, $\beta = 0.8$, $\gamma = 10$, $\phi = 1$.

Error correction		Δs_{t-i}				Δs^*_{t-i}			
μ	δ	λ_1	λ_2	λ_3	λ_4	ω_1	ω_2	ω_3	ω_4
−0.004	−1.01	0.48	0.16	0.1	0.05	0.00	−0.01	0.02	0.01
−10.2	−20.7	46.1	13.9	8.5	5.3	0.4	−0.9	1.4	1.1

Table 8.18. Error-correction model: $C = 5$, $\beta = 0.9$, $\phi = 1$, $\gamma = 0.5$.

Error correction		Δs_{t-i}				Δs^*_{t-i}			
μ	δ	λ_1	λ_2	λ_3	λ_4	ω_1	ω_2	ω_3	ω_4
−0.003	−1.11	0.32	0.19	0.14	0.1	0.02	0.01	0.00	0.01
−7.7	−5.5	30.5	18.2	12.7	9.06	1.8	0.6	0.1	1.1

8.11 Appendix: Additional Results for the EC Model

In Tables 8.16–8.18 we show the EC model for selected parameter values.

9

Official Interventions in
the Foreign Exchange Markets

9.1 Introduction

Can the central bank influence the course of the exchange rate movements by intervening in the foreign exchange market? This question has been analyzed in great detail in the economics literature (for surveys, see Sarno and Taylor 2001; de Haan et al. 2005). No consensus seems to have emerged from the extensive research on this question: two broad schools of thought have developed. The first is based on the efficient-market model. It can be summarized as follows (see Mussa 1981; LeBaron 1999). In an efficient market, the exchange rate reflects current and expected future fundamentals. As a result, the central bank can only hope to influence the exchange rate if, by its interventions, it influences current fundamentals, or if these interventions signal future changes in fundamentals. This seems to rule out sterilized interventions as a tool to influence the exchange rate. Sterilized interventions are purchases and sales of foreign exchange by the central bank that are done in such a way as to leave the domestic money stock unchanged.[1] Thus, since these interventions do not affect fundamentals, the exchange rate will not be affected, except if the interventions signal something about the future fundamentals. It is, however, difficult to see how this could happen. Since sterilized interventions are designed to leave current fundamentals unchanged, it is difficult to imagine that they could affect future fundamentals. The corollary of this analysis is that only interventions that change current or future fundamentals (unsterilized interventions) can affect the exchange rate. Thus, if say the central bank wants to stop an appreciation of the domestic currency, it will have to sell the domestic currency and buy the foreign

---

[1] The way a central bank achieves this can be described as follows. Suppose the European Central Bank (ECB) buys U.S. dollars to stop the downward slide of the dollar in the foreign exchange market. This intervention implies that the ECB will sell euros in exchange for the dollars. The effect of this intervention is that the stock of money in the Eurozone increases, leading to a downward pressure on the interest rate. The ECB can offset this by performing the opposite operation in the Eurozone money market. It will do this by open market operations, i.e., by buying back euros in exchange for securities. As a result, the initial money stock is restored. Thus, the ECB "sterilizes" the monetary effect of the interventions in the foreign exchange market.

currency, and allow the money-loosening effect of this intervention to operate. As a result, the sales of the domestic currency will lead to a drop in the domestic interest rate. This drop will make it attractive to again hold the foreign currency, thereby helping to stop its decline in the foreign exchange market.

There is one channel through which, even in the efficient-market model, sterilized interventions can influence the exchange rate: the risk premium channel. When a central bank buys domestic currency and sells foreign exchange, it changes the composition of domestic and foreign currency assets held by the private sector (see Dominguez and Frankel 1993). As a result, it also affects the risk premium on domestic currency assets. This could potentially alter the course of exchange rate movements. There is a consensus, however, that this effect is weak (see Sarno and Taylor 2001), so it cannot easily be used to affect the exchange rate in a predictable manner.

The upshot of the efficient-market view of the effectiveness of intervention is that unsterilized intervention works, while sterilized interventions are largely futile exercises. Two factors have tended to undermine this view. First, central banks intervene regularly and, when they do, they overwhelmingly use sterilized interventions. This suggests either that central banks fail to understand economic theory, or that the efficient-market view is not the correct framework in which to think about the effectiveness of foreign exchange market interventions. The second factor is the empirical evidence. While, during the 1980s, little evidence could be found that sterilized interventions affect the exchange rate, the empirical studies of the 1990s were able to find significant effects of sterilized interventions. The empirical studies of Dominguez and Frankel (1993a,b) have been influential in this regard. More recent research has tended to corroborate these studies (see Beine et al. 2003; Beine and Lecourt 2004; Kubelec 2004).

All this has led to a reevaluation of the effectiveness of foreign exchange market interventions. It has also led to a revival of an older view that is well represented by Williamson (1983), which stresses that foreign exchange market interventions, even when fully sterilized, can affect the exchange rate.

This chapter explores the issue of the effectiveness of official interventions in the foreign exchange market. We will use the model presented in the previous chapters as our workhorse. We will introduce a third actor in the model, i.e., the central bank, and we will specify its behavior in the market.

9.2   Modeling Official Interventions in the Foreign Exchange Market

The model presented in Chapter 3 allows for an easy way to introduce the interventions of the central bank. In this model agents allocate their wealth as between domestic and foreign assets. This portfolio allocation leads to a demand for foreign assets which has to equal the (exogenous) supply. This then leads to a market clearing level of the exchange rate (see equation (3.6)). We reproduce this market clearing exchange rate here:

$$s_t = \left(\frac{1+r^*}{1+r}\right) \frac{1}{\sum_{i=1}^{N} w_{i,t}/\sigma_{i,t}^2} \left[\sum_{i=1}^{N} w_{i,t} \frac{E_t^i(s_{t+1})}{\sigma_{i,t}^2} - \Omega_t Z_t\right] + \epsilon_t. \qquad (9.1)$$

The supply of foreign assets Z_t is determined by the current account position, i.e., a surplus (deficit) in the current account increases (decreases) the supply of foreign assets. The supply of foreign assets, however, can also be influenced by the intervention activities of the central bank. More specifically, when the central bank sells foreign exchange, it increases the supply of foreign assets Z_t. This will generally put downward pressure on the exchange rate. This can also be seen from equation (9.1): the sign of Z_t is negative. Conversely, when the central bank buys foreign exchange, it reduces the supply of foreign assets, putting upward pressure on the exchange rate.

It can be useful to analyze the impact effect of a surprise change in foreign assets on the exchange rate. We obtain this by isolating the effect of a change in Z_t in equation (9.1). Setting the expectational terms equal to zero, and using the definition of Ω_t (see equation (3.7)) we obtain

$$\Delta s_t = -\left(\frac{\mu}{1+r}\right) \frac{1}{(w_{c,t}/\sigma_{c,t}^2) + (w_{f,t}/\sigma_{f,t}^2)} X_t, \qquad (9.2)$$

where $X_t = \Delta Z_t/N$, i.e., the supply of foreign assets per capita. As before, we have also assumed that there are only two types of agent, i.e., chartists and fundamentalists (denoted by the subscripts 'c' and 'f', respectively).

Equation (9.2) makes it clear that the effect of a foreign exchange market intervention on the exchange rate will be difficult to predict *ex ante* because it depends on the weights the chartists and fundamentalists have in the market, together with the forecast errors they have made in the past. In other words, the effect of interventions will depend on the market structure and the risk perceptions at the time of the intervention. Since these factors change continuously, the effect of interventions will also change.

It should also be stressed that we analyze the effects of sterilized interventions here, i.e., interventions that are not allowed to affect domestic money market conditions, including the domestic interest rate. Thus, we analyze interventions that do not affect the fundamentals.

We explore in the following way the issue of how this type of intervention affects the exchange rate. We start by presenting simulations of the model of Chapter 3, using the standard set of parameters. We assume that the central bank temporarily increases the supply of foreign assets (per capita) by 0.01 in the first period. The resulting exchange rate is shown in Figure 9.1 with intervention ($X = 0.01$) and without intervention ($X = 0$). In both simulations we assume exactly the same

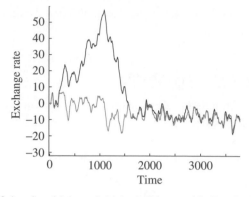

Figure 9.1.   Sensitivity to initial conditions, with $C = 5$, $\beta = 0.9$,
$\gamma = 1$, $\phi = 0$, and $\rho = 0.5$. Black line, $X = 0$; gray line, $X = 0.01$.

stochastic realization of the exogenous fundamental. The result is quite remarkable. We find that the sale of foreign exchange has the effect of eliminating the bubble that arises in the pure floating environment ($X = 0$). Thus, it appears that relatively small sales of foreign exchange can be quite effective in eliminating bubbles.

The problem with this conclusion is that it is extremely difficult to know *ex ante* whether the intervention will have this beneficial effect. We show this by repeating the same experiment as in Figure 9.1 but assuming in each experiment a different realization of the exogenous stochastic realization of the fundamental variable. We show the results in Figure 9.2. We first concentrate on parts (a) and (b). These show examples of interventions of the same magnitude in two different stochastic realizations of the fundamental. We find that sometimes the intervention has no effect on the emerging bubble (see part (a), which shows that the emergence of the bubble is essentially unaffected by the interventions). Something similar happens in part (b).

Part (c) shows an example where the interventions actually create a (negative) bubble, while there are none in the freely floating regime. Admittedly, this is an artificial result because we assume that the central bank has sold foreign exchange. This can then trigger a negative bubble when, in the absence of intervention, the exchange rate is declining. Note, however, from part (d) that a sale of foreign exchange can sometimes prevent a negative bubble. This seems to occur in part (d) when the intervention eliminates a positive bubble that (in the absence of intervention) leads to an undershoot and a negative bubble.

From the previous discussion we can conclude first that an intervention in the foreign exchange market (a once-and-for-all sale of foreign exchange) *can* have a very strong effect on the exchange rate and, second, that we do not know *ex ante* whether it will have this effect. Sometimes, intervention is very effective; at other times it fails completely to prevent a bubble from occurring. This result is related to the "sensitivity to initial conditions" character of the dynamics of the model. Small

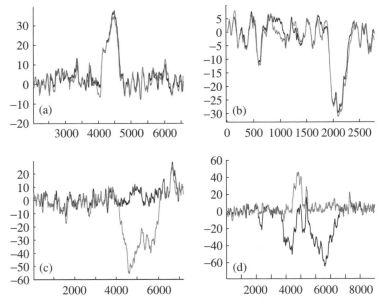

Figure 9.2. Sensitivity to initial conditions, with $C = 5$, $\beta = 0.9$, $\gamma = 1$, $\phi = 0$, and $\rho = 0.5$. Black line, $X = 0$; gray line, $X = 0.01$.

shocks can have a very pronounced effect, but we do not know *ex ante* when they have these effects.

The large degree of unpredictability in the effects of interventions can be illustrated in a different way. We define the effect of the intervention as the difference between the freely floating exchange rate ($X = 0$) and the exchange rate obtained with intervention ($X = 0.01$), assuming the same underlying stochastics of the fundamental. We show a few examples in the time domain (Figure 9.3). We find that these effects are highly unpredictable. In some simulations, there appears to be very little effect on the exchange rate, while in other simulations, using exactly the same parameters but a different stochastic realization of the fundamental, the same intervention has a dramatically large effect on the exchange rate. The same conclusion can be drawn from the representation of the effect of the intervention in the frequency domain (Figure 9.4). We observe that the frequency distributions of the effects of the same intervention in different stochastic realizations the fundamentals differ profoundly. We conclude from all this that there is an indeterminacy surrounding the effects of interventions in the foreign exchange market, making it extremely difficult for the authorities to predict how a particular intervention applied in a particular environment will affect the exchange rate. It should therefore not be surprising that central banks often hesitate to intervene in the market.

Our results make sense of this hesitation. There are certainly episodes during which interventions have been very successful in turning around the market. At

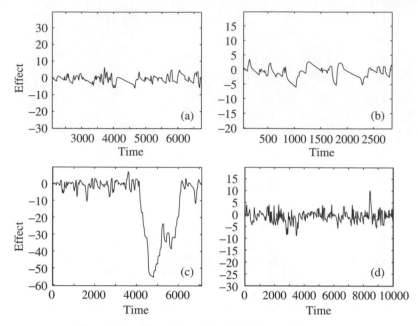

Figure 9.3. The effect of shock in X on exchange rate,
with $C = 5$, $\beta = 0.9$, $\gamma = 1$, $\phi = 0$, and $\rho = 0.5$.

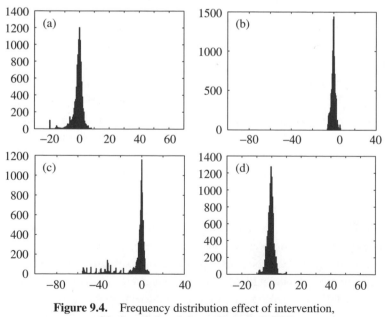

Figure 9.4. Frequency distribution effect of intervention,
with $C = 5$, $\beta = 0.9$, $\gamma = 1$, and $\rho = 0.5$.

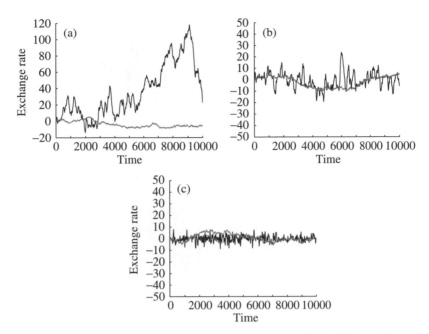

Figure 9.5. Market and fundamental exchange rates, with $C = 0, \beta = 0.9, \gamma = 5, \rho = 0.5,$ $\phi = 0, \mu = 1$, and (a) $\epsilon = 0$, (b) $\epsilon = 0.01$, (c) $\epsilon = 0.1$. Gray lines denote fundamental rate; black lines denote exchange rate.

other times, seemingly similar intervention activities have utterly failed to move the market. Central banks are aware of this and are therefore reluctant to use an intervention instrument that is both powerful and highly unpredictable in its effects.

The reason it is so difficult to predict the effect of a particular intervention is made clear by our model. We have shown that the effect of a sale (purchase) of foreign exchange depends on the weights chartists and fundamentalists have in the market at the time of the intervention. Since these weights vary continuously, so will the effect of such sales (purchases). (See Neely and Weller (2001) on this issue.)

It should be stressed that this conclusion holds for discretionary intervention activities.

9.3 Rule-Based Interventions in the Foreign Exchange Market

From the preceding discussion, one may get the impression that official interventions in the foreign exchange markets are not very attractive policy instruments. We have to analyze, however, whether systematic interventions, i.e., interventions that are conducted using a particular rule, can be made to overcome the indeterminacy problem detected in the previous section.

We will investigate this by analyzing some simple intervention rules. The simplest rule we consider is the "leaning-against-the-wind" intervention rule, in which

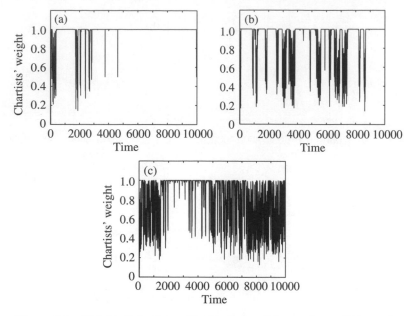

Figure 9.6. Weight of chartists, with $C = 0$, $\beta = 0.9$, $\gamma = 5$, $\rho = 0.5$, $\mu = 1$, and (a) $\epsilon = 0$, (b) $\epsilon = 0.01$, (c) $\epsilon = 0.1$.

the central bank is continuously in the market, smoothing the movements of the exchange rate. We specify this rule as follows:

$$\Delta Z_t = \epsilon(\Delta S_{t-1}), \tag{9.3}$$

where $\epsilon \geqslant 0$. Thus, when the exchange rate increases (decreases), the central bank sells (buys) foreign exchange in the market, so that the supply of foreign assets increases (decreases). The parameter ϵ measures the intensity with which the central bank performs these operations. Note that, as in the case of the private agents, the current exchange rate is not in the information set of the central bank. The current exchange rate is the market clearing exchange rate that will be the outcome of the decisions of both the private agents and the central bank, but is not known when agents make their decision.

We now implement this simple intervention rule by substituting equation (9.3) into equation (9.1) and solving the model numerically, as we have done in the previous chapters. We show some results of simulating the model in the time domain in Figure 9.5, using the same parameter configuration as in the previous section. Part (a) shows the exchange rate in the absence of any intervention ($\epsilon = 0$). This is the freely floating exchange rate solution that we have analyzed in previous chapters. It exhibits the large movements of the exchange rate around its fundamental. Parts (b) and (c) show the exchange rate for increasing intensity of intervention. In part (b) we assume that $\epsilon = 0.01$ and in part (c) that $\epsilon = 0.1$. We find that, as ϵ increases, the exchange rate is forced to move more closely around its fundamental. Thus, it appears that this simple rule is capable of eliminating the bubble equilibria that are responsible for the periods of large disconnection of the exchange rate from its fundamental in a freely floating environment. As a result, the application of this rule ensures that the exchange rate better reflects the underlying fundamental.

The remarkable aspect of this result is that the central bank does not need to have information about the underlying fundamental. All it has to do is to "lean against the wind," i.e., when the exchange rate is moving up, the bank should slow it down; when the exchange rate is moving down, the bank should push it up without trying to steer it towards a particular target. This behavior of the central bank appears to be sufficient for the market (i.e., the fundamentalists) to keep the exchange rate close to its fundamental. The reason for this surprising result is that this "leaning-against-the-wind" strategy of the central bank reinforces the mean-reverting dynamics in the market, thereby strengthening the hand of the fundamentalists at the expense of the "trend chasers" (chartists). This stabilizes the market and reduces the probability of the emergence of bubbles. Thus, the effect of this intervention is that the exchange rate follows the movements of the underlying fundamentals more closely.

In order to shed more light on the question of why a simple intervention rule works so well, we plot in Figure 9.6 the weights of the chartists that correspond to the three simulations in Figure 9.5. We observe that, in the free-float scenario (Figure 9.6(a)), the weight of the chartists is often close to 1. This feature of the free-float solution was analyzed in detail in Chapters 2 and 3. From parts (b) and (c) we conclude that, as the intensity of interventions increases (increasing ϵ), the weight of chartists tends to decline (the weight of fundamentalists increases). This is confirmed in Table 9.1, where we show the average weight of the chartists corresponding to the three scenarios. We see that, in the free-float simulation, the chartists have on average a weight of 90% in the market (the fundamentalists' weight is then 10%), while in the scenario of intense intervention ($\epsilon = 0.1$) the average weight of the chartists declines to 76% (the average weight of fundamentalists increases to 24%). Thus, when the central bank successfully stabilizes the exchange rate so that it closely reflects the fundamentals, the fundamentalists have, on average, a higher share in the market than when the central bank does not intervene. In other words, systematic interventions by the central bank change the structure of the foreign exchange market, i.e., they reduce the importance of chartists and increase the importance of fundamentalists. Thus, the "leaning-against-the-wind" intervention rule of the central bank creates an environment in which the fundamentalists are more active, thereby keeping the exchange rate close to its fundamental. The reason why this is made possible is that the intervention rule increases the mean-reverting forces in the market thereby making fundamentalists forecasting rules more profitable. We show this in Table 9.1, where we present the average profits of chartists and fundamentalists in the three scenarios corresponding to Figures 9.5 and 9.6. We

Table 9.1. Mean profits and weights of fundamentalists and chartists.

	ϵ		
	0	0.01	0.1
Mean profit (fundamentalists)	0.0010	0.0045	0.0081
Mean weight (fundamentalists)	0.1	0.13	0.24
Mean profit (chartists)	0.1099	0.0971	0.0888
Mean weight (chartists)	0.9	0.87	0.76

find that in the intervention scenarios ($\epsilon = 0.01$ and $\epsilon = 0.1$) the fundamentalists make significantly more profits than in the free-float scenario ($\epsilon = 0$). The reverse is true for the chartists' profits. This confirms that the intervention rule of the central bank increases the relative profitability of fundamentalist forecasting rules, thereby enhancing the position of fundamentalists in the market.[2] Thus, the stabilizing effect of the intervention rule comes about indirectly, i.e., it makes fundamentalist forecasting more attractive, thereby allowing the market to discover the fundamental value of the exchange rate more effectively.

Another way of interpreting this result is as follows. We have seen that bubbles occur because of a failure of arbitrage by fundamentalists. The intervention strategy of the central bank helps to eliminate this market failure. It does this by increasing, on average, the profitability of forecasting rules based on mean reversion (fundamentalism). As a result, agents using fundamentalist forecasting rules will, on average, be more willing to arbitrage.

9.4 Target Intervention

In the previous section we analyzed a very simple intervention rule that does not require the central bank to use information about the underlying fundamental. The drawback is that the central bank must intervene continuously in the foreign exchange market. An alternative rule, the so-called target intervention rule, has been advocated by John Williamson (see Williamson 1983; Williamson and Miller 1987). This implies that the central bank only starts intervening when the exchange rate deviates sufficiently from its fundamental value (when the exchange rate is "misaligned"). The advantage of this policy rule is that the central bank does not always have to be active in the market. However, it implies that the central bank must have knowledge of the fundamental. We implement this rule as follows:

$$\Delta Z_t = \begin{cases} \epsilon(\Delta S_{t-1}) & \text{if } |S_{t-1} - S^*_{t-1}| > M, \\ 0 & \text{if } |S_{t-1} - S^*_{t-1}| \leqslant M, \end{cases}$$

where M is the degree of misalignment.

---

[2] Note that, even in the intervention scenarios, chartism remains more profitable than fundamentalism.

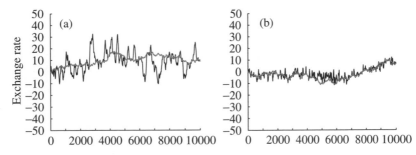

Figure 9.7. Market and fundamental exchange rates, with $C = 0$, $\beta = 0.9$, $\gamma = 5$, $\phi = 0$, $\rho = 0.5$, $M = 3\text{STD}$, and (a) $\epsilon = 0.01$, (b) $\epsilon = 0.1$. Gray lines denote fundamental rate; black lines denote exchange rate.

Thus, if the deviation of the exchange rate from its fundamental exceeds M (either in a positive or negative sense), the central bank starts to intervene. The intervention is then of the leaning-against-the-wind type that we have also used in the previous section. This is important for, as Williamson and Miller have stressed, the limit (M) at which the central bank starts to intervene should not be a rigid border that cannot be transgressed (like in a fixed exchange rate system). Instead, it is a soft border, i.e., the central bank announces that it starts intervening at that border without committing itself to keeping the exchange rate within the border.

We implemented this "soft" target intervention policy by setting $M = 3 \times$ standard deviation of the fundamental, S_{t-1}^*. Admittedly this is a little arbitrary, but we will analyze how sensitive the results are to this choice. We then simulated the model and we show some results in Figure 9.7. The most striking feature of these results is their similarity with the results obtained when the central bank is continuously intervening (see Figure 9.5). Thus, the target intervention system produces the same kind of exchange rate stabilization as the more active intervention system of the previous section.

The previous results are sensitive to the choice of the target band. We show this in Figure 9.8, which presents simulations of the exchange rate and its fundamental, assuming increasingly large target bands. Unsurprisingly, it may be seen that, when the target band increases, the stabilizing properties of interventions are reduced.

9.5 Is Intervention Sustainable?

We analyzed the effectiveness of simple intervention rules and concluded that they can be tailored to be surprisingly effective in eliminating bubbles in the exchange market. But are such interventions sustainable? In other words, is such intervention not going to lead to unsustainable depletions (or accumulations) of international reserves of central banks? The question is important because, if the answer is positive, the use of intervention policies will have to be abandoned. In order to check whether this is the case we computed the stock of international reserves

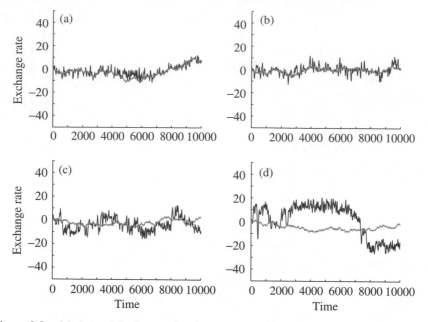

Figure 9.8. Market and fundamental exchange rates, with $C = 0$, $\beta = 0.9$, $\gamma = 5$, $\phi = 0$, $\epsilon = 0.1$, $\rho = 0.5$, and (a) $M = 3$STD, (b) $M = 10$STD, (c) $M = 20$STD, (d) $M = 50$STD. Gray lines denote fundamental rate; black lines denote exchange rate.

of the central bank, and we checked whether this stock has a tendency to grow or to shrink over time. We first show the evolution of the stock of international reserves (per capita) in Figure 9.9. This is the stock of international reserves that corresponds to the intervention scenario of Figure 9.5(c). We observe that this stock is fluctuating a lot and appears to have a strong mean reversion. Thus, starting with a given stock of international reserves (which in the simulation was normalized to zero) we tend to return to this initial stock of reserves. This is in fact not surprising. The leaning-against-the-wind interventions operate symmetrically in the long run.

A simple unit root test on the series plotted in Figure 9.9 confirms this conclusion. The ADF test statistic is $-15.130\,47$ (with a critical value at the 1% level of -3.4342). As a result, we can reject the hypothesis that the stock of international reserves exhibits a unit root. Thus, this intervention rule does not lead to unsustainable accumulations or decumulations of international reserves.

9.6   Conclusion

In an efficient market, sterilized interventions are futile exercises. They should not affect the exchange rate. Yet, when central banks intervene in the foreign exchange markets, they overwhelmingly use sterilized interventions, i.e., interventions that do not affect domestic monetary conditions. Does this mean these central banks do not understand economic theory? The results of this chapter show that central bankers

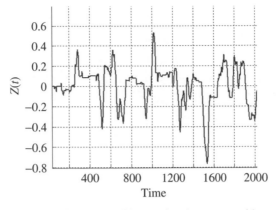

Figure 9.9. Stock of international reserves, with
$C = 0$, $\beta = 0.9$, $\gamma = 5$, $\rho = 0.5$, and $\epsilon = 0.1$.

understand the workings of the foreign exchange markets better than the efficient-market theorists. We have shown that, in our model, simple intervention rules of the leaning-against-the-wind type can be quite effective in eliminating bubbles and crashes in the exchange rate. Our results also vindicate a long-standing proposal of John Williamson and Marcus Miller to use target intervention rules (with a soft band). Finally, occasional interventions without the use of a clear rule have been shown to be powerful but very unpredictable in their effects.

10

Chaos in the Foreign Exchange Markets

10.1 Introduction

In the previous chapters we regularly encountered a very special dynamics: chaotic dynamics. In this chapter we analyze its nature. In addition, we study the conditions in which it arises. Finally, we also study the empirical relevance of chaotic dynamics.

10.2 What Is Chaos?

This is not a book on chaos. We will therefore limit ourselves to a very short and simplified discussion of chaos. We will base the discussion here on De Grauwe et al. (1993), where more technical detail can be found.[1]

Chaotic dynamics is created in nonlinear deterministic models. There is no commonly agreed definition of chaos. We define chaos here to be a seemingly random and irregular signal generated by a deterministic process with the following properties.

The first property is that the process that generated a chaotic signal exhibits sensitivity to initial conditions, i.e., the solutions for two sets of (marginally different) initial conditions start diverging after some time and become entirely different.

A second property is the existence of a "strange attractor." This attractor defines the trajectory of the solution in the phase space. For example, in a model consisting of one nonlinear differential equation (like the logistic model: $x_t = \lambda x_{t-1}(1-x_{t-1})$) the attractor can be a fixed point (there is one solution). It can also be a limit cycle (e.g., a two-period cycle in which the solutions oscillate between two values in a perfectly predictable way). Finally, it can be a strange attractor in which the number of solutions is infinite, and in which the solutions oscillate in a less than perfectly predictable manner. Which of the three types of solution will prevail depends on the parameters of the model. (In the logistic model we have a fixed point for $1 < \lambda < 3$ and a two-period solution for $3 < \lambda < 3.45$; for larger values of λ we obtain four-period solutions, eight-period solutions, and so on,

---

[1] For an easily accessible discussion, see Peters (1991). One of the "fathers" of chaotic dynamics is Mandelbrot (see Mandelbrot 1983). A more advanced introduction is Baker and Gollub (1990). For a survey of chaotic models used in finance, see Hommes (2005).

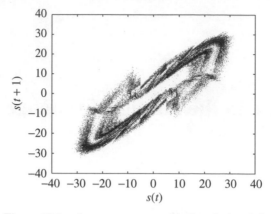

Figure 10.1.   Strange attractor, with $C = 5$, $\psi = 0.2$,
$\beta = 0.95$, $\gamma = 10$, $\phi = 0$, $\rho = 0.5$, and $\epsilon = 0.1$.

until the critical value $\lambda = 4$, when we have infinitely many solutions that are contained in the strange attractor.) The characteristic of the strange attractor is that it leads to a trajectory of the dynamic variables that never repeats itself. In this sense we can say that the solution of a chaotic system is aperiodic, i.e., the cyclical movements never repeat themselves. Each cycle is unique. This feature is one of the fascinating aspects of chaotic dynamics especially because it is generated by a perfectly deterministic system. We show an example of a strange attractor generated in our model for particular parameter values (to be discussed later) in Figure 10.1. The figure describes the movements of the exchange rate in the (s_{t+1}, s_t)-plane. The collection of points defines the trajectory of solutions for the exchange rate. For other values of the parameters we can obtain a singular fixed-point solution. In that case we would only have one point in the (s_{t+1}, s_t)-plane. When the solution is a two-period cycle, we would have two points in the (s_{t+1}, s_t)-plane.

An important characteristic of a strange attractor is that it has a fractal dimension. By that we mean that the dimension of the geometric figure constituting the strange attractor is a noninteger number (e.g., 1.46). An interesting implication of a geometric figure with a fractal dimension is that it exhibits self-similarity, i.e., the whole figure is a magnification of its parts, and details in the figure are reductions of the whole figure. The visually most spectacular features of self-similarity are obtained in the Mandelbrot set (see Mandelbrot 1983).

Chaos can be detected in different ways. We will use the largest Lyapunov exponent (which measures the rate of divergence of nearby trajectories) as a measure of chaos: a positive largest Lyapunov exponent indicates chaos (see Rosenstein et al. (1992) and De Grauwe et al. (1993) for a discussion of Lyapunov exponents). Since we have access to the equations generating chaos (and thus we know the dimension of the system), it is relatively simple to estimate the largest Lyapunov exponent from the following expression:

$$\lambda_1(i) = \frac{1}{T-1} \sum_{t=1}^{T-1} \ln \frac{d_t(i)}{d_t(0)}, \tag{10.1}$$

where $d_t(i)$ is the (Euclidean) distance between the tth pair of nearby trajectories after i iterations, and $d_t(0)$ is the reinitialized distance between two trajectories at each point t.[2]

There are other characteristics of chaos, e.g., ergodicity, that we do not discuss here. The reader is again referred to De Grauwe et al. (1993).

10.3 Conditions for Chaos to Occur

Under what conditions does the model produce a chaotic dynamics? This is the question we answer in this section. From the previous section, we remember that there are several different ways to detect a chaotic dynamics. Here we will analyze how strange attractors emerge and we will compute the Lyapunov exponents. We also stressed in the previous section that chaotic dynamics is characterized by sensitivity to initial conditions, so we will therefore also analyze this. It should be borne in mind, however, that this sensitivity is not a characteristic found only in chaotic dynamics. As was shown in the previous chapters, one also obtains sensitivity to initial conditions with systems that generate fixed-point solutions when the basins of attractions have a fractal nature.

As before, our analysis is based on numerical simulations. We will use the model of Chapters 5 and 6, and study how the emergence of chaos in the model depends on some parameters of the model.

A first result of this analysis is that the emergence of chaos crucially depends on the size of the "feedback parameters" in the model. We have two "feedback parameters."[3] The first one, ϕ, measures the sensitivity of risk aversion to the degree of misalignment. We call it a feedback parameter because, as the exchange rate tends to deviate from the fundamental, it sets in motion a return movement towards the fundamental. The mechanism that engenders this is that, when $\phi > 0$, an increasing misalignment makes the fundamentalists less risk averse, so that they become more willing to arbitrage. The second "feedback parameter" is ϵ, which measures the intensity with which the current account reacts to misalignments. Thus, when $\epsilon > 0$, increasing deviations of the exchange rate from its fundamental lead to increasing supplies of net foreign assets, thereby driving the exchange rate back to its fundamental value.

---

[2] Note that, since we have a ten-dimensional system, the (Euclidean) distance between the two nearby trajectories is computed for the 10 variables at each point t in time.

[3] In fact, there is a third feedback parameter. This governs the intensity with which the central bank operates in the foreign exchange market.

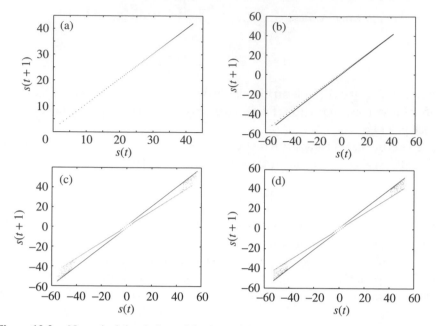

Figure 10.2. Numerical simulations of the deterministic part of the model. Strange attractor: $C = 5$, $\psi = 0.2$, $\beta = 0.95$, $\gamma = 5$, $\rho = 0.5$, and $\epsilon = 0$. (a) $\phi = 0.1$, (b) $\phi = 0.5$, (c) $\phi = 1$, (d) $\phi = 4$.

The first important result we obtain is that, when both these feedback parameters are zero, chaotic dynamics does not emerge. In that case, we obtain fixed-point solutions, one of which is the fundamental solution and the others are nonfundamental (bubble) solutions. These were analyzed in detail in Chapters 2 and 3. Again note that we found sensitivity to initial conditions in this case when the basins of attraction have fractal boundaries. Thus, in order to obtain chaotic dynamics, one of the two feedback parameters has to be positive. We now turn to a systematic analysis of how increasing values of these parameters produce "routes" to strange attractors.

10.3.1 "Routes" to Strange Attractors: The Influence of ϕ

This section contains numerical simulations of the deterministic part of the model that show how a stable steady state becomes chaotic for increasing values of the parameter ϕ. We show the evidence in Figure 10.2. We present the attractors in the phase space in Figure 10.2(a)–(d) for increasing values of ϕ starting with $\phi = 0.1$. Remember that the phase space collects the points in the (s_{t-1}, s_t)-plane.[4] Parts (e)–(h) show the exchange rate in the time domain for two different

---

[4] The phase space in our model has a dimension greater than 2 (see Chapter 3). As a result, the points in the plane with ordinates (s_{t-1}, s_t) should be interpreted as projections of the phase space in the plane (s_{t-1}, s_t).

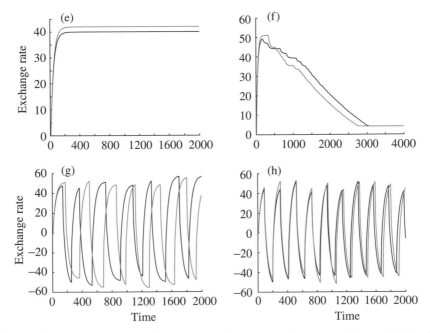

Figure 10.2. (*Cont.*) Numerical simulations of the deterministic part of the model. Sensitivity to initial conditions: $C = 5$, $\beta = 0.95$, $\gamma = 5$, $\rho = 0.5$, and $\epsilon = 0$. (e) $\phi = 0.1$, (f) $\phi = 0.5$, (g) $\phi = 1$, (h) $\phi = 4$. Black line, without shock; gray line, with shock.

initial values of the exchange rate. Starting with the smaller value of ϕ ($\phi = 0.1$), we find that the exchange rate converges to a fixed point that is a nonfundamental equilibrium. The fact that the convergence is towards a nonfundamental equilibrium is due to the selection of parameters. There are other parameter values that will produce a convergence to a fundamental equilibrium. We show an example in Section 10.8. Note also that the results obtained for the small value of ϕ are qualitatively not different from the case when $\phi = 0$ (not shown here).

Figure 10.2 shows how the nature of the attractors changes fundamentally when ϕ increases. When $\phi = 0.5$ the exchange rate is attracted to a fundamental equilibrium.[5] Further increases in ϕ lead to the emergence of strange attractors. In the case of $\phi = 1$, the exchange rate is caught up in an attractor that leads to switches between low and high values at low frequency. As ϕ increases further, these switches become more frequent, creating a high degree of turbulence in the exchange rate movements. We also note that, in all these cases, there is sensitivity to initial conditions, i.e., a small difference (of 0.1) in the initial exchange rate leads

---

[5] It should be stressed that the exact value of ϕ at which this happens depends on the other parameters of the model. It also depends on the initial conditions. One interesting result is that two slightly different initial conditions can produce, in one case, convergence to a fundamental and, in the other case, convergence to a nonfundamental equilibrium. We show an example in Section 10.9.

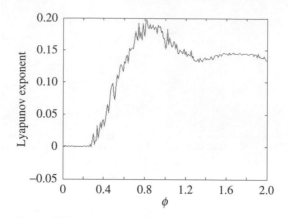

Figure 10.3. Lyapunov exponent as a function of ϕ, with $C = 5$, $\beta = 0.95$, $\rho = 0.5$, and $\epsilon = 0$.

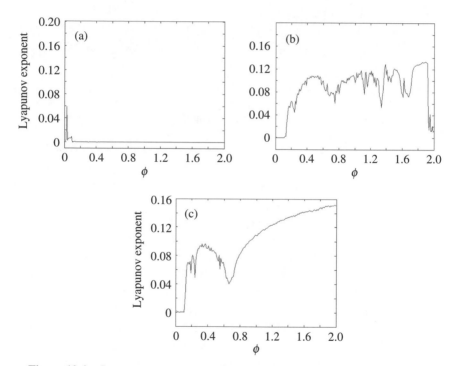

Figure 10.4. Lyapunov exponent as a function of ϕ, with $C = 5$, $\gamma = 1$, $\rho = 0.5$, $\epsilon = 0$, and (a) $\beta = 0.8$, (b) $\beta = 0.9$, and (c) $\beta = 0.95$.

to a different time path of the exchange rate. The exchange rate remains attracted by the same strange attractor.

Figure 10.2 provides only a visual indication of the existence of a chaotic dynamics. One can detect the existence of chaos more rigorously by calculating the largest

Lyapunov exponent as defined in the previous section. We have set $i = 1$, which is a conservative measure, i.e., we compute the distance at each iteration. We show the results of computing the largest Lyapunov exponents in Figure 10.3. This confirms the visual impression of Figure 10.2, i.e., for sufficiently high values of ϕ the largest Lyapunov exponent becomes positive. Note that, for low values of ϕ, the Lyapunov exponent is zero. This result is due to the coexistence of fixed-point attractors. In the absence of chaos, we obtain one separate fixed point for each initial condition (see Figure 10.2). This means that, when computing the Lyapunov exponent for two nearby trajectories, we will find that these trajectories keep a constant distance in the steady state. As a result, the largest Lyapunov exponent must also be zero.

The exact value of ϕ at which a chaotic attractor emerges depends on the other parameters of the model and on the initial conditions. We show the importance of the other parameters of the model, concentrating on β in Figure 10.4. We find that, for small values of β ($\beta = 0.8$), no chaotic attractor emerges within the range $0 \leqslant \phi \leqslant 2$. For higher values of β one obtains chaotic attractors.

10.3.2 *"Routes" to Strange Attractors: The Influence of ϵ*

In this section we analyze the routes to strange attractors produced by changes in our second feedback parameter. This is ϵ, which measures the intensity with which the supply of foreign assets reacts to deviations of the exchange rate from its fundamental. In Figure 10.5 we present, in a similar way to that in the previous section, the attractors for increasing values of ϵ. For sufficiently small values, the exchange rate converges to a nonfundamental equilibrium.[6] There is a range of values of ϵ for which the exchange rate is attracted to a fundamental equilibrium (Figure 10.5(b)). This figure also illustrates that the initial conditions also determine whether the exchange rate converges to a fundamental or a nonfundamental equilibrium. It can be seen that for one initial condition the steady-state solution is a fundamental equilibrium (solid line), while for the other initial condition (which differs only by 0.1) the steady-state solution is a nonfundamental equilibrium (dotted line).

There is a range of values of ϵ for which chaotic attractors emerge. This is shown for the cases between $\epsilon = 0.04$ and $\epsilon = 0.1$. For these values of ϵ we find strange attractors that produce extreme turbulence and strong sensitivity to initial conditions. One of the characteristics of these strange attractors is the phenomenon of intermittency, i.e., the exchange rate tends to move in and out from the orbit described by the strange attractor (see, for example, Hommes 2001, p. 152). This feature is shown in Section 10.9, where we present the exchange rate in the time domain for the same parameter configuration as in Figure 10.5(d).

Finally, for sufficiently high values of ϵ (in Figure 10.5(e) we show the case where $\epsilon = 0.5$), the strange attractor disappears and the exchange rate converges to

---

[6] The same comment should be made here as in the previous section, i.e., the convergence will occur to a fundamental equilibrium when the parameters β and γ are sufficiently small.

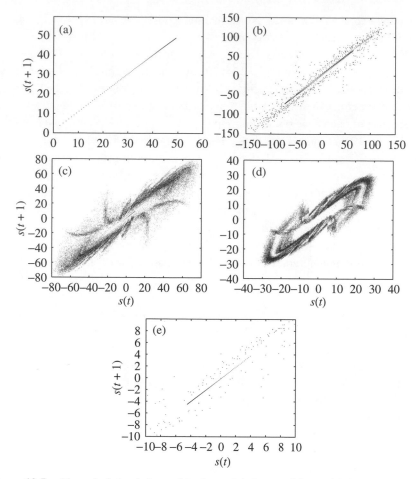

Figure 10.5.   Numerical simulations of the deterministic part of the model. Strange attractor: $C = 5$, $\psi = 0.2$, $\beta = 0.95$, $\gamma = 1$, $\rho = 0.5$, and $\phi = 0$. (a) $\epsilon = 0.01$, (b) $\epsilon = 0.02$, (c) $\epsilon = 0.04$, (d) $\epsilon = 0.1$, (e) $\epsilon = 0.5$.

a fundamental equilibrium (located inside the transaction-cost band). These effects of changing the parameter ϵ are summarized in the Lyapunov exponents shown in Figure 10.6. We observe that, for small values of ϵ, the Lyapunov exponent is zero, indicating that the exchange rate converges to a fixed point (fundamental or nonfundamental). There is an intermediate range of values of ϵ for which the Lyapunov exponent is positive, indicating the existence of a strange attractor. For large values of ϵ, the Lyapunov exponent tends to return to zero. As before, the exact values of ϵ that trigger changes in the dynamic regime depend on the other parameters of the model.

We conclude from the analysis of Figure 10.5 that changing the feedback parameter ϵ produces a very rich dynamics, characterized by great complexity and different

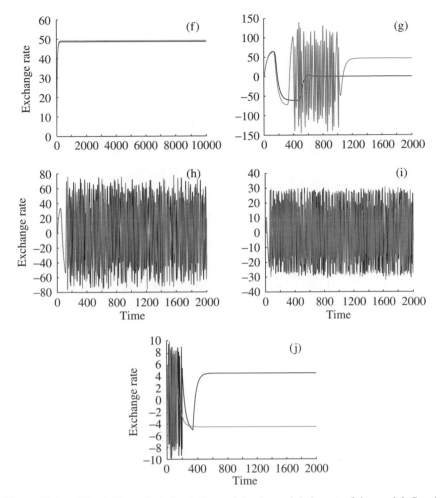

Figure 10.5. (*Cont.*) Numerical simulations of the deterministic part of the model. Sensitivity to initial conditions: $C = 5$, $\beta = 0.95$, $\gamma = 1$, $\rho = 0.5$, and $\phi = 0$. (f) $\epsilon = 0.01$, (g) $\epsilon = 0.02$, (h) $\epsilon = 0.04$, (i) $\epsilon = 0.1$, (j) $\epsilon = 0.5$. Black line, without shock; gray line, with shock.

outcomes for the equilibrium to which the exchange rate converges. When stochastics is added to the model this feature creates the potential for frequent switches in dynamic regimes.

10.4   Foreign Exchange Market Intervention and Chaos

In Chapter 9 we analyzed the effectiveness of foreign exchange market interventions. We found that these interventions introduce a feedback mechanism that fundamentally changes the dynamics of the foreign exchange market. It is therefore worthwhile studying how the intensity of the interventions affects the emergence

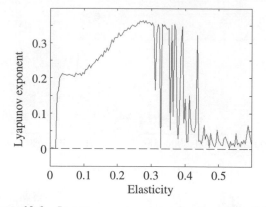

Figure 10.6.   Lyapunov exponent as a function of elasticity,
with $C = 5$, $\beta = 0.95$, $\rho = 0.5$, and $\phi = 0$.

of chaotic attractors. In Chapter 9 we introduced two types of intervention: leaning-against-the-wind and target interventions. We will maintain the same distinction here.

10.4.1   *Leaning-against-the-Wind Interventions*

In this intervention strategy, the central bank is continuously in the market, buying the foreign currency when it is depreciating and selling it when it is appreciating. Thus, this intervention strategy introduces a feedback mechanism, the strength of which is measured by the parameter ϵ (elasticity). We proceed as before and present the attractors in the phase space for increasing values of ϵ (see Figure 10.7). We also show the sensitivity to initial conditions in the time domain. We find results that are very similar to those obtained in the previous sections: for small values of ϵ, the model generates fixed-point solutions that can be either nonfundamental or fundamental equilibria. There is an intermediate range of values of ϵ that lead to chaotic attractors. Note that, in the simulation presented in Figure 10.7(d), the initial conditions can lead the exchange rate into a strange attractor or a fixed-point solution. This is an example of extreme sensitivity to initial conditions: a very small difference in the initial value of the exchange rate has a dramatic effect on the future movements of the exchange rate. Finally, with a sufficiently high value of ϵ, the strange attractor disappears and the exchange rate is always attracted by the fundamental equilibrium: sensitivity to initial conditions disappears. Thus, a sufficiently intense intervention activity by the central bank ensures that the exchange rate remains in the neighborhood of the fundamental. In a way, it can be said that, quite paradoxically, these interventions contribute to the efficiency of the exchange markets, in that they help the market to ensure that the exchange rate reflects the underlying fundamental value.

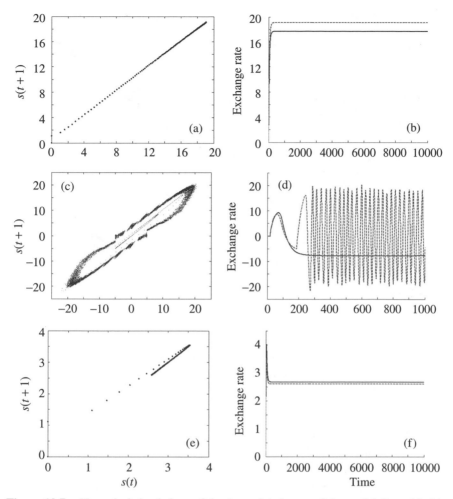

Figure 10.7. Numerical simulations of the deterministic part of the model. Parts (a), (c), and (e) show results for the strange attractor: $C = 5$, $\psi = 0.2$, $\beta = 0.95$, $\gamma = 1$, $\phi = 0$, and $\rho = 0.5$. (a) $\epsilon = 0.05$, (c) $\epsilon = 0.1$, (e) $\epsilon = 0.2$. Parts (b), (d) and (f) show the sensitivity to initial conditions: $C = 5$, $\psi = 0.2$, $\beta = 0.95$, $\gamma = 1$, $\phi = 0$, and $\rho = 0.5$: (b) $\epsilon = 0.0.5$, (d) $\epsilon = 0.1$, (f) $\epsilon = 0.2$. Black line, without shock; dotted gray line, with shock.

10.5 Target Intervention

In the second type of intervention the central bank defines a band around the fundamental, within which it will not intervene. Conversely, when the exchange rate is driven outside this band, the central bank intervenes. It then sells the foreign currency when it continues to increase, and buys it when it continues to decline. In this intervention the width of the band matters. We present numerical simulations assuming a relatively large band of $M = 6$ which is larger than the transaction-cost band of $M = 5$. (In an appendix (see Section 10.10) we present and discuss

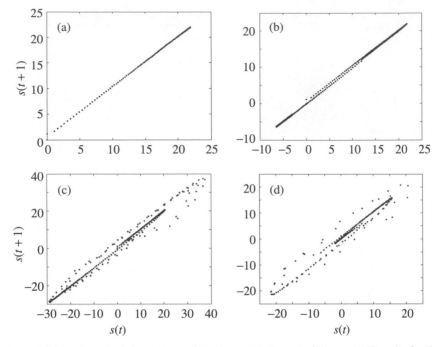

Figure 10.8. Numerical simulations of the deterministic part of the model. Results for the strange attractor: $C = 5$, $\psi = 0.2$, $\beta = 0.95$, $\gamma = 1$, $M = 6$, and $\rho = 0.5$. (a) $\epsilon = 0.05$, (b) $\epsilon = 0.07$, (c) $\epsilon = 0.1$, (d) $\epsilon = 0.2$.

simulations where we assume that the intervention band is smaller than the transaction-cost band.) We show the results in Figure 10.8. The results are similar to those obtained in the leaning-against-the-wind strategy (see Section 10.4.1), i.e., for small values of ϵ we have convergence to a fixed point (fundamental or nonfundamental); for sufficiently large values of ϵ the exchange rate converges to a fundamental equilibrium. There are some differences though. In particular, while, in the leaning-against-the-wind strategy (see Figure 10.7), there is an intermediate range of values of ϵ for which we obtain a chaotic attractor, this is no longer the case in the target intervention regime. For example, when $\epsilon = 0.1$, we obtain a chaotic attractor in the leaning-against-the-wind strategy, while such an attractor is absent in the target intervention We obtain some initial turbulence for high values of ϵ, a feature that is not present in the leaning-against-the-wind intervention.

10.6 Empirical Relevance of Chaotic Dynamics

We have shown that our model generates a chaotic dynamics for certain parameter values. This feature is interesting, even exciting. The question, however is whether chaotic dynamics is observed in reality. Much empirical analysis has been done to investigate this (see, for example, De Grauwe et al. 1993; Guillaume 2000;

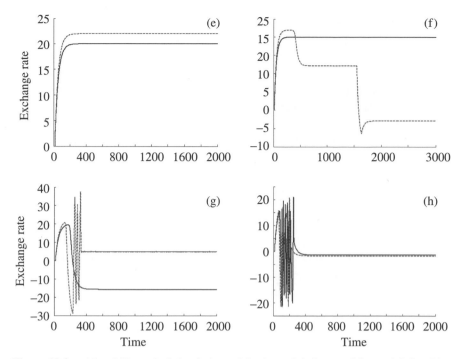

Figure 10.8. (*Cont.*) Numerical simulations of the deterministic part of the model. Sensitivity to initial conditions: $C = 5$, $\beta = 0.95$, $\gamma = 1$, $\phi = 0$, $M = 6$, and $\rho = 0.5$. (e) $\epsilon = 0.05$, (f) $\epsilon = 0.07$, (g) $\epsilon = 0.1$, (h) $\epsilon = 0.2$. Black line, without shock; dotted gray line, with shock.

Schittenkopf et al. 2001). The consensus that emerges from this analysis is that the empirical evidence in favor of chaotic dynamics is relatively weak. De Grauwe et al. (1993) find that most of the time the hypothesis of the existence of chaotic dynamics in the foreign exchange markets must be rejected. There are only a few episodes where chaotic dynamics can be detected in the data, e.g., the GBP/USD rate during the period 1973–81 and the JPY/USD rate during the period 1971–72. De Grauwe et al. stress that it is generally difficult to find conclusive evidence for the existence of chaotic dynamics because the available techniques do not separate the exogenous noise from chaos (see Brock 1986). This lack of strong evidence for the existence of chaos has been confirmed by Guillaume (2000) and Schittenkopf et al. (2001).

In a way, the lack of evidence for chaos should not be surprising. The chaotic attractors create cyclical movements in the exchange rate with high frequency and large amplitude (see, for example, parts (d) and (i) of Figure 10.5). In other words, chaotic attractors create extreme short-term turbulence. There are not many periods in which such extreme turbulence can be observed. The important message of the previous analysis, however, is that sometimes such strong turbulence can occur.

While the evidence for the existence of chaotic attractors is weak, there is ample evidence for the existence of nonlinearities in the exchange rate dynamics. We have illustrated these nonlinearities in Chapter 8. These have to do with volatility clustering and fat tails. These arise because of the prevalence of sensitivity to initial conditions, which in turn follow from the fact that the exchange rate can switch from one type of equilibrium to another. These switches then create turbulence in the market. The empirical evidence that such nonlinearities exist is overwhelming. We have argued that our model naturally generates these nonlinearities. The surprise is that one does not need chaotic dynamics to generate these nonlinear features. The possibility that sometimes the exchange rate can get embroiled in a chaotic dynamics just reinforces these nonlinear features.

10.7 Conclusion

In this chapter we have analyzed the conditions under which chaotic dynamics can arise in our model. We found that certain combinations of parameter values generate chaotic dynamics, e.g., a large chartist extrapolation parameter together with strong feedback parameters. Thus, if chartists strongly extrapolate past exchange rate changes into the future and if, in addition, there is a strong effect of exchange rate changes on the current account, then chaotic dynamics can occur. Another combination is a strong extrapolation by chartists and a strong sensitivity of fundamentalists' risk perception to misalignments.

The empirical evidence for the existence of chaotic dynamics is weak. This has much to do with the fact that it is difficult to separate noise from chaotic dynamics in real-life data. It may also have something to do with the fact that, most of the time, the feedback mechanisms that create chaos, i.e., the current account and the endogeneity of risk perceptions, are weak. Thus, chaotic dynamics, although possible, remains a rare phenomenon in the foreign exchange market.

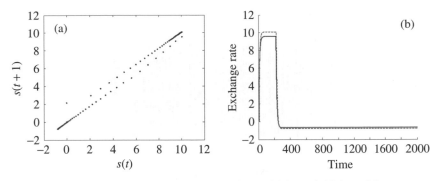

Figure 10.9. (a) Strange attractor and (b) sensitivity to initial conditions. For both parts, $C = 5$, $\psi = 0.2$, $\beta = 0.8$, $\gamma = 1$, $\phi = 0.1$, $\rho = 0.5$, and $\epsilon = 0$.

10.8 Appendix: Sensitivity to Parameter Values

In this appendix we show that the exchange rate converges to a fundamental equilibrium for small values of β and γ. The results in this appendix (see Figure 10.9) should be compared with the results in Figure 10.2(a), which show convergence to nonfundamental equilibrium when $\beta = 0.95$ and $\gamma = 5$. These results confirm those discussed in previous chapters showing how, for small shocks in initial conditions, the exchange rate converges to a fundamental equilibrium and, for large shocks, it converges to a nonfundamental equilibrium.

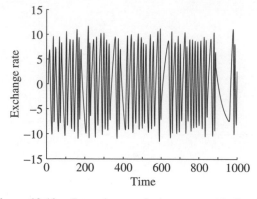

Figure 10.10.   Intermittency phenomenon, with $C = 5$,
$\beta = 0.95$, $\gamma = 1$, $\phi = 0$, $\rho = 0.5$, and $\epsilon = 0.1$.

10.9   Appendix: Intermittency Phenomenon

The numerical simulation presented in Figure 10.10 illustrates a recurrent feature of chaotic dynamics which has been called intermittency. This is a dynamics in which the exchange rate is moving in and out of the orbits described by the strange attractors. The frequency with which this happens depends on the parameter values and the initial conditions.

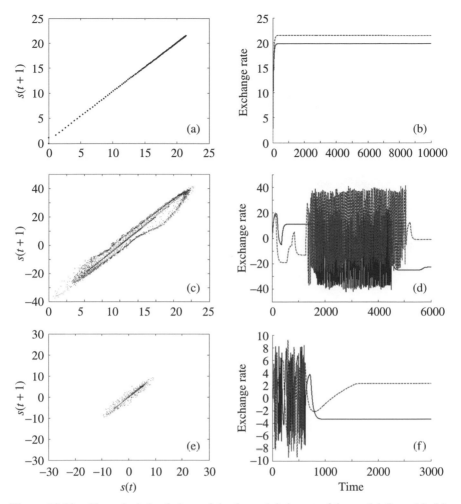

Figure 10.11. Numerical simulations of the deterministic part of the model. Parts (a), (c), and (e) show results for the strange attractor: $C = 5$, $\psi = 0.2$, $\beta = 0.95$, $\gamma = 1$, $\rho = 0.5$, and $M = 2$. (a) $\epsilon = 0.05$, (c) $\epsilon = 0.1$, (e) $\epsilon = 0.2$. Parts (b), (d) and (f) show the sensitivity to initial conditions: $C = 5$, $\beta = 0.95$, $\gamma = 1$, $\phi = 0$, $\rho = 0.5$, and $M = 2$. (b) $\epsilon = 0.0.5$, (d) $\epsilon = 0.1$, (f) $\epsilon = 0.2$. Black line, without shock; gray line, with shock.

10.10 Appendix: Target Intervention with Small Target Band

In this appendix we present results obtained in the target intervention regime when we assume that the target band (TB) is small relative to the transaction-cost band. We set TB $= 2$. The results of the simulation of the model are shown in Figure 10.11. Surprisingly, we now obtain a strange attractor for intermediate values of ϵ, creating a lot of short-term turbulence.

11
Conclusion

The rational-expectations–efficient-market (REEM) model has provided the dominant mode of thinking about asset markets for at least three decades. This impressive intellectual construction continues to be highly influential and is the only model that is taken seriously in academic teaching about price formation in asset markets (including the exchange market). In a way, this is surprising, because the accumulating empirical evidence is not favorable for the REEM model. Many of its predictions have been refuted by the data. In particular, the prediction that asset prices only change because of news in underlying fundamentals should be rejected. In addition, many empirical phenomena observed in asset markets, e.g., volatility clustering, fat tails in the distribution of the returns, and the profitability of chartist rules, remain unexplained by the REEM model.

This state of affairs teaches us that, for a theory to be discarded by its users, it is not sufficient for it to be refuted by the data. In the absence of an alternative theory, the former one remains in place, even if it is rejected by the empirical evidence. The conditions for a new theory to take the place of the old one are not only that it should be better at predicting the data, but that it must also satisfy the conditions of internal consistency and elegance in order to become respectable.

In this book we have attempted to provide an alternative mode of thinking about the exchange market. Our source of inspiration has been the behavioral finance literature. The basic philosophy of our modeling approach can be summarized as follows. The starting point is that agents experience a cognitive problem when they try to understand the world in which they live. They find it difficult to collect and to process the complex information with which they are confronted. As a result, they use simple rules ("heuristics") to guide their behavior. They do this not because they are irrational, but rather because the complexity of the world is overwhelming. Thus, the agent we propose is very different from the rational agent assumed to populate our economic models, who is able to comprehend the full complexity of the world, i.e., who has a brain that can contain and process all the information embedded in the world in its full complexity.

The second component in our modeling approach was to discipline the behavior of our agents, i.e., to impose a criterion that allows some behavioral rules to survive and others to disappear. Thus, in this second stage, we assumed that agents regularly evaluate the behavioral rules they use, and that they do this by comparing the utility of the rule they are using with the utility of other rules. If it turns out that this other rule gives them more satisfaction, they are willing to switch to that other rule. In this sense one can say that rationality is introduced in the model. Rationality should, however, be understood in a different way than in the REEM model. It is a selection mechanism based on trial and error, in which imperfectly informed agents decide about the best behavior based on their past experiences. This trial-and-error strategy is probably the best possible strategy in a very uncertain world.

We formalized these ideas in the context of simple models of the foreign exchange market. This formalization has been greatly influenced by the important literature on nonlinear dynamics. This is becoming increasingly influential and was surveyed recently by Hommes (2005).

The ensuing model allowed us to generate results that closely mimic the main dynamic features observed in the foreign exchange market. First, our model predicts that the exchange rate will be disconnected from its underlying fundamentals for most of the time. Obstfeld and Rogoff (2000) called the disconnect phenomenon one of the major puzzles in international finance. Our model predicts that the disconnect phenomenon is a natural outcome in a world where agents find it difficult to understand the underlying model and use trial-and-error methods in their forecasting strategies. It is as if the trial-and-error learning strategies lead to a never-ending groping of the market towards the fundamental exchange rate. At the same time, the model predicts that, in the long run, the exchange rate is cointegrated with its fundamental. The speed with which the exchange rate returns to the fundamental, however, turns out to be slow, on average. This slow average convergence of the exchange rate towards its fundamental has also been confirmed by the empirical evidence.

Second, the model predicts that, frequently (but unpredictably), the exchange rate will be involved in a bubble-and-crash dynamics. The bubbles arise because of the self-fulfilling character of extrapolative forecasting rules: when these rules turn out to be profitable, they attract newcomers who reinforce the upward (or downward) movement, making these even more profitable, attracting newcomers, and so on. We showed, however, that, in a stochastic environment, the attraction exerted by the fundamental variables overcomes the temporary forces of speculative bubbles, leading to a crash.

Third, in our model, the extrapolative forecasting rules (chartism and technical analysis) that do not take into account information about the fundamental exchange rate do surprisingly well and, on average, create more profits than fundamental-based forecasting rules do. The reason why this happens is that these extrapolative rules create noise, which generates additional profits in a self-fulfilling way. Thus, our model predicts that chartist rules are profitable. This has also been observed empirically in the foreign exchange market. The implication is that chartist fore-casting rules survive in the long run. This prediction contradicts the prediction made by Milton Friedman that these forecasting rules are unprofitable in the long run and that they tend to disappear.

Fourth, our model mimics the other empirical regularities observed in the for-eign exchange markets, i.e., the existence of fat tails in the exchange rate returns, and of volatility clustering. The phenomenon of fat tails implies that very large changes in the exchange rate occur with a frequency that cannot be explained by a normal distribution. The interesting feature of our model is that it generates these fat tails endogenously. It does not assume volatility clustering to be present in the distribution of the shocks in the fundamentals. Similarly, the model generates the phenomenon of volatility clustering, which implies that periods of tranquillity and turbulence alternate in an unpredictable manner. The main reason why we obtain these results is that the model produces different equilibria (attractors). In a stochas-tic environment, small disturbances can lead the exchange rate to be attracted by a new equilibrium, leading to large changes in the exchange rate and, under certain conditions, to clustering of volatilities.

The disconnect phenomenon and the occurrence of bubbles and crashes have much to do with failures of arbitrage. We analyzed the sources of these failures and how they affect the dynamics of the exchange rate. We concentrated on two sources of arbitrage failures. The first is the existence of risk aversion. This analysis led to the conclusion that the existence of risk aversion, which prevents fundamentalists from exploiting profit opportunities when bubbles emerge, lies at the heart of the disconnect puzzle. Thus, paradoxically, bubbles and crashes occur because agents who use fundamentalist forecasting rules are too risk averse, and therefore fail to act on their beliefs. The second source of arbitrage failures arises from transaction costs in the goods markets that weaken the mean reversion in the real exchange rate.

Sensitivity to initial conditions is a pervasive force in our model. It explains why large changes in the exchange rate occur, and why there is volatility clustering. It also has important implications for our understanding of how shocks in the fundamentals (the news) affect the exchange rate. Our main finding here is that news in the fundamentals has an unpredictable effect on the exchange rate. Sometimes news strongly affects the exchange rate; at other times the same news has no effect whatsoever. In addition, it is essentially unpredictable when news will have an effect and when it will not. The fundamental reason for this indeterminacy in the effect of news is that there is no unique equilibrium to which the exchange rate will converge. For example, when the exchange rate is involved in a bubble at the moment the news reaches the market, the news may not affect the exchange rate at all, while, at more tranquil times, the same news will strongly affect the exchange rate. The unpredictability of the effect of news in the fundamentals on the exchange rate is also observed in reality. For example, there is a lot of evidence suggesting that news in the fundamentals (like inflation differentials, the current account, economic growth) has unpredictable effects on the euro/USD exchange rate (see De Grauwe 2000). There have been periods during which news in the U.S. current account had no effect whatsoever on the euro/USD rate. At other times, the same news about the U.S. current account had very strong effects on the exchange rate. Similar phenomena have been observed with other fundamental variables. Our model allows us to understand why the unpredictability of the effects of news is the rule rather than the exception.

We have also used our model to analyze the effects of official interventions in the foreign exchange market. In an efficient market, sterilized interventions are futile exercises. They should not affect the exchange rate. And yet, when central banks intervene in the foreign exchange markets, they overwhelmingly use sterilized interventions, i.e., interventions that do not affect domestic monetary conditions. Is it possible that central banks do not understand economic theory? The results of our analysis show that central bankers understand the workings of the foreign exchange markets better than the efficient-market theorists. We have shown that, in our model, simple intervention rules of the "leaning-against-the-wind" type can be quite effective in eliminating bubbles and crashes in the exchange rate. The reason for this result is that the central bank's intervention strategy reinforces the mean-reverting dynamics in the market, thereby strengthening the hand of the fundamentalists at the expense of the "trend chasers" (chartists). This stabilizes the market and reduces the probability of the emergence of bubbles. Thus, the effect of this intervention is that the exchange rate follows the movements of the underlying fundamentals more closely. In a way, it can be concluded, quite paradoxically, that by intervening in the foreign exchange market the central bank makes the market look more efficient.

Much research remains to be done to provide a fully convincing alternative to the REEM model. Such an alternative model will also have to take into account recent discoveries about how the human brain functions. It is now increasingly recognized by psychologists and neuroscientists that there are two (interacting) cognitive processes at work in our brains. The first one is based on intuition and emotion. The second is based on explicit reasoning. The latter also functions as a monitoring process, evaluating the quality of the mental processes as a whole. In the light of these discoveries, the now popular microfoundation of macromodels appears to be increasingly problematic. Humans certainly do not take decisions using the process of reasoning in isolation. The emotional and intuitive process is of crucial importance for allowing the reasoning process to lead to rational decisions.

Economists' scientific defense of the rational agent hypothesis has always been that this is an "as if" proposition that should be judged by its capacity to generate powerful empirical predictions. This is fair enough. However, it has to be admitted today that this hypothesis does not deliver the powerful predictions, at least not in the foreign exchange market. As a result, it is no longer acceptable to maintain this hypothesis, and it is time to incorporate new insights that are provided by other scientific fields.

We claim that the two-stage modeling approach used in this book, based on the use of simple intuitive rules (first stage) that are then evaluated rationally in a second stage, comes closer to a correct microfoundation of macroeconomics than the REEM model. However, it remains a crude approximation. As a result, the task of convincing the profession that a new paradigm is in the making remains a challenging one.

References

Abreu, D. and M. Brunnermeier. 2003. Bubbles and crashes. *Econometrica* 71:173–204.

Anderson, S., A. de Palma, and J.-F. Thisse. 1992. *Discrete Choice Theory of Product Differentiation*. Cambridge, MA: MIT Press.

Azariadis, C. and R. Guesnerie. 1984. Sunspots and cycles. CARESS Working Paper 83-22R, University of Pennsylvania.

Bacchetta, P. and E. van Wincoop. 2003. Can information heterogeneity explain the exchange rate determination puzzle? NBER Working Paper 9498.

Bachelier, L. 1900. *Théorie de la Spéculation*. Paris: Gauthiers-Villars.

Baker, G. and J. Gollub. 1990. *Chaotic Dynamics: An Introduction*. Cambridge University Press.

Barberis, N. and R. Thaler. 2002. A survey of behavioural finance. NBER Working Paper 9222.

Beine, M. and C. Lecourt. 2004. Reported and secret interventions in the foreign exchange market. *Financial Research Letters* 1:215–225.

Beine, M., S. Laurent, and C. Lecourt. 2003. Central bank intervention and exchange rate volatility: evidence from a switching regime analysis. *European Economic Review* 47:891–911.

Blanchard, O. J. 1979. Speculative bubbles, crashes and rational expectations. *Economics Letters* 3:387–389.

Blanchard, O. J. and S. Fischer. 1989. *Lectures on Macroeconomics*. Cambridge, MA: MIT Press.

Blanchard, O. J. and M. W. Watson. 1982. Bubbles, rational expectations and speculative markets. In *Crisis in Economic and Financial Stucture: Bubbles, Bursts, and Shocks* (ed. P. Wachtel). Lanham, MD: Lexington Books.

Brock, W. 1986. Distinguishing random and deterministic systems: an expanded version. *Journal of Economic Theory* 90:168–195.

Brock, W. and C. Hommes. 1997. A rational route to randomness. *Econometrica* 65:1059–1095.

——. 1998. Heterogeneous beliefs and routes to chaos in a simple asset pricing model. *Journal of Economic Dynamics and Control* 22:1235–1274.

Brunnermeier, M. 2001. *Asset Pricing under Asymmetric Information: Bubbles, Crashes, Technical Analysis, and Herding*. Oxford University Press.

——. 2004. Learning to reoptimize consumption at new income levels: a rationale for prospect theory. *Journal of the European Economic Association* 2:98–114.

Cheung, Y. W. and M. Chinn. 2001. Currency traders and exchange rate dynamics: a survey of the U.S. market. *Journal of International Money and Finance* 20:439–472.

Cheung, Y. W. and D. Friedman. 1997. Individual learning in normal form games: some laboratory results. *Games and Economic Behavior* 19:46–76.

——. 1998. A comparison of learning and replicator dynamics using experimental data. *Journal of Economic Behavior & Organization* 35:263–280.

Cheung, Y. W., K. S. Lai, and M. Bergman. 2001. Dissecting the PPP puzzle: the unconventional roles of nominal exchange rate and price adjustments. *Journal of International Economics* 64:135–150.

Cheung, Y. W., M. Chinn, and I. Marsh. 2004. How do U.K.-based foreign exchange dealers think their market operates? *International Journal of Finance & Economics* 9:289–306.

Cutler, D., J. Poterba, and L. Summers. 1988. What moves stock prices? NBER Working Paper 2538.

Damasio, A. 2003. *Looking for Spinoza: Joy, Sorrow, and the Feeling Brain*. New York: Harcourt.

Dawid, H. 1999. *Adaptive Learning by Genetic Algorithms: Analytical Results and Applications to Economic Models*, 2nd edn. Springer.

De Boeck, J. 2000. The effect of macroeconomic "news" on exchange rates: a structural VAR approach. Mimeo, University of Leuven.

De Grauwe, P. 2000. Exchange rates in search of fundamentals: the case of the euro–dollar rate. *International Finance* 3:329–356.

De Grauwe, P., H. Dewachter, and M. Embrechts. 1993. *Exchange Rate Theories: Chaotic Models of the Foreign Exchange Markets*. Oxford: Blackwell.

De Grauwe, P., R. Dieci, and M. Grimaldi. 2005. Fundamental and nonfundamental equilibria in the foreign exchange market. A behavioural finance approach. CESifo Group Working Paper 1431.

De Haan, J., S. Eijffinger, and S. Waller. 2005. *The European Central Bank: Credibility, Transparency, and Centralization*. Oxford University Press.

De Long, J., B. Bradford, A. Schleifer, and L. Summers. 1990. Noise trader risk in financial markets. *Journal of Political Economy* 98:703–738.

Dewachter, H. 2001. Can Markov switching models replicate chartists' profits in the foreign exchange markets. *Journal of International Money and Finance* 20:25–41.

Dewachter, H. and M. Lyrio. 2005. The economic value of technical trading rules: a nonparametric utility-based approach. *International Journal of Finance & Economics* 10:41–62.

De Vries, C. G. 2000. Fat tails and the history of the guilder. *Tinbergen Institute Magazine* 4:3–6.

Dominguez, K. and J. Frankel. 1993a. Does foreign exchange intervention matter: the portfolio effect. *American Economic Review* 83:1356–1369.

———. 1993b. *Does Foreign Exchange Intervention Work?* Washington, D.C.: Institute for International Economics.

Dornbusch, R. 1976. Expectations and exchange rate dynamics. *Journal of Political Economy* 84:1161–1176.

Dumas, B. 1992. Dynamic equilibrium and the real exchange rate in a spatially separated world. *Review of Financial Studies* 5:153–180.

Ehrmann, M. and M. Fratzscher. 2005. Exchange rates and fundamentals: new evidence from real-time data. *Journal of International Money and Finance* 24:317–341.

Engel, C. and J. Rogers. 1995. How wide is the border? International Finance Discussion Paper 498, Board of Governors of the Federal Reserve System, Washington, D.C.

Epstein, S. 1994. Integration of the cognitive and psychodynamic unconscious. *American Psychologist* 49:709–724.

Evans, G. and S. Honkapohja. 2001. *Learning and Expectations in Macroeconomics*. Princeton University Press.

Evans, M. and R. Lyons. 1999. Order flow and exchange rate dynamics. NBER Working Paper 7317.

Fama, E. 1965. The behavior of stock market prices. *Journal of Business* 38:34–105.

———. 1970. Efficient capital markets: a review of theory and empirical work. *Journal of Finance* 25:383–417.

Fama, E. 1991. Efficient capital markets. II. *Journal of Finance* 46:1575–1613.

Faust, J., J. Rogers, E. Swanson, and J. Wright. 2002. Identifying the effects of monetary policy shocks on exchange rates using high frequency data. International Finance Discussion Papers, No. 739, Board of Governors of the Federal Reserve System, Washington, D.C.

Flood, R. and A. Rose. 1995. Fixing exchange rates: a virtual quest for fundamentals. *Journal of Monetary Economics* 36:3–37.

Frankel, J. 1979. On the mark: a theory of floating exchange rates based on real interest differentials. *American Economic Review* 69:610–622.

Frankel, J. and K. Froot. 1986. The dollar as a speculative bubble: a tale of fundamentalists and chartists. NBER Working Paper 1963.

———. 1990. Chartists, fundamentalists and trading in the foreign exchange market. *American Economic Review* 80:181–185.

Frankel, J. and A. Rose. 1994. A survey of empirical research on nominal exchange rates. NBER Working Paper 4865.

Franses, P. H. and D. van Dijk. 2000. *Nonlinear Time Series Models in Empirical Finance*. Cambridge University Press.

Friedman, M. 1953. The case for flexible exchange rates. In *Essays of Positive Economics*. Chicago University Press.

Fudenberg, D. and D. K. Levine. 1998. *The Theory of Learning in Games*. Cambridge, MA: MIT Press.

Garber, P. M. 2000. *Famous First Bubbles*. Cambridge, MA: MIT Press.

Gaunersdorfer, A. and C. Hommes. 2000. A nonlinear structural model for volatility clustering. CeNDEF Working Paper 00-02, University of Amsterdam.

Gaunersdorfer, A., C. Hommes, and F. Wagener. 2003. Bifurcation routes to volatitlity clustering. CeNDEF Working Paper 03-03, University of Amsterdam.

Gilbert, D. T. 2002. Inferential correction. In *Heuristics and Biases* (ed. T. Gilovich, D. Griffin, and D. Kahneman), pp. 167–184. Cambridge University Press.

Goodhart, C. 1989. News and the foreign exchange market. LSE Financial Markets Group Discussion Paper 71.

Goodhart, C. and L. Figliuoli. 1991. Every minute counts in the foreign exchange markets. *Journal of International Money and Finance* 10:23–52.

Guillaume, D. 2000. *Intradaily Exchange Rate Movements*. Dordrecht: Kluwer Academic.

Hammond, K. R. 1996. *Human Judgment and Social Policy: Irreducible Uncertainty, Inevitable Error, Unavoidable Injustice*. Oxford University Press.

Haskel, J. and H. Wolf. 2001. The law of one price: a case study. *Scandinavian Journal of Economics* 103:545–558.

Hayek, F. A. 1945. The use of knowledge in society. *American Economic Review* 35:519–530.

Hommes, C. H. 2001. Financial markets as a nonlinear adaptive evolutionary systems. *Quantitative Finance* 1:149–167.

———. 2005. Heterogeneous agents models in economics and finance. In *Handbook of Computational Economics II: Agent-Based Computational Economics* (ed. K. Judd and L. Tesfatsion), Handbooks In Economics Series. Elsevier.

Huisman, R., K. Koedijk, C. Kool, and F. Palm. 2002. The tail-fatness of FX returns reconsidered. *De Economist* 150:299–312.

James, J. 2003. Simple trend-following strategies in currency trading. *Quantitative Finance* 3:C75–C77.

Johansen, A. and D. Sornette. 1999. Modeling the stock market prior to large crashes. *European Physical Journal* B 9:167–174.

Johansen, S. 1991. Estimation and hypothesis testing of cointegration vectors in Gaussian vector autoregressive models. *Econometrica* 55:1551–1580.

Kahneman, D. 2002. Maps of bounded rationality: a perspective on intuitive judgment and choice. Nobel Prize Lecture, December 8, Stockholm. (Available at http://nobelprize.org/economics/laureates/2002/kahneman-lecture.html.)

Kahneman, D. and A. Tversky. 1973. Prospect theory: an analysis of decisions under risk. *Econometrica* 47:313–327.

———. 2000. *Choices, Values and Frames.* Cambridge University Press.

Kahneman, D., J. Knetsch, and R. Thaler. 1991. The endowment effect, loss aversion and status quo bias. *Journal of Economic Perspectives* 5:193–206.

Kilian, L. and M. Taylor. 2003. Why is it so difficult to beat the random walk forecast of exchange rates? *Journal of International Economics* 60:85–107.

Kindleberger, C. 1978. *Manias, Panics, and Crashes. A History of Financial Crises.* New York: John Wiley.

Kirman, A. 1993. Ants, rationality and recruitment. *Quarterly Journal of Economics* 108:137–156.

Kirman, A. and G. Teyssière. 2002. Microeconomic models for long memory in the volatility of financial time series. *Studies in Nonlinear Dynamics and Econometrics* 5:137–156, 281–302.

Koedijk, K., P. Stork, and C. de Vries. 1992. Foreign exchange regime differences viewed from the tails. *Journal of International Money and Finance* 11:462–473.

Krugman, P. 1987. Pricing to market when the exchange rate changes. In *Real Financial Linkages among Open Economies* (ed. S. Arndt and D. Richardson). Cambridge, MA: MIT Press.

Kubelec, C. 2004. FOREX trading strategies and the efficiency of sterilized intervention. Mimeo, Bank of England.

LeBaron, B. 1992. Technical trading profitability in foreign exchange markets in the 1990s. Working Paper (July), University of Wisconsin–Madison.

———. 1999. Technical trading rule profitability and foreign exchange intervention. *Journal of International Economics* 49:125–143.

Lee, C., A. Shleifer, and R. Thaler. 1991. Investor sentiment and the closed-end fund puzzle. *Journal of Finance* 46:75–109.

Lux, T. 1998. The socio-economic dynamics of speculative markets: interacting agents, chaos, and fat tails of return distributions. *Journal of Economic Behavior & Organization* 33:143–165.

Lux, T. and M. Marchesi. 1999. Scaling and criticality in a stochastic multi-agent model of a financial market. *Nature* 397:498–500.

———. 2000. Volatility clustering in financial markets: a microsimulation of interacting agents. *International Journal of Theoretical and Applied Finance* 3:675–702.

Lux, T. and S. Schorstein. 2005. Genetic learning as an explanation of stylized facts of foreign exchange markets. *Journal of Mathematical Economics* 41:169–196.

Lux, T. and D. Sornette. 2002. On rational bubbles and fat tails. *Journal of Money, Credit and Banking* 34:589–610.

Lyons, R. 2001. *The Microstructure Approach to Exchange Rates.* Cambridge, MA: MIT Press.

McCallum, J. 1995. National borders matter: Canadian–U.S. regional trade patterns. *American Economic Review* 85:615–623.

Mandelbrot, B. 1963. The variation of certain speculative prices. *Journal of Business of the University of Chicago* 36:394–419.

Mandelbrot, B. 1983. *The Fractal Geometry of Nature*. New York: Freeman.

———. 1997. *Fractals and Scaling in Finance*. Springer.

Meese, R. and K. Rogoff. 1983. Empirical exchange rate models of the seventies: do they fit out of sample? *Journal of International Economics* 14:3–24.

Menkhoff, L. 1997. Examining the use of technical currency analysis. *International Journal of Finance & Economics* 2:307–318.

———. 1998. The noise trading approach—questionnaire evidence from foreign exchange. *Journal of International Money and Finance* 17:547–564.

Michael, P., R. Nobay, and A. Peel. 1997. Transaction costs and nonlinear adjustment in real exchange rates: an empirical investigation. *Journal of Political Economy* 105:862–879.

Moore, M. and M. Roche. 2005. A neo-classical explanation of nominal exchange rate volatility. In *Exchange Rate Economics, Where Do We Stand?* (ed. P. De Grauwe). Cambridge, MA: MIT Press.

Mussa, M. 1981. *The Role of Official Intervention*. New York: Group of Thirty.

Neely, C. and P. Weller. 2001. Technical analysis and central bank intervention. *Journal of International Money and Finance* 20:949–970.

Obstfeld, M. and K. Rogoff. 1996. *Foundations of International Macroeconomics*. Cambridge, MA: MIT Press.

———. 2000. The six major puzzles in international macroeconomics: is there a common cause? NBER Working Paper 7777 (July).

Peters, E. E. 1991. *Chaos and Order in the Capital Markets: A New View of Cycles, Prices and Market Volatility*. New York: John Wiley.

Pratt, J. 1964. Risk aversion in the small and in the large. *Econometrica* 32:122–136.

Rosenstein, M., J. Collins, and C. De Luca. 1992. A practical method for calculating largest Lyapunov exponents from small data sets. Unpublished manuscript, Department of Biomedical Engineering, Boston University.

Sargent, T. 1993. *Bounded Rationality in Macroeconomics*. Oxford University Press.

Sarno, L. and M. Taylor. 2001. Official interventions in the foreign exchange markets: is it effective, and if so, how does it work? *Journal of Economic Literature* 39:839–869.

———. 2002. *The Economics of Exchange Rates*. Cambridge University Press.

Schittenkopf, C., G. Dorffner, and E. Dockner. 2001. On nonlinear, stochastic dynamics in economics and financial time series. *Studies in Nonlinear Dynamics and Econometrics* 4:101–121.

Schulmeister, S. 2005. The interaction between technical currency trading and exchange rate fluctuations. Unpublished manuscript, Austrian Institute of Economic Research, Vienna.

Sercu, P., R. Uppal, and C. Van Hulle. 1995. The exchange rate in the presence of transaction costs: implications for tests of relative purchasing power parity. *Journal of Finance* 50:1309–1319.

Shiller, R. 1989. *Market Volatility*. Cambridge, MA: MIT Press.

———. 2000. *Irrational Exuberance*. Princeton University Press,

Shleifer, A. 2000. *Introduction to Behavioural Finance*. Oxford: Clarendon.

Shleifer, A. and R. Vishny. 1997. The limits to arbitrage. *Journal of Finance* 52:35–55.

Simon, H. 1957. *Models of Man*. New York: John Wiley.

Sloman, S. A. 2002. Two systems of reasoning. In *Heuristics and Biases* (ed. T. Gilovich, D. Griffin, and D. Kahneman), pp. 379–396. Cambridge University Press.

Sornette, D. 2003. *Why Stock Markets Crash*. Princeton University Press.

Stanovich, K. and R. West. 2000. Individual differences in reasoning: implications for the rationality debate. *Behavioral and Brain Sciences* 23:645–665.

Stanovich, K. and R. West. 2002. Individual differences in reasoning: implications for the rationality debate. In *Heuristics and Biases* (ed. T. Gilovich, D. Griffin, and D. Kahneman), pp. 421–440. Cambridge University Press.

Taylor, M. and H. Allen. 1992. The use of technical analysis in the foreign exchange market. *Journal of International Money and Finance* 11:304–314.

Taylor, M., D. Peel, and L. Sarno. 2001. Nonlinear mean reversion in real exchange rates: towards a solution to the purchasing power parity puzzles. *International Economic Review* 42:1015–1042.

Thaler, R. 1994. *Quasi Rational Economics*. New York: Russell Sage Foundation.

Tirole, J. 1982. On the possibility of speculation under rational expectations. *Econometrica* 50:1163–1181.

Tversky, A. and D. Kahneman. 1981. The framing of decisions and the psychology of choice. *Science* 211:453–458.

Wei, S.-J. and J. Kim. 1997. The big players in the foreign exchange market: do they trade on information or noise? NBER Working Paper 6256.

Werner, T. and C. Upper. 2004. Time variation in the tail behaviour of bunds futures returns. *Journal of Futures Markets* 24:387–398.

Williamson, J. 1983. *The Exchange Rate System*. Washington, D.C.: Institute of International Economics.

———. 1985. *The Exchange Rate System*. Policy Analyses in International Economics, Vol. 5. Washington, D.C.: Institute for International Economics.

———. 1994. *Estimating Equilibrium Exchange Rates*. Washington, D.C.: Institute for International Economics.

Williamson, J. and M. Miller. 1987. *Targets and Indicators: A Blueprint for the International Coordination of Economic Policy*. Washington, D.C.: Institute of International Economics.

Index